W9-DCF-607

# AUGUSTINE
# AND
# THE ARIANS

# AUGUSTINE AND THE ARIANS

## The Bishop of Hippo's Encounters with Ulfilan Arianism

William A. Sumruld

Selinsgrove: Susquehanna University Press
London and Toronto: Associated University Presses

© 1994 by Associated University Presses, Inc.

All rights reserved. Authorization to photocopy items for internal or personal use, or the internal or personal use of specific clients, is granted by the copyright owner, provided that a base fee of $10.00, plus eight cents per page, per copy is paid directly to the Copyright Clearance Center, 27 Congress Street, Salem, Massachusetts 01970. [0-945636-46-6/94 $10.00+8¢ pp, pc.]

BR
1720
.A9
S86
1994

Associated University Presses
440 Forsgate Drive
Cranbury, NJ 08512

Associated University Presses
25 Sicilian Avenue
London WC1A 2QH, England

Associated University Presses
P.O. Box 338, Port Credit
Mississauga, Ontario
Canada L5G 4L8

The paper used in this publication meets the requirements of the American National Standard for Permanence of Paper for Printed Library Materials Z39.48-1984.

**Library of Congress Cataloging-in-Publication Data**

Sumruld, William A., 1952–
    Augustine and the Arians : the Bishop of Hippo's encounters with Ulfilan Arianism / William A. Sumruld.
        p.   cm.
    Includes bibliographical references and index.
    ISBN 0-945636-46-6 (alk. paper)
    1. Augustine, Saint, Bishop of Hippo.   2. Arianism.   3. Trinity—History of doctrines—Early church, ca. 30–600.   4. Jesus Christ—History of doctrines—Early church, ca. 30–600.   5. Ulfilas, Bishop of the Goths, ca. 311–381—Influence.   6. Maximinus, Bishop, fl. 427.   7. Goths—Religion.   8. Algeria—Church history.   9. Hippo (Extinct city)—Church history.   I. Title.
    BR1720.A9S86   1994
    273'.5—dc20                                                            92-50684
                                                                                CIP

PRINTED IN THE UNITED STATES OF AMERICA

# CONTENTS

# PREFACE

The origins of this book are to be found in an assignment for a doctoral seminar led by Dr. James Leo Garrett at Southwestern Baptist Theological Seminary. Given the task of translating the *Contra Sermonem Arianorum* by Augustine of Hippo, the writer soon discovered that no published monographs about Augustine's opposition to Arianism were available. Further investigation revealed that no dissertations on that subject had been written in the United States, and no books on the topic were listed with the Library of Congress. The most he could find were a few scattered paragraphs in biographies, in translations of Augustine's *Epistulae* and *Retractationes,* in patrologies, and in historical and theological studies. The information and analysis were shockingly sparse. In these, he found surprisingly little comment made about the *Contra Sermonem Arianorum* or the important *Collatio cum Maximino Arianorum episcopo.* The importance of these works to Augustine was garnered from his own comments on the *Contra Sermonem Arianorum* in the *Retractationes* and from the comments of his contemporary and disciple, Possidius, in his *Vita Sancti Aurelii Augustini.*[1] The English biographies that gave the most space to this controversy reserved almost all of their all-too-brief comments for the bishop's rather frustrating experiences with Pascentius,[2] who was by far the theological and intellectual inferior of Maximinus and the anonymous author of *Sermo Arianorum.*

While translating the *Contra Sermonem Arianorum,* the writer realized the need for a better understanding of the Arianism it opposed. English works generally assumed that the heresy all but disappeared after the Council of Constantinople in A.D. 381. A few noted its continued existence in the Roman army and among the Germanic tribes but assigned it little significance. Those studies that covered Western Roman and barbarian Arianism were very few. French scholarship showed, by far, the greatest interest in the field, as a quick review of the bibliography will reveal.

Based on these preliminary studies, the writer began to feel that he had a topic which could make some small contribution to Augustinian studies. He began the long and arduous task of reading and analyzing Augustine's own anti-Arian works, pertinent comments in the bishop's other works, and those Arian works available to him. Most of the sources have not been published in English and were available almost exclusively in the *Patrologiae Latinae* and its *Supplementum*. Augustine's major anti-Arian works are usually listed as the *Contra Sermonem Arianorum*, the *Collatio cum Maximino Arianorum episcopo,* and the *Contra Maximinum Arianorum episcopum*. A minority of scholars will sometimes also list the *De Trinitate*. With these, a few of his letters, such as number 238 to Pascentius, his sermons, and some brief excerpts from a few of his other works are on rare occasions listed under this category. Where available, more recent critical editions were consulted. All translations of these and of the secondary works are the writer's own unless otherwise indicated.

This book would have been impossible without the help and encouragement of many people. Mrs. Susan Alexander taught me to read Latin. Professors William R. Estep and James Leo Garrett of Southwestern Baptist Theological Seminary convinced me that my research was worthy of a book. John and Rochelle Jee, Richard Molpus, and Molly Rose Koontz provided some technical support for the original typing. My mom and dad never lost faith in me. I wish my mother had lived to see the completion of this project. She would have been so proud. John McCance and his library staff at College of the Southwest were very helpful during the final stages of research. The administration, faculty, and staff at College of the Southwest encouraged me to finish. The editors and staff at both Susquehanna and Associated University Presses have been patient and very helpful during the final preparation of this manuscript. A final thanks must go to my lovely wife, Kay. Without her patience, love and understanding, I never would have completed this project.

# INTRODUCTION

Christianity has always been attentive to historical concerns. Most of its doctrinal clarifications, through the centuries, have come not as purely theological exercises but in response to some external or internal pressure. Therefore, valid analysis of Christian documents or artifacts must proceed with a historical awareness of the events, customs, social problems, literature, and expressed attitudes of the culture and epoch in which they were produced.[1]

While theoretically, historical technique emphasizes one's separation from the past, there is a genuine connection between the researcher and the reality the text seeks to portray. If this were not so, one could not speak intelligibly about the object of study. This merging of horizons is the hermeneutical problem. Only when one experiences, however imperfectly, the question for which his text seeks an answer does he begin to understand the text.[2] To aid the reader in this necessity, chapter 1 provides a brief overview of some of the more significant social and political forces in the era of crisis for the late Western empire.

Chapter 2 furnishes a background for understanding the Gothic, or Ulfilan, Arianism that Augustine faced in his last debate. In chapter 3, a discussion of Roman Africa and the events surrounding Augustine's contacts with Arianism will appear. In chapter 4, Augustine's last great debate and one of his last works will receive rather close scrutiny. With them in the chapter will be a reconstruction of Augustine's role in the collapse of Roman Africa. The fifth chapter will be devoted to a review of the major theological arguments of Augustine's debate with Maximinus and an evaluation of his theology in contrast with that of the Ulfilans. In the Conclusion, the many strands of his study will be taken up again in an effort to answer some important questions. One area of focus will be the social, political, and military context for Augustine's conflict with the Gothic Arians. There also will be a final estimation of the specific type of Arianism he encountered. Along with these issues will be a review of the bishop's encounters with this type of Arianism. Finally, there will be an evaluation of the conflict's effects on his theology.

Possidius, Augustine's contemporary and biographer, noted that writing the *Contra Maximinum Arianorum episcopum,* probably begun in 428, occupied the whole space of the bishop's remaining days (Vita 17). Yet the anti-Arian writings are neglected in most major interpretations of Augustine's Christological and Trinitarian thought. Even when they are cited, few scholars resist the temptation to disregard their historical and textual integrity, merely lumping them with the bishop's earlier statements, such as the *De Trinitate.*[3]

This can lead to serious hermeneutical distortion. Augustine's thought tended to be progressive and was often so polemically or dialectically oriented that positions maintained at one time might differ significantly from later views. This problem has been the bane of many eminent scholars. One must avoid the mere collation of his views without regard to context and chronology.

The best scholarship has long been divided on whether there was general continuity to Augustine's thought or change of a radical nature. The two extremes are represented by Etienne Gilson and Odilo Rottmanner. Gilson saw change only on minor points, while Rottmanner believed that anyone who failed to see the radical character of change in Augustine's thought would never truly understand his theology.[4] Most scholarship today favors seeing at least some change in Augustine's thought. Scholars seem prepared to admit that his thought on the will and predestination were at least more carefully defined due to the Pelagian controversy, and that his views on toleration were modified by conflict with the Donatists.[5] Therefore, unless there is a careful investigation of his anti-Arian works in their historical context, modern scholarship runs the risk of an incomplete understanding of Augustine's Trinitarian and Christological thought. Valid and "serious scholarship of St. Augustine's thought involves familiarity with the period in question, with its trends of thought, social organization, and its political, cultural, and religious problems."[6]

The problems of Trinity and Christology are again the topic of debate in some circles.[7] Many theologians seem to feel that the Trinitarian dogmas and confessions need reappraisal and reevaluation in the light of modern philosophy and psychology, with their heavy stress on function and evolution, process, relativity, and contingency. They want to make Trinitarian and Christological doctrines more "immediately relevant to modern man's way of thinking and living."[8]

Augustine, in his final years, confronted those who rejected the orthodox Trinitarian conception of God. He and his brethren in the orthodox clergy waged a successful campaign that not only checked the spread of Arianism but led to its eventual demise. Perhaps one may discover in the study of Augustine's anti-Arian works some clues to their success. Certainly a study of the final conclusions of one of theology's master thinkers could be of value to today's discussion.

The researcher aims to provide a needed reconstruction of Augustine's encounters with Arianism. He also hopes to answer several important questions about the dating of some of Augustine's works.

# AUGUSTINE
# AND
# THE ARIANS

# 1

# FIFTH-CENTURY CONTEXT

## Introduction

The barbarian crises of the fifth-century Roman West are one of the major watersheds of history. Historians have long debated the complex phenomenon commonly referred to as the "Decline and Fall of the Roman Empire."

In the 1920s and 1930s, the traditional view of the Germanic barbarians was challenged. The long-accepted approach had emphasized the dissimilarities of German and Roman life and the disappearance of Roman civilization in the fifth and sixth centuries. The challengers claimed that the Germanic "invasions" were relatively minor in their effect on European government and society. Leading proponents of this approach were the Austrian scholar Alfons Dopsch and the famous Belgian economic historian Henri Pirenne. Dopsch, in his massive *Economic and Social Foundations of Western Civilization,* used what appears to be special pleading, tortured misreading of texts, and what now seems dubious archeological evidence to argue that there was almost no difference of cultural and economic level between the Germans and the inhabitants of the empire. Henri Pirenne also argued against any disastrous break in the social and economic development of the empire during the barbarian invasions. Instead, he attributed any cataclysmic disruption to the Islamic expansion of the eighth century. Norman F. Cantor gives an apt, if satirical, evaluation of their work when he says, "The Germans in Dopsch's work appear as good Austrian burghers ready to sit down for a bit of Wiener Schnitzel and Löwenbrau with their fortunate Roman hosts."[1]

In an attack led by French scholarship, the Dopsch-Pirenne interpretation has been overwhelmingly rejected. Scholarship has returned to the earlier view of the disastrous consequences of the fifth-century crisis. As Cantor notes, E. Salin knocked the props from under Dopsch's view of German cultural attainments the archaeological side.[2] Pierre Paul Coucelle, in his brilliant *Histoire littéraire grandes invasion Germaniques,* demonstrated that one must take seriously the views of contemporaries on the importance of the invasions and the significance of German actions. Robert Latouche nailed the coffin lid shut on the Dopsch-Pierenne view and restored the central importance of the Germanic invasions with his exceptional general history of the migrations and settlements of the barbarians.[3]

There simply is not enough room here to give adequate attention to the complex phenomenon commonly referred to as the "Decline and Fall of the Roman Empire." The review of some elements of the Western crisis are, however, essential to an understanding of Augustine's context with regards to the Ulfilan Arian threat.

### An Ancient Empire

Modern writers and researchers sometimes seem to forget that the Roman empire was an ancient society, dependent upon primitive systems of communication, economy, and agriculture. The famous Roman roads passed through towns that derived almost all of what the inhabitants ate, wore, and lived in from a radius of some thirty miles. They knew that if their harvest ever failed, they faced a winter of starvation. For many months every year, all central control of the military, economy, and politics of much of the Roman world simply vanished. The passes filled with snow, the great Roman roads sank into the mud, the stores of fodder dwindled at the posting-stations, the little boats rocked at anchor, and the distance between the emperor and his subjects tripled.[4]

## A Society in Collapse

### The Revenue Crisis

The Western empire was a society in collapse in which "too few producers supported too many idle mouths."[5] The primitive state of agriculture, a manpower shortage, and an increasing demand for goods and services (the legacy of the barbarian incursions of the third century), created a spiraling fiscal crisis. Debasement of coinage began under the Severians. Organized inflation, monetary manipulation, and all the usual financial games resorted to by governments in economic trouble were unable to alleviate the problem. Insane fiscal demands resulted in widespread tax evasion. Even threats of direct penalties could not stop it. The cost of living rose constantly. Price-fixing edicts, the first dated A.D. 301, could not halt it. The situation grew so bad that poor parents often felt themselves driven to infanticide. Many also sold their children into slavery. In 315 the problem was so bad in Italy that Constantine ordered immediate aid in the form of food and clothing, by law, for the raising of newborns whose parents could not meet their needs.[6]

A marked deterioration of the efficiency and honesty of public officials destroyed the possibility of justice for those who were poor and prevented an appropriate response to the economic and military crisis.[7] The government of the West seemed especially susceptible to problems of corruption for three reasons: excessive centralization of government; the existence of a wealthy, powerful, and selfish aristocracy; and the loss of men of the highest moral character to church positions.[8]

### Lack of Patriotism

There had never been great surges of patriotism for the empire. As A. H. M. Jones has noted, "The Roman empire seems never to have evoked any active patriotism from the vast majority of its citizens."[9] But at its core there had always been a cadre of men willing to sacrifice for the general welfare. In the late empire, however, one of the most depressing signs of decline is the obvious and almost complete absence of public spirit. Officials and ordinary citizens alike seemed quite indifferent toward unceasing outrage toward the imperial majesty and periodic ravagings of the provinces. But they would permit no meddling with their faith or pleasures.[10]

One factor that helped to insure a lack of popular military resistance to the barbarians was that the empire's urban citizens were accustomed to being defended by a professional army. For reasons of internal security, it had long been illegal for the citizenry to bear arms. Therefore, the long tradition of a professional force that handled all military matters adversely affected their outlook. They looked to the army for protection, but this time the army would fail them.

Social injustice and economic ruin eroded the peasantry's loyalty to the empire. They help to account for the peasant revolts that rocked the empire since an intolerable despotism, unable to preserve law and order in the face of the barbarian menace, demanded more and more revenue. The feared *Bacaudae* were merely poor wretches who, in despair from being pillaged and murdered by unjust judges and cruel landowners, became, like the barbarians, armed plunderers or else welcomed the barbarian plunderers as liberators from their tax burdens.[11]

## Army Quality and Size

Although the cause of the empire's demise was primarily military, it did not derive from a decline in the quality of the field armies *(comitatenses)*. Under good leadership, they could still defeat barbarian forces that far outnumbered them. And while some, even during the late empire itself, have questioned the reliability of Germanic soldiers in the regular army, they were both efficient and reliable, good soldiers who often rose from the ranks to positions of command. As A. H. M. Jones has said, "There is no hint in our sources that Germans recruited into the regular army and properly administered were ever unreliable."[12]

It is difficult to estimate accurately the forces defending the Roman empire. Were it not for the *Notitia dignitatum,* the task would be impossible. In appendix 2 of his *Later Roman Empire, 284–602,* Jones has provided an important analysis of this valuable document along with some helpful commentary. The *Notitia dignitatum* offers invaluable information on the military organization of the late empire. It seems to have been written or thoroughly revised right after the split of the empire in 395. The portion concerning the Western forces was revised at about the time of the death of Honorius, A.D. 423. Some of the material was left unrevised, and it is likely that some clerical errors occurred. However, careful analysis, combined with the realization that Roman units were often well below their "paper strength" and an awareness of the events of the crisis and their effects, allows one to make a somewhat reliable estimate of the force levels maintained.

The closest estimates may vary from as much as thirty thousand to fifty thousand for the *limitanei* (border guards), and by a somewhat smaller margin for the *comitatus* (field army). Jones estimates the *comitatus* at about one hundred thirty-six thousand and the *limitanei* at approximately one hundred thousand in A.D. 423. Bury, on the other hand, estimates the *comitatus* at about one hundred thousand and the *limitanei* at slightly under that. Either could well be correct or both could be slightly off the real figures. About a third of the *comitatus* was stationed in Italia. There were also *comitatenses* in Hispania, Gallia, Illyricum, Africa, and, until it was abandoned, in Britannia. After the invasions, the largest of these forces operated in Gallia. There were *limitanei* in most of the border provinces, the greatest concentrations being in Germania, Illyricum, Gallia, and

Britannia. In Africa, the *limitanei* were incorporated into the *comitatus* to give a total force of about twenty thousand.

To modern ears these numbers might seem quite adequate for the defense of the empire. But when one considers the vastness of the empire, the difficulties and slowness of ancient transport and communication systems, the unpredictability of the barbarians, the disruption caused by the "native" tribes and disgruntled peasants, he or she begins to see the woeful inadequacy of the late imperial army of the West for its assigned task. Once the border was breached by the barbarians and they had spread across Gallia, Italia, and Hispania, it became next to impossible to force them out of the empire. When imperial troops defeated a barbarian concentration, the barbarian force would merely splinter into smaller bands and continue to raid Roman villas and towns. Without a patriotic, loyal citizenry ready to take up arms to defend it, the empire was doomed. The army was good at its job, but it did not have the resources to defend a crumbling empire. Once the tax base was destroyed by the devastation and loss of control of many of the principal provinces, the army itself would deteriorate.

## The Barbarian Foederati

The relationship of the "tribal" groups, called *foederati,* with the central Roman authority was one of the great problems of the period. It is difficult to avoid confusion when using the term *foederati.* Originally it meant those bound by a definite treaty of alliance, a *foedus.* These, during the republic and early empire, were client states outside the boundaries of the empire, who provided soldiers as a term of their treaty. The soldiers themselves were called *foederati.* Later treaties, which included bribes purchasing immunity from barbarian raids, still required the use of these soldiers in Roman's defense. The term *foederati* could also designate bodies of troops drawn indifferently from various foreign peoples. These units were probably the most efficient soldiers of their day and a part of the regular army.[13] But, in the late fourth and early fifth centuries some groups designated *foederati* proved to be instrumental in the destruction of the Western empire. These were the barbarian tribes who wandered across the Roman provinces. They would often seek to profit at the empire's expense through military adventurism but later profess loyalty in order to maintain their privileges.[14]

Surprisingly, the Romans seldom tried to rid themselves of the wandering Germans, since they considered them an indispensable reservoir of troops for enrollment into imperial Roman service.[15]

They constituted the major forces of the barbarian invasions. Reliance on the federated tribes for the defense of the empire was a serious mistake. By the time of Valentinian III, barbarian auxiliaries were used on a large scale in practically every campaign. In Roman eyes, "Such a policy spared the manpower of the Empire, and the barbarians were good fighting material ready to hand, whereas the process of training Roman recruits was slow and painful."[16]

## Cultural and Religious Chauvinism

Contempt for the barbarian was deeply ingrained in the Roman soul.[17] The upper classes were especially plagued with cultural chauvinism. They were quite as patronizingly superior to their less educated countrymen as to the barbarians. This increasing differentiation of the social classes was an outstanding feature of late Roman society. The gap grew with regard to property ownership, political influence, and legal status. There were many legal privileges of rank and title that were highly valued, and they steadily became more florid and bombastic.[18]

The key to the patronage and approval of the upper class was erudition and rhetorical eloquence. This feature of Roman chauvinism would prove to be one of the major barriers to the assimilation of the barbarians, who were not rejected as equals because they were Germans. Race had almost nothing to do with the Roman reluctance to accept the barbarians as equals, but cultural diversity made a great deal of difference to the Romans. As Robert Austin Markus remarks, "Roman aristocratic society may have been snobbish but it was not often racist."[19] Germans could and did enter the charmed circle, provided they were willing to abandon their own culture and conform to the values of the dominant classes of Roman society.

When in the fourth and fifth centuries the Roman cultural aristocracy drifted into Catholicism, Christianity simply became part of their culture. Many could not even imagine a Christianity outside the parameters of Roman culture and society. "The whole traditional development of Christianity, its urban structure and now its classical culture made the notion of a barbarian Christian odd to them."[20]

By the beginning of the fifth century, nothing seemed to qualify a man for episcopal office, in Roman eyes, as much as wealth and social standing. Soon the majority of Western bishops belonged to the wealthy families who were the traditional leaders of Roman society.[21] The major exception, perhaps, was Roman Africa, where some of the "middle class" were becoming bishops. This was due in part to the influence of Augustine and his ascetic community, which served as sort of a seminary for future bishops. It was a notable exception but an exception nonetheless.

Many Christian leaders became part of the old aristocracy and, thus, prisoners of their own status. They seldom recognized the needs of the oppressed peasants and failed to find remedies even when they did. For many of them, the preservation of Roman literary culture would become, during the crisis, the paragon of Roman patriotism.[22] They joined the old pride of the aristocrat with the intolerant Catholicism of the post-Theodosian era.

Their instinctive identification of Roman with Catholic and of Arian with barbarian "reinforced the divisions created by the invasions with religious barriers" and helped to prevent the peaceful assimilation of barbarians into Roman society.[23]

In the final analysis, barbarian loyalty to Arianism circumvented their full Romanization. Although other factors such as race, custom, and language were barriers, "these gaps were easily bridgeable as compared with the gap in belief."[24] Even those barbarians in the regular army of the empire would be unable to overcome the separateness that the religious difference imposed. Religion was the primary barrier to "continuity" between the empire and the later barbarian kingdoms. The Goths, as a separate people, might very soon have ceased to exist had they not also been Arians. Their legal remains demonstrate how their customary way of life became at once, and heavily, influenced by Roman usage. Intermarriage, again, was bound to dilute not only their blood but also their language. For many Goths of the second and succeeding generations, Latin was their mother tongue.[25]

Peter Brown is in agreement with this assessment. He has isolated religious intolerance on the part of orthodox Romans as the primary reason for the failure to assimilate the barbarians. He claims that the only form of continuity between Roman and barbarian of which anyone was conscious in the later empire was a common adherence to Catholic orthodoxy, and that this was denied to some of the most effective Western Mediterranean states by a wall of dumb hatred. Brown also chides Warren C. Hollister for ignoring this fact in his attempt to find "continuity" between the Roman empire and the barbarian kingdoms.[26]

## Fall of the West

While many of the factors discussed above contributed to the empire's failure during the crisis, they did not occasion it. The Eastern government, facing the same problems, persisted for another thousand years. The failure to assimilate the barbarians was instrumental in bringing an end to the ancient world. Most of the reasons usually given for the decline of the Western empire were problems for the Eastern empire as well, though sometimes to a slightly milder degree. A. H. M. Jones, in his massive study of the late empire, has shown that "in most matters no significant distinction can be traced."[27]

The experiences of East and West differed in two respects. The East, with a larger population and a healthier social and economic structure, was better able to withstand the strains imposed upon it by the crisis. More importantly, the West was "more exposed to barbarian onslaughts which in persistence and sheer weight of numbers far exceeded anything which the Empire had previously to face."[28] Although the Persian problem would later become severe for the Eastern empire, in the 240 years between Diocletian and Justinian only 40 were actually spent in a state of war with the Persians, and most of those were filled with truces and negotiations rather than with fighting.[29] The East had less than half the frontier to guard from the barbarians. The straits of the Dardanelles and the defenses of the city of Constantinople provided it with a second bulwark that the West lacked. Jones aptly summarized the West's dilemma:

> It was beyond the resources of the Western empire to contain a simultaneous attack on the Rhine and the upper Danube, and when the front line was breached by such a double assault, as it was in the early fifth century, there was no satisfactory second line of defense.[30]

In fact, the strength of the East in this regard contributed to the problems experienced by the West. Unable to penetrate the defenses of the East and having exhausted the resources of Illyricum, the Visigoths under Alaric and later the Ostrogoths under Theodoric would feel compelled to move west into Italy. All realized that Constantinople was too tough a nut to crack. Even Attila the Hun would grow tired of ravaging the Balkans and march west.

The barbarians were the primary cause for the collapse of the Western government. A. Piganiol summed it up very succinctly:

> Roman Civilization did not die a natural death. It was assassinated.[31]

Each military disaster played its role in a dance of death. One by one, the provinces were ravaged or came under the control of the barbarians.[32] Loss of tax revenue brought greater military weakness and the eventual loss of more provinces. A virtually bankrupt Western government was forced to rely increasingly upon the doubtful loyalty of its barbarian federates. By 444, the treasury was unable to meet necessary expenses.[33]

But this military/economic "assassination" could not have occurred if a loyal Roman populace had vigorously opposed the barbarian incursions. There simply were not enough barbarians to overwhelm them. Although the barbarians played a key role in the complicated demise of the empire, it was not overwhelmed by huge hordes of them working in concert with a unified plan of conquest. These popular myths must be laid aside if any adequate understanding of the barbarians' role in the fifth-century crisis is to be obtained. These migrating tribes were a minority, probably no more than 5 percent of world population, about five hundred thousand out of an estimated world population of one hundred million. Evidence for the population of the largest tribes seems to support this. At their entry into Spain, the mighty Visigoths numbered less than one hundred thousand. When they crossed into Africa, the united Vandals and Alans numbered only some eighty thousand. The Burgundians, one of the larger groups, seem to have numbered about twenty-five thousand, of whom only about five thousand were warriors. In Italy, at the height of their power, there were only about one hundred thousand Ostrogoths in a population of six or seven million. Further evidence of their minority status is the relative insignificance of their ethnic contribution to the areas they "conquered." The Germanic physical type is today scarcely ever found in any regions of the old empire. The survival of Latin languages all over Roman Europe, except in the frontier regions of the old empire where the Germans were relatively concentrated, is further evidence of their minority status.[34] But while they never achieved a majority in any conquered province, their migrations had the effect of destroying the Roman empire in the West.

Roman society alienated the very forces which could have preserved it. The Roman peasantry scattered throughout the empire, and the unassimilated tribesmen within the provincial frontiers of Roman Africa, Hispania, and Britannia, embittered by their treatment at the hands of the empire, proved eager to tolerate or even to join in the destruction of Roman power and influence. The tribesmen, as yet untouched by Christianity, had been a constant danger for centuries. They had been held back from rebellion and plunder mainly by their oaths and by fear of Roman retribution. Once Roman power declined, they were quick to join in ravaging their provinces. The crushing burden which Rome placed on its peasant class had alienated their loyalty. Major peasant revolts often coincided with the extension of Germanic barbarian power, as in the revolts between 415 and 441 in modern Brittany, the Loire Valley, and the Ebro Valley.[35]

## The Role of the Great Military Disasters

Three great military disasters, each following the other by about thirty years, contributed to the demise of Roman power. Each triggered a chain of dire consequences. The first of these was the disaster at Edirne. Fearing subjugation by the ferocious Huns, the Visigoths pleaded for permission to cross into the empire as Roman allies.[36]

With the blessing of the emperor Valens, they made a peaceful crossing of the Danube in A.D. 376. Only seeing the interests of the moment, courtiers had persuaded the emperor that good fortune had brought a vast army of allies from afar and that now some of the tax revenue usually reserved for the upkeep of the army could be diverted to other purposes.[37] But by 378 the Visigoths were in open revolt against the empire. When corrupt officials cheated and abused them, the hot-tempered tribesmen responded by ravaging the countryside. Valens, obligated to take the field against them, hurried to battle without sufficient preparation and without his cavalry. His defeat and death, in a field near modern Adrianople, on 9 August A.D. 378, forever shattered the myth of Roman invincibility. Two-thirds of his army was utterly destroyed. In the words of Henry Melvill Gwatkin, "The everlasting Empire shook from end to end."[38] Adrianople had shown that these pretended auxiliaries themselves constituted a dire threat to the empire.[39]

Theodosius, the highly capable successor of Valens, was barely able to pacify the Visigoths. He could not expel them.[40] At his death in A.D. 395, the empire was split between the guardians and advisors of Theodosius's two incompetent sons. The obligations of empire became pawns in strong men's games of power, position, and influence. As H. Daniel-Rops has commented, "Possibly Renaissance Italy is the only other period containing such singular careers, where men gambled with power and death, triumph and assassination as if in a game of dice."[41]

During this period of calamities, Germans would become the real masters of the empire's affairs. They already filled the elite corps of the army and most of the posts of command. Goths were especially eager to enroll in the Roman army. From this point on, effective military rulers either were barbarians or were reliant on barbarian support.[42]

The second great disaster resulted from a conflict between two romanized Germans. Alaric, an ambitious Visigothic leader, was angered when he failed to receive what he considered proper recognition. He threatened to ravage Italy with his Visigoths. His first assault was defeated by the deft manuevering of Stilicho, a romanized Vandal in command of the Western empire's defenses. When, in 406, Alaric again threatened Italy, Stilicho stripped the Rhine frontier of troops in order to block his advance. As a consequence, barbarians along the Rhine soon enjoyed an overwhelming local superiority.[43]

On the night of 31 December A.D. 406, the Vandals and a number of other tribes swept across the lightly guarded and probably frozen Rhine River near modern Mainz and into Gaul.[44] This marked the turning point in the first century of the Germanic invasions. Accused of treason, probably falsely, Stilicho was executed. But the emperor soon discovered he had no general capable of replacing him. The ravage of Gaul and Spain continued without any effective Roman intervention, and Alaric sacked Rome. Less than thirty-three years after the Rhine crossing, Gaul, Spain, and North Africa had all been lost by the empire.

The death knell of the Western empire would come with the loss of Roman Africa. While Illyria, Gaul, Spain, and Italy had already been ravaged by German depredations, Roman Africa remained prosperous, the sheet anchor of Roman fortunes in the West. As early as A.D. 68, the cutting off of grain from Africa resulted in famine at Rome. By 383 there was utter dependence upon African grain, not only in Rome but also in most of the large cities of northern Italy.[45] With harvests devastated by marauders, possession of the African granaries was essential to the survival of the Western government. Without them there would not be enough grain to bribe *foederati* or to supply military forces.

Again, rivalry and personal ambition played significant roles in a Roman tragedy. Aetius, *magister equitum* (master of cavalry) in Gaul, desired supreme military authority and saw in Boniface a dangerous rival. He persuaded Felix, the *magister militum* (master of soldiers), that there was some doubt about the loyalty of Boniface, *comes Africae et domesticorum* (count of Africa and of the household).[46]

The emperor Constantine had created this new nobility, the *comites,* or counts. The title was bestowed upon those who, like Boniface, were employed in positions of trust and eminence in a military or civil capacity. The word *comes* means "companion." *Comites do-*

*mesticorum* was the title used to designate both the military commanders of the various field armies and the special administrative representatives of the emperor.[47] As count of Africa and commander of the African *comitatus,* Boniface rightfully held the title through two different positions. This is what made the threat of possible treason on his part particularly worrisome to the central authority. Africa was, after all, the last major unravaged imperial possession.

Felix, fearing that Boniface was trying to separate the vital African provinces from the rest of the empire and make them his private domain, urged Galla Placidia, the empress regent, to recall him. Meanwhile, Aetius, feigning friendship for the African *comes,* urged him to resist her summons. Furious at the accusation of treason, Boniface refused to return meekly and face these charges. So, in 427, he was declared an "enemy of the Republic."[48]

Galla Placidia immediately sent an army under the generals Mavortius, Gallionis, and Sanoecis to subdue Boniface. The African *comes* destroyed this force and then sent a message to Gunderic, the Vandal king, begging his help against the imperial forces. Perhaps Boniface had known Gunderic earlier and was basing his estimates of Vandal reaction on this knowledge. This is probable since Boniface had been in Spain in 422. Boniface's wife was very likely an Arian Vandal from Spain and was, quite possibly, a relative of Gunderic.[49]

In 428 a second Roman force, under the romanized Goth Segisvultus, landed in North Africa. Segisvultus, appointed to replace Boniface as *comes Africae,* succeeded in seizing Carthage and possibly Hippo Regius.[50] Meanwhile, the Vandal king Gunderic died and was replaced by the unscrupulous Gaiseric. The new king used Boniface's appeal to the fallen Gunderic as an excuse to invade Africa. It is not unlikely that Boniface was very surprised by Gaiseric's actions.[51]

Only by uniting forces could the Romans hope to save Roman Africa. Placidia sent her agent, Darius, to regain Boniface's allegiance. Darius achieved a reconciliation and concluded a truce with Gaiseric. The truce was, however, of short duration. From May to June 430, Gaiseric was able to enter Numidia, defeat Boniface, and besiege him in Hippo Regius. In July 431 the siege was lifted when new forces arrived from Italy and Constantinople under the command of Aspar, the leading general of the Eastern empire. Aspar and Boniface joined forces, fought a battle, and were defeated by Gaiseric's Vandals. Hippo was soon retaken, along with most of the rest of Africa. Only Carthage and Cirta remained in Roman hands.[52]

Aetius continued to seek the supreme power. By 429 he had gained such prestige from his successes against the Goths and Franks that he was able to extort the highest military command from Placidia. After replacing Felix, Aetius had Felix killed for suspicion of treachery. Galla Placidia lost all trust in her new *magister militum*. At her request, Boniface brought his *comitatus* to Italy in 432. Placidia received him with favor, deposed Aetius, and gave the highest post to Boniface, at the same time conferring on him the status of patrician. Aetius refused to yield, and soon civil war raged in Italy. Boniface defeated Aetius in battle, but was mortally wounded and soon died. Although Sebastian, Boniface's son, succeeded him, Aetius soon returned with a Hunnic force and made Placidia dismiss Sebastian and reappoint himself as the supreme commander. From this time until he was assassinated by Valentinian III and his chief eunuch, Aetius was the real ruler of the Western empire. Aetius, thus, became the unchallenged shaper of Rome's military policies and in 435 made peace with the Vandals by ceding Mauretania and Numidia to them.[53]

Gaiseric, however, never intended the settlement to be final. On 19 October A.D. 439 he took Carthage. This conquest of Roman Africa was a major turning point in the history of the invasions. It was the beginning of the last act.[54] The Vandals formed piratical fleets and cut off sea communications between Italy and the rest of the empire, making it next to impossible to reinforce and supply imperial armies in Gaul and Spain.[55] Sicily was ravaged from 440 to 442. In 442 the Vandals were ceded the Western empire's richest African provinces in return for Mauretania.[56] With the Sicilian granaries ravaged and supplies of grain from Africa cut off, Italy faced perpetual starvation.

The loss of Africa had sealed the empire's fate. The recruiting field for some of the finest horses and horsemen in the imperial army was lost. The losses in revenue to the central government meant that it had little money for the waging of war.

## The Gothic Arian Threat and the Catholic Reaction

Church historians and historical theologians have often ignored the persistence of Arianism into the seventh and eighth centuries. The sect is usually relegated to the status of a footnote. Perhaps it lacks the drama of the conciliar conflicts between A.D. 325 and 381.

When this later Arianism is discussed at all, it is usually portrayed as a bare survival, a mere shadow of its former self.

But Gothic Arianism was a dangerous adversary for Western Catholicism. The Gallic bishop Sidonius Apollinaris ably expressed the typical reaction of Catholic churchmen to the barbarians in this regard: "I must confess that, formidable as the mighty Goth may be, I dread him less as the assailant of our walls than as the subverter of our Christian laws."[57] Rising from the ashes of its defeat at Constantinople and Aquileia, Homoian Arianism in its Ulfilan form, as the religion of barbarian soldiers and conquerors, would seek to reign once again in Ravenna, Carthage, and Toulouse.[58] The Roman army itself was now largely composed of German barbarians and was "the one element in the Roman social order where Arianism had continued to flourish."[59] The barbarians in the army and the federated tribes would become the protectors of a resurgent Arian movement. Just how serious the threat of this Ulfilan Arianism was still perceived to be, even as late as the sixth century, is indicated by the emphasis given to refuting it in the Athanasian Creed. This creed, though it bears the name of the fourth-century Greek father, was written in the West between A.D. 520 and 530. While on the surface the creed opposes both Sabellianism and Arianism, the material dealing with Sabellianism seems to be present only for the sake of completeness. The author's real concern seems to be the Homoian Arianism of Ulfila, the Arianism that found its authoritative expression in the creed of Seleucia-Rimini.[60] As J. N. D. Kelly notes, it was a kind of Arianism to which Catholic congregations would be particularly susceptible since it used Catholic-sounding formulae, acknowledged Christ as Lord and God, offered him worship, and glossed over the issue of consubstantiality with the Father by saying Christ was "like" the Father in all things.[61] He believes "the Athanasian Creed itself was shaped by the reaction to Gothic and Vandal Arianism."[62] Whatever modern writers may think about the inevitability of Catholic orthodoxy's victory, the contemporary church leaders of the Roman West considered Ulfilan Arianism a serious threat.

At the same time orthodoxy was beginning to lose some of its state protection through the collapse of Roman authority, Homoian teachers found protection among barbarians of the same faith.[63] The special status of the barbarian *foederati* made them excellent protectors.[64] Because Roman law concerned only the Romans, the barbarians could remain privileged heretics in the midst of an officially orthodox empire. Even the most intolerant of Byzantine sovereigns never disdained the services of stout misbelievers like Aligern or

Harold Hardrada. Justinian, for example, never ventured to meddle with the beliefs of his Gothic soldiers.[65]

The barbarians also served throughout the regular military establishment of the empire and were thus able to preserve their dogmas and religious practices, not only in the military camps and in the provinces but also in the palace itself. However great Roman police surveillance may have been, it was very difficult to put a stop to the Roman practice of Arianism when the barbarians were free to practice the same cult. It would have been very perilous to wrest other Arians away from the protection of these rude coreligionists and dangerous, in the extreme, to demand that the edicts of the prince be obeyed in the presence of a force of *foederati*. Therefore, because of increasing government pressure against Romans who professed Arianism, contacts between Roman and Gothic Arians became continually more frequent and intimate. Although the Arians would never have another Constans or Valens backing them with the power of the central government, they could count on barbarian help and could thus flaunt some of the imperial laws.

The Roman Arians, however, requested too much of their new protectors. They expected either the elevation of an Arian to imperial dignity, the repeal of all laws persecuting their sect, prevention of the enforcement of anti-Arian laws, or all three. But as Revillout noted, their protectors lacked the patience to vanquish systematically these difficulties, and they constantly contradicted their own efforts in this regard for the sake of gain or ambition.[66]

Wherever the Goths went, however, they made strenuous efforts to convert local populations to Arian views.[67] They became militant bearers of their creed among the other Germanic peoples.[68] The Goths preached their gospel with great ability, especially on the village level.[69] Gothic Arianism spread among the barbarians with astonishing rapidity. The Visigoths were responsible for the conversion of the Ostrogoths, Gepids, Vandals, Alans, Rugii, Heruli, and Sciri, and, temporarily, the Burgundians, Spanish Suevi, and Lombards.[70] Aside from the Franks and Anglo-Saxons, who both remained pagan, initially all the barbarian peoples who entered the empire during the fifth century were Arians, right down to the latecomers.[71]

As the importance of barbarian forces grew, so did Arian boldness. Many natives feared that the barbarians would attempt to enforce their Arianism on a Catholic population. In the midst of that fear, some of the Catholic clergy fled their posts and some even defected to Arianism.[72] Perhaps they saw it as a path to influence over dangerous military forces.

With the orthodox population temporarily demoralized, the Arians, at first, did have some success among the Catholic laity. During this period of upheaval, the Arians grew bold enough to attack the orthodox practitioners in oratory, even mocking their processions on the streets. As mentioned above, some even began to call openly for the repeal of the imperial laws that proscribed their faith.[73] In general, however, Visigothic missions had very little success in converting Romans directly from Catholicism. The Arians, therefore, began to develop methods to take over the Catholic organization in an area. Their idea seems to have been that control of the Catholics' organizational structure would lead to massive Roman conversions in the long term.

The direct method, used most consistently by the Vandals, included the seizing of church buildings and the proscription of orthodox clergy. It was usually accompanied by violence and the refusal to allow Catholics to build churches. Sidonius Apollinaris has left a harrowing picture of the position of the Catholic communities in Visigothic Gaul at this time. Their church buildings were falling into disrepair and their clergy had been beheaded.[74] This method of repression was resented by the Catholic laity and left Arian clergy isolated and hated.

The indirect method was the attempted substitution of Arian for Catholic bishops, by guile and outward legality. This was usually done by either corrupting or intimidating episcopal elections. Sometimes an Arian hid in the midst of an orthodox clergy (a sort of religious fifth column) in order to arrive more surely at an episcopate. Others sought to convert prelates by fair or foul means from Nicene to Arian faith. This was the most successful means of converting Catholics to the Arian faith, for once the people had accepted an Arian bishop, it was an easy matter to draw them into the heresy. Only after their kingdoms were established and pacified did the Goths and other Arian peoples abandon missionary efforts among the Romans.[75]

Catholics soon fought back with what weapons were at their disposal. Most of their efforts were aimed at maintaining the loyalty of their own congregations. Education was the key feature of their program. They produced a number of anti-Arian works. Most were merely simplifications of what the great Eastern Fathers had already written. Catholic leaders also sought to confound their adversaries in public. They would invite an Arian to a solemn conference, which would quickly turn into a debate with the most eloquent of the orthodox bishops. A record of the conference would then be published for the instruction of others. Augustine's debate with Maximinus is one example of this methodology at work. Since these methods sometimes proved too intellectualy elevated for their people, the bishops often tailored their appeals to the simplest members of their congregations. As time went on, they used sermons and hymns as their chief means of indoctrinating the laity against Arianism. Even this proved inadequate. Orthodox laymen, it seems, were so gullible that once they accepted the credentials of a heretical bishop, they could easily be led by him into Arianism.[76]

The most successful tactic seems to have been the prevention of any contact with Arians. When Arianism appeared in a neighboring bishopric, the orthodox bishops noted the "treachery" and would quickly name a new pastor to replace the heretic. Clergy grew so suspicious that anyone who voluntarily contacted a barbarian was automatically suspect. Priests were sometimes excommunicated for even dining with Arians.[77] Those who married a suspected Arian or allowed their children to be baptized as Arians were also often condemned.[78] One bishop, Fulgentius of Ruspe, warned his people:

> Never enter their churches to pray. They are not churches of God but caves of robbers, a shop for souls, and the entrance of Hell. Therefore all sons of God who want to be his heirs should pray to their Father within the bosom of their Mother and not go to this stepmother, who seeks to kill them all.[79]

Another weapon in the Catholic arsenal was the effective use of propaganda. It was the first of their weapons to have noticeable success among the Arians themselves. The courage of those Africans who were martyred by the Vandals made particularly effective evidence for the Catholic faith's validity. Coupled with the comparatively recent development of the cult of saint worship and the veneration of relics, it was specially geared to appeal to barbarian sensibilities.[80]

Eventually the Catholic program would achieve a total victory, but early in the fifth century this was not yet apparent. The Catholics would spend a number of anxious years insuring the victory of orthodoxy in the West.

# 2

# THE RISE OF ULFILAN ARIANISM

## Introduction

It is a serious mistake to speak of Arianism as if it were a unified cult under a single leader. The divisions within Arianism were real, though sometimes doctrinally shallow. Some Arians were as ready to condemn one another as they were the orthodox.

During most of Augustine's life, his knowledge of Arianism was academic, gleaned from orthodox refutations of the heresy. Only near the end of his life did he face a direct Arian challenge. The Arianism he faced was very different from that written of in the refutations. He would encounter neither the classical Arianism of Arius and Eusebius of Nicomedia nor the hard-driving rationalism of Aetius and Eunomius. The Arianism that Augustine faced was the Homoian Arianism of the Ulfilans.

The course of Arianism's history in the Eastern empire is relatively well known. A number of excellent studies are available. Some attention, however, must be given to the Homoian Arianism of Illyricum, since this was the variety of Arianism from which sprang the Ulfilan Arianism that most influenced the Germanic barbarians.

## Historical Background

*Homoian Arianism*

Arianism first came to the borders of Gothia during the exiles of Arius and Eusebius of Nicomedia to the Danubian regions of Illyricum. Their presence soon resulted in the almost wholesale adhesion of the regions' bishops of Arian views.[1]

Two students of Arius, the bishops Ursacius of Singidunum and Valens of Mursa, soon took an active role in the Arian controversy. They brought charges against Athanasius in the Council of Tyre in

A.D. 335, charges that Valens later retracted as false before Pope Julius in A.D. 347. Joined by their fellow Arian Germinius of Sirmium, Valens and Ursacius also became the chief theological advisers of the emperor Constantius. When Constantius, who had ruled the Eastern provinces and the Danubian region since 337, became sole emperor in 350, his advisers urged him to force on the West the results of the Council of Tyre, in which Athanasius had been condemned. At councils in Arles (353) and Milan (355), the emperor's Illyrian counselors achieved their goal by threatening the Western bishops with exile.

In 356 the Danubian Arians, led by the emperor's advisers, met in a council at Sirmium. Also present were Mark of Arethusa and George of Alexandria (Arian usurper of Athanasius's seat in Alexandria). A doctrinal statement issued by the council, the so-called Blasphemy of Sirmium, forbade all mention of the term *substance,* especially the phrases *homoousios* and *homoiousios* because of their extrabiblical character, in Trinitarian speculation and emphasized the subordination of the Son to the Father.[2] The council claimed that the use of such technical terms caused confusion and division, not clarification. Their position was soon endorsed, under compulsion, by the aged Ossius of Cordova, Constantine's advisor at Nicaea. It would develop into the Homoian "orthodoxy" of Seleucia and Rimini.[3]

There are those who argue with the reconstruction of events given above. Although his study of Western Arianism is excellent in many regards, Michel Meslin contends that the primary purpose of this first generation (Valens of Mursa, Ursacius of Singidunum, and Germinius of Sermium) was the resolution of religious turmoil, and that they showed no real interest in providing a theological solution to the Trinitarian problem. He admits, however, that in this period it is often difficult to distinguish doctrinal activity from ecclesiastical politics.[4] Meslin thinks that only in the last part of the fourth century did the Homoians of Illyricum actually begin to become Arians (Palladaius, Secundianus, Maximinus, and so on).[5] His conlusions fly in the face of the opinions of their contemporaries, Hilary of Poitiers in the West and Athanasius of Alexandria in the East. The two aspects, ecclesiastical politics and Trinitarian theology, were inextricably bound. Meslin, as J. D. Burkhard notes, "underestimates their consciousness of the theological questions in play and the creeds which had been proposed."[6] The second creed of Sirmium in 351 was either composed by or had the approval of Valens and Ursacius, and it "reveals a subordinationist doctrine that is but a very little distinguished from classical Arianism."[7] If one compares anathemas

18 and 26 (according to the enumeration of Athanasius) with the preceding formulas, their pronounced subordinationism is unavoidably evident. Meslin's off-hand conclusion that they held a "conservative orthodoxy" is far too magnanimous.[8]

Constantius summoned the bishops of the East and West to two councils in A.D. 359: one at Seleucia for the Eastern bishops, the other at Ariminium (Rimini) for the Western bishops. The Danubian Arians had convinced the emperor that only by excluding questions of substantial relations between the Father and the Son could a document ever be written to which all parties could subscribe.[9]

The theological parties at this time were finally relatively easy to distinguish. The Homoians were those who rejected use of the term *substance (ousios)*, yet agreed that the Son was "like" the Father. The Homoiousians were those who still wanted to use the term *substance* but shrank from the complete identity of Father and Son implied in the term *homoousios*. The Neo-Arians, sometimes called Anhomoians, rejected any likeness between Father and Son except a likeness of will. The Homoousians wanted the reinstatement of the decisions at Nicaea in 325. They insisted that the Father and the Son are "of the same substance."

The chief forces at Seleucia, besides the Homoians, were the homoiousians and the Neo-Arians, while the Danubian Homoians faced a very strong Homoousian force at Rimini. At both councils the Homoians fought an uphill battle. At Seleucia, debate almost degenerated into a shouting match between the various factions. At Rimini, the Homoousian majority strongly resisted the Homoianism being imposed on them. Only by the skillful use of political coercion and deceit were the Homoians able to win acceptance for a revised form of their creed. This revision excluded the phrase "in all things" with respect to the Son's likeness to the Father. Thus, the crucial phrase of the 10 October creed was the formula that the Son is "like the Father who generated him according to the Scriptures." Because of the great variations in opinions and large numbers of bishops attending, Rimini's formulations and definitions were forced to be vague. The formula drawn up by the council of Rimini in 359 also rejected use of the terms *ousia* and *hypostasis* as unscriptural. The council also insisted that the term *homoios* (like) be used in any discussion of the relationship between the Father and Son.[10]

In January 360 there was yet another council, this time in Constantinople. Seventy-two bishops, mainly from the East but including a few Western Homoians, such as Valens, Ursacius, and Ulfila—the national bishop of a Gothic colony in Illyricum—ratified the Homoian formulas of the previous year and pronounced all other formulas—future or past—null and void. In order to rid the church of further controversy surrounding the terms *essence* and *hypostasis* (which were crucial to the theology of the Homoousians, Homoiousians, and Heteroousians or Neo-Arians), it was declared that they were never again to be used in discussion about God.[11] One outcome of these events was the transformation of Neo-Arianism from an ecclesiastical party to an independent sect. The moderated Arianism of the Homoians had prevailed.[12]

On the way to Constantinople from Antioch on 3 November A.D. 361 Constantius died. After a brief period of uncertainty under the emperors Julian the Apostate and Jovian, by 363–64 Valentinian I, in the West, and Valens, in the East, succeeded to the imperial throne.

The West was already moving toward total rejection of the results of Rimini. Soon, outside of Illyricum, the only Western bishopric that remained in Arian hands was Milan. The emperor Valentinian (364–75), who affected a position of neutrality in these matters, protected its status.[13] At the Council of Milan in 355, the city had received as its bishop an Arian named Auxentius. Despite the efforts of the Catholics (he was condemned at Rimini in 359, Paris in 360, and, along with Valens of Mursa and Ursacius of Singidunum, at Rome in 372), this prominent supporter of Arianism would retain his see until his death in either late 373 or early 374.

Orthodoxy made advances even in the Danubian provinces all through the 360s and the 370s. Athanasius confidently assured Jovian in 363 and the African bishops in 369 that the true faith was professed in the Danubian provinces and in Greece, among other areas. The "old guard" was passing off the scene. The last document referring to Valens of Mursa and Ursacius as living persons dates from 371. It is not known who succeeded Valens, but Ursacius was succeeded as bishop of Singidunum by one of his priests named Secundianus, who would later be one of those condemned at the council of Aquileia. Even so, the area remained a hotbed of Arianism.[14] Germinius of Sirmium, for example, in 366, published and defended a clearly subordinationist Christology, which recalls the position professed in 357, at the most extreme point in his evolution of theses properly Arian.[15]

At the death of Auxentius of Milan near the end of 374, the Nicenes and the Arians each sought to elect one of their own as bishop. With violent conflict imminent, a government official named Ambrose was sent to keep the peace. In a surprising move, he was chosen by both sides as bishop. He soon became the uncompromising champion of Nicene orthodoxy in the West.[16]

Ambrose took over a church that had been led by an Arian bishop for nineteen years, a church in which a significant number of the clergy and laity were Arian. His neutrality, as a representative of Valentinian, is probably what made his unanimous choice possible. As a thoroughly Nicene bishop, he soon faced a difficult task of house cleaning. Ambrose assaulted Arianism's Illyrian strongholds. In spite of strong opposition, he forced the installment of a Nicene bishop in Sirmium. Although he had no real authority for such intervention, he knew well the Danubian political and religious terrain. The new bishop of Milan had resided many years at Sirmium before being named governor of a province. Therefore, on the eve of the death of the emperor Valens, Ambrose stood ready to assault the last bastions of Roman Arianism in Illyricum. Ambrose's actions in Sirmium, an Arian stronghold, may have coincided with a regional council in Ilyricum, in which six Arian bishops were deposed. This council of Sirmium did not mark the end of Arian influence in Illyricum. In spite of the sentences of deposition pronounced on this occasion, it yet restored some Arian bishops to their seats, notably Palladius of Ratiara and Secundianus of Singidunum.[17] Michel Meslin doubts the existence of this council,[18] but to do so and remain consistent is to doubt also all the Arian councils of the 350s, including that of Tyre, where Athanasius was deposed, since the evidence for all these councils is fundamentally equal.

Valens, a simple Pannonian soldier of peasant stock, had strongly favored a moderate Homoian Arianism. Baffled by the confused state of the Eastern churches, he was only too willing to follow the advice of Eudoxius, the Homoian bishop of Constantinople.[19]

Though he seems to have preferred a rather strict Arianism, Valens had reason to favor the Homoians over the Neo-Arians. The Neo-Arians backed their friend Procopius in his revolt against Valens. They were confident of the pretender's patronage. Had the rebellion succeeded, Neo-Arian history would have turned out rather differently. In A.D. 367 Eunomius was exiled and his estate confiscated when Valens learned that he had sheltered the rebellious Procopius.[20] Only by the intercession of Valens of Mursa, who evidently felt that the Neo-Arian position was not wholly incompatible with the Homoian settlement, was the Neo-Arian Eunomius restored to the empire. He was, however, refused a court audience. In 370 he was again sent into exile.[21] His efforts to arianize Cappadocia had evidently drawn the ire of Basil of Caesarea, whose patron was the praetorian prefect Modestus. While still in exile, probably in 378 or thereabouts, Eunomius published his answer to the *Contra Eunomium* by Basil of Caesarea. He entitled it *Apologia Apologiae*. The first two books were written in 378. A third came out sometime between 380 and 382. Thomas A. Kopecek believes that a fourth and a fifth book came out sometime after that. Only fragments of the first three are extant (quoted in Gregory of Nyssa's *Contra Eunomium*).[22] As previously noted, Augustine responds to some of Eunomius's arguments in the *De Trinitate* and, therefore, was likely a reader of the works against him by the Cappadocians.

## The Rise of Ulfilan Arianism

Although Christianity had already penetrated Gothia, two men played very important roles in both the entry of the Visigoths into the empire and their conversion to Homoian Arianism. They were the emperor Valens and Ulfila, the famous apostle to the Goths.

Christianity was probably first introduced to the Goths by those in subjection to them. The first efforts at their conversion may have been made by Cappadocian war prisoners gathered in their third-century raids or, perhaps, by Roman merchant adventurers or even volunteer missionaries. Whichever it was, their first Gothic adherents appear to have been in the lower classes of Gothic society. By 325 Catholic Christianity, at least, had a church functioning there. Theophilus, bishop of Gothia, was among those who signed the acts of the Council of Nicaea. (Gothia is the name often used by ancient authors for the regions controlled by the Goths, especially that territory which they controlled before their entry into the empire.) Perhaps this early adherence to Nicaea by a Gothic bishop accounts for the belief, widespread among fourth- and fifth-century churchmen, that the Goths at first professed the orthodox faith and were only later deceived into accepting the Arian heresy.[23] This was also perhaps the reason for Orosius's false confidence that the Visigoths would soon abandon Arianism for the Catholic faith.[24]

Also important to the earliest spread of Christianity among the Goths is the treaty which Constantine forced on them in about 332. The treaty favored contacts with Christianity and coincided with a great sweep of the Christian faith through the Romano-Dacian population of Gothia's border regions.[25]

By 369 there were at least three different Christian minorities among the Goths. They included a few orthodox Christians, the followers of a banished schismatic named Audaeus, and the Arians.

Audaeus, originally from Syria, was an arrogant and rigorous censor of the vices and luxury of the clergy. He emphasized asceticism and taught that God had material being, since the man formed in his image is composed of both body and soul. Among the barbarians, Audaeus founded a very strict monastic order. His followers were much noted for their austerity and personal piety. In doctrine they were far closer to the Catholics than to the Arians. This group did not survive the persecution of 369–72.[26]

There is, unfortunately, no means of knowing which of the three groups (Catholic, Audaean, or Arian) had won the greatest following in Gothia before the second wave of persecutions, which erupted in about 369. While Christians were probably a minority, their numbers were growing and all their communities vital. The Arians, however, constituted the most important group for the future of Gothic Christianity, since they alone survived the holocaust with their organizational structure intact. Ulfila's early service as a lector and his ordination as bishop presupposes a thriving, if small, Christian community. Certainly this included Christian captives and their families, but it probably also included some of their Gothic overlords. It was not ancient church practice to ordain a bishop for missionary work among pagans, but rather for care of new converts in an already established church.[27]

Many scholars have failed to take note of what this writer refers to as "the Illyrian connection." This is unfortunate, since its recognition goes far in accounting for the rise of Gothic Arianism. The Roman diocese of Illyricum, as noted above, was one of Arianism's greatest strongholds. From its borderlands came the Danubians, who, along with the followers of Acacius, forced the Homoian settlement on a reluctant church. As leaders of the Homoian party and court clerics, the Illyrians wielded great power and influence on the course of the empire's religious history. Considering their proximity to Gothia, it would have been remarkable indeed if the Goths had converted to the Nicene faith upon their entrance into the empire.

One man more than any other would come to symbolize Gothic Arianism. He was largely responsible for shaping the mass movement of the Visgoths into Arianism. His name was Ulfila.[28] The more one studies Ulfila and the brand of Homoian Arianism he promoted, the less likely one is to simply identify it as "Gothic." Some of his later students, such as Auxentius, bishop of Durostorum, were not Visigoths at all, but Romans. Because of the political realities of late Roman society, however, many of them became the religious leaders of Visigothic congregations. This coupled with the fact that Ulfila's brand of Arianism became the faith of most of the invading Germans led to the identification of Ulfilan Arianism with the Goths.[29]

Ulfila was born in about 311. His mother's parents were Cappadocians, and his father was probably a Goth. Raised in a Christian home, the young Ulfila entered the clergy and became a lector (reader). This function testifies to a knowledge of languages that his probable family origins affected, since the Scriptures had not yet been translated into the Gothic language.[30] Soon the young man began to translate the Bible from Greek into the Gothic language.

In this early, and possibly orthodox, phase, he seemed to have little interest in dogmatic theology. But, from the very beginning, he preferred to reduce the major doctrines of Christianity to simple formulas for the sake of his converts.[31]

In the second month of 341, at about thirty years of age, Ulfila was ordained the first Arian bishop of Gothia. He was consecrated by Eusebius of Nicomedia.[32] Ulfila had come to the imperial court in the company of a Gothic embassy, perhaps as a translator.[33] The adoption of a basically Arian theological stance must have begun some time before, possibly through Illyrian influence. Some scholars, like Henry Melvill Gwatkin, claim that Ulfila was "only accidentally an Arian."[34] Charles Christopher Mierow, the translator of Jordanes's *Gothic History,* holds this view. He stipulates that "Ulfilas was an Arian because while his theological ideas were being formed, Arianism of one kind or another—for there were many varieties— was orthodoxy at Constantinople, and Athanasius was denounced there as a dangerous heretic."[35]

The young bishop returned to his efforts in Gothia until, in about the seventh year, disaster struck. The first great persecution in Gothia ravaged the churches. There were quite a few martyrs. The Catholics suffered greatly from this wave of persecution. It is commonly believed that in one incident some twenty-six of them were burned in their church building.[36]

Ulfila felt constrained to lead a great number of his people into Roman territory. He was received with honor by Constantius, who permitted the exiles to establish themselves at the foot of Mount Haemus, near Nicopolis, in Moesia Inferior. It was in this colony that Ulfila was to spend the remaining thirty-three years of his episcopate.[37] For this feat Constantius called Ulfila "the Moses of our time" (Aux. Scol. 37).[38] And although Ulfila seems never to have returned to Gothia, he remained the official representative of Gothic Christianity to the empire.

Ulfila may have taken part in a number of councils, but his presence is only attested at the Council of Constantinople in A.D. 360.[39] It was there that the famous "apostle to the Goths" subscribed to the formulas of Rimini.[40]

Between the two great persecutions of the Goths, Ulfila exerted great influence on the second generation of Homoian Arian bishops. His creed and his life became the exemplars of orthodoxy for the Danubian authors of the *Scolia Arriana* in *Concilium Aquileiense.* He was held up as a role model and an authoritative figure by Auxentius (Scol. 35–41). Maximinus, when pressed in debate, resorted to quoting his creed found in the *Scolia* (Coll.. 4).[41] Analysis of his creed and the theologies of the various authors of the *Scolia* reveals almost no variance in thought. The homogeneity of thought found in these authors—Ulfila, Auxentius of Durostorum, Palladius of Ratiara, and Maximinus—can be traced to their participation in the same theological school, that of Ulfila.[42]

The second great persecution began in A.D. 369, when the Goths suddenly found themselves at war with Rome. The pagan chiefs of the Goths feared that the small Christian community of Gothia would aid the Romans.[43] Their solution to this potential problem was the destruction of the Christian minority. When persecution erupted, Ulfila's church in Nicopolis acted as a support group for further refugees.[44] The organizational structures and leadership of the Catholics and the Audaeans were shattered by almost three years of intense persecution, but the headquarters for Gothic Arianism was safe at the foot of Mount Haemus in Moesia.

From 369 to the late 370s, there was little contact between Ulfila's group and Gothia. But when the Visigothic leaders began to realize that their only hope of escaping Hunnic domination was immigration into the empire, lines of communication were reopened. Gryson believes that this renewal of contact in the late 370s helps to explain why the immigrants became Arians in an epoch when the empire was moving toward a thoroughgoing Nicene stance.[45]

The Visigothic leaders quickly placed the influential Ulfila at the head of their deputation to the emperor. As the deputation proceeded toward Antioch, where Valens held court, they were daily assailed with strong Arian solicitations. Ulfila had already given his own assent to the Council of Rimini, and he pledged the Gothic *foederati* to the same, yet the Roman Arians insisted that only a second, and more formal, consent to the symbol of Rimini would allow the Goths access to the emperor. After their arrival in Syria, the emperor himself seemed to attach great political importance to a formal conversion of the Visigoths to Homoian Arianism. He seemed convinced that nothing else could insure their loyalty and fidelity. Promises, flatteries, and presents, along with the reasoned arguments of Arian theologians, were used to persuade Ulfila's delegation. The bishop himself sought to convince them to accept the emperor's faith. When the delegation expressed doubts, he assured them that the controversies over Arianism were no more than quarrels over words.[46] The account of these events has been altered slightly from the picture painted by the orthodox historians Sozomen and Theodoret. This writer believes that the Gothic bishop had a real loyalty to the decisions at Rimini. Without this presupposition much of the reconstruction of events would be incomprehensible. The assumption of Ulfila's genuine faithfulness to Rimini is strongly supported by the testimony of Auxentius, his student (Scol. 34–41).

Perhaps if the Goths had felt less pressed, they could have received more favorable terms from the emperor without a change of religion. Little did they realize that the Romans were no less eager to welcome them into Moesia than they were to obtain those dwellings. But they did not know the secret desires of the emperor and so leapt to the bosom of Arian faith. The emperor then appointed priests to aid Ulfila in the conversion and indoctrination of the Visigothic nation.[47]

The Goths soon accepted the spiritual leadership of Ulfila. His Homoian form of Arianism would eventually become an expression of their national identity. Later, under Ataulf, the Goths were often referred to as "Ulfilan Arianists."[48] This Gothic Arianism would preserve Homoian beliefs virtually unchanged through the fifth and sixth centuries,[49] which may explain why some of the later Gothic theologians often seem to lack originality. This particular variety of the sect would eventually become the form of Christianity accepted not only by the Goths but also by the Vandals, Burgundians, Suevi, and other barbarian tribes.[50]

### Theodosius

The defeat of Valens by the Goths at Edirne was as much a tragedy for Roman Arianism as for Roman military prestige; for both it marked the beginning of the end.

When Valens died in January A.D. 379, Gratian, the Western emperor, placed on the Eastern throne a Spanish-born general named Theodosius.[51] By 10 January A.D. 381, Theodosius had issued a law which forbade "the heretics" from using the churches and denied them the right of assembly in the towns. His edict spoke specifically of "the Photinian pestilence, the poison of the Arian sacrilege, and the crime of the Eunomian perfidy."[52]

By May 381 the Nicenes and Neo-Nicenes (Homoiousians who had decided that they could live with the term *homoousios* after all) met in a council in Constantinople. They officially sanctioned the Nicene Creed of 325 and explicitly anathematized Neo-Arianism and Homoianism.[53] Responding to the council's request that its decisions be given the force of law, Theodosius issued a proclamation on 19 July A.D. 381 which effectively forbade all Homoian and Neo-Arian meetings.[54]

However, attempts to implement the new anti-heresy laws caused such an uproar that, by the summer of 383, Theodosius invited all the sects to a general conference in Constantinople. Theodosius had decided to try free debate.[55] He naïvely assumed that the Christian bishops and theologians, as men of good will, would quickly establish doctrinal unity and achieve peace in the church. But the Nicene bishop of Constantinople, Nectarius, was terrified at the prospect of debate. This theological neophyte suggested that dialectics be avoided. Instead, the leader of each group should try to prove his theological case by appeals to the Ante-Nicene Fathers.

Nectarius's plan resulted in a babel of confusion. Even within each party, no one could agree on how to apply the ancient truth to the contemporary problem. The distressed Theodosius canceled the discussions. He demanded a written statement of basic tenets from each of the parties. After reviewing their statements, he decided to approve only the Nicene statement. He condemned the others and the parties that had proposed them.[56] Then, with a new edict, he completely outlawed Arianism.[57]

### The Council of Aquileia

The Council of Aquileia was a major turning point in the history of Western Arianism. It witnessed the end of a Western Homoianism free of barbarian protection and patronage.

When in July 379 Gratian returned to Milan from establishing Theodosius as the Eastern emperor, he granted audiences to Ambrose for the sake of theological discussions. These meetings resulted in a law, signed on 3 August, that expressly prohibited as heretical every form of worship found outside the Catholic Church. Ambrose was quickly propelled into a fierce literary duel with Palladius, bishop of Ratiara.[58]

Aquileia was originally intended as a general council, with the purpose of settling some geographic and administrative problems caused by Illyricum being split between the Western and Eastern governments, though it still functioned as an ecclesiastical unit. Aquileia, an Italian town on the Adriatic shore, was chosen as the site for the meeting. But the Nicene party, both East and West, sensed the potential danger of a general council and exercised its political influence to avoid it. Ambrose, wanting not a council but a heresy trial, persuaded Gratian to cancel the instructions given previously and dissuade other bishops from journeying to Aquileia. This made the synod at Aquileia a meeting largely confined to bishops of northern Italy, with no invitations issued to those in other regions.[59]

Assured by Gratian that Eastern bishops would be present, Palladius and his friend Secundianus, the bishop of Singidunum, traveled to Aquileia. At first the Arians of Illyria were quite pleased with the proposal, for they counted on support for their side from many with similar views in the East. Many there favored the formulas of Rimini and Seleucia (formulas deemed most satisfactory specifically because of their lack of theological precision in expressing the union).[60] Palladius sought a large Eastern representation because he hoped for their aid. In the East, the Arians had held first rank all during the reign of the emperor Valens. Palladius probably thought that in spite of the changes going on at the top of the empire, he could still find a number of partisans there. He soon discovered that he had been deceived.[61]

The council convened in September 381. The only persons who attended were twelve bishops from northern Italy, five from southern Gaul, two deputies from Africa, and four strongly Nicene bishops from Illyria. The more wary Arians had stayed away, but Palladius felt himself honor-bound to participate.[62] Before he quite knew what had happened, he found himself in the role of defendant.[63]

Palladius, already an old man, had been a priest for eleven years and a bishop for thirty-five. He had ascended to the seat of Ratiara in 346 and had been ordained in 335. He was probably born in the early fourth century. Little is known of his activities prior to his controversy with Ambrose.[64]

At matins on 3 September 381, a meeting was scheduled that Palladius seemed to believe was a private, unofficial conference. It gathered in a little hall annexed to the basilica. There were only about ten people present. Among them were the Homoians Palladius of Ratiaria, Secundianus of Singidunum, and the priest Attalus of Poetovio.[65] The bishop who presided sat alone on an elevated dais. At his side, a separate chair was reserved for Ambrose.[66] The seating itself should have made it evident to Palladius that this was not to be a free discussion between equals but a legal investigation. The account of the meeting, given below, is based primarily on the Arian *Scolia* to the acts of the Council of Aquileia.

Ambrose tried to force Palladius to give his opinion of a letter from Arius to Alexander of Alexandria. Palladius replied that he had not come to examine documents or to judge the faith of the dead. He said his purpose in coming had been to exchange ideas on theses of the faith. He demanded that the laity be permitted to follow the debate.

Ambrose refused by declaring that the laity ought not to be established as judges of bishops. Palladius countered that if bishops were ordained on the testimony of the laity, then there was no reason why they should not assure, by their attendance, that the bishops remain faithful to the rule of faith.

Ambrose then drew attention back to the letter and asked if the word *creature,* which was employed in the text, was appropriate to the Son of God. Palladius responded that it was never applied that directly in the Scriptures. Ambrose demanded that the two Arian bishops sign a formal condemnation of the letter of Arius. Palladius refused.

Ambrose brought out the previously hidden stenographic clerks *(notarii),* and the trial started. He began a systematic interrogation of Palladius on the thesis of Arius's letter. He demanded that Palladius state clearly whether he believed that the Son of God is or is not eternal. Palladius refused to respond to the demand, noted the absence of the Eastern bishops, and accused his accusers of preventing, by their maneuvers, such a council as the emperor had called. He protested that it was not up to him to prove anything, and that they did not have the authority to examine him.

Ambrose ignored the Arian's protests. He countered that failure to condemn the doctrine of Arius proved Palladius's heresy. The bishop of Milan, without further delay, pronounced an anathema on those who deny the eternity of the Son.

Palladius, realizing that his judges were intent on carrying the trial to its end, began to defend his faith. He refused to apply the terms *true, good,* or *powerful* to the Son in the same sense as to the Father. On each point, after a brief verbal duel, Palladius's subordinationist faith earned him an anathema.

Palladius rose abruptly and attempted to leave the hall. He was physically restrained. Palladius denounced the intrigues of the council, questioned the integrity of the stenographers, and again demanded the presence of lay auditors.

Ambrose then turned to the Arian priest Attalus and the bishop

Secundianus. If he expected to find less resistance, he was quickly disappointed. Attalus also questioned the council's authority.

Finally Ambrose decided to conclude. He pronounced his sentences and invited his colleagues to do the same. Palladius and his companions were declared to be demoted from the priesthood, and Catholic successors were named for them. The council then wrote to the Eastern and the Western emperors, informed them of the sentence which had been pronounced, and asked for an assurance of their execution.

They also denounced a particularly dangerous Illyrian bishop, Julianus Valens. Valens had been driven from his church at Pettau on a charge of high treason. He not only fraternized with the Goths, but now, with Milan itself as his base, he was carrying on Arian propaganda in Italy and consecrating like-minded persons as bishops, contrary to the law.[67]

With the emperor's assent, Syagrius, the *praefectus praetorio,* took energetic measures against the condemned Arians Palladius and Secundianus.[68] The angry Palladius responded by publishing a protest. He attacked Ambrose and demanded a public debate. It was to be conducted for forty days in the Roman senate in the presence of Christian biblical scholars, pagans, and Jews. Ambrose ignored Palladius's demands. The two Illyrians also tried to use the influence of their patron, the Gothic bishop Ulfila, to gain an audience with Theodosius in Constantinople. But Ulfila died shortly after reaching the capital, and their appeals fell on ears of stone.[69]

A young Arian bishop named Maximinus wrote an angry polemic, but he could only rage; he could not alter the results.[70] From this point on, the only active Arians who could preserve their liberty did so with the protection of Gothic arms. Illyrian and Gothic Arianism would soon be forced to merge.

With Gothic help, on 23 January A.D. 386, the Arians at the Western court were able to get a law passed that was very favorable to their faith. Valentinian II (375–92), influenced by his mother, Justina, and the Arian bishop Mercurinus Auxentius (elected in 384), allowed the right of assembly to all Christians who subscribed to the Homoian doctrine established at the Council of Ariminium in 359 and the Council of Constantinople in 360.[71]

But when Theodosius became the emperor of the West in 392, he fought to insure Homoianism's absolute illegality there as well. By the time of his death in 395, Roman Homoianism had been reduced to a state of marginal survival by the councils of Aquileia and Constantinople. Other forms of Roman Arianism were well on the way to becoming historical curiosities.[72] Soon Roman Arianism would end. But Ulfila's brand of Homoianism would continue to retain its hold on the Goths and Teutons.[73]

# The Theology of Ulfilan Arianism

*Introduction*

The Ulfilans were less concerned with metaphysical speculation than the Neo-Arians, or even the early followers of Arius. They tended to derive their views directly from subordinationist scriptural texts instead of from logic.[74]

They considered themselves theological moderates, holding the biblical middle ground between unreasonable extremes. They recoiled in horror from the Neo-Arian insistence that the Son was "unlike" God, but rather like a Father who is merely the expressed will of God.[75] They insisted on a divine but subordinate Son who was like the Father, yet refused the Homoiousians' "in all respects." To their minds, the Catholic orthodoxy of Ambrose and Augustine had plunged itself hopelessly into a new Sabellianism in which all distinction between Father, Son, and Spirit was lost.

They feared that human speculation had almost shipwrecked the faith and therefore desired to forbid extrabiblical words from official creeds. They felt that all that was needed was a simple affirmation of the Son's similarity to the Father "according to the Scriptures."

Like the first Arians, the Homoian school of Ulfila considered itself the defender of the traditional faith of the Church.[76] Like them, the early Arians had believed that the concept of the substantial unity of Father and Son was a heretical and illogical innovation with dangerous overtones of ditheism or Sabellian modalism.[77] They intensely resented any claim that Arius was the author of their faith. He was but one witness among many. For example, Maximinus said that it was not the bishops, like Eusebius of Caesarea and Eusebius of Nicomedia, who had followed Arius, but Arius who had followed the bishops (Scol. 11).

While they denigrated theological speculation and claimed a simple biblicism, the Ulfilans did exhibit a distinctive and surprisingly uniform theology. They may not have realized it, but the philosophical underpinnings of their Arianism predisposed them to an emphasis on subordinationist texts and a subordinationist understanding of all major Christian doctrines. It is best, therefore, to view their theology in the context of other Arian groups.

*Trinity*

The varieties of Arianism had the same basic conception of God. They assumed God's absolute unity of being, simplicity of essence, and isolation from the world of finite beings. These attributes belonged to his substance as impersonal and eternal properties constitutive of his definition and were not contingently separable. R. D. Williams believes this view could have been derived from the *Isagoge* or *Categories* of Porphyrian Aristotelianism.[78] Arians usually appealed to ingeneracy as the distinguishing mark of God's Deity.[79]

For Arius and his colleagues, the terms *Father* and *Son* were descriptive designations for individuals who are unique and particular subsistents. But in spite of this clear distinction between the *Logos* as attribute and the Son as first creature, Arius frequently mixed the terms *Logos* and *Son*. When he did so, he usually commented that the Son was designated as *Logos* according to grace.[80] The Son, as an *ousia* (a proper subject for predication), has his own essential characteristics which must of necessity be different from those of the essentially eternal and ungenerated Father.[81] The Son cannot inalienably or by nature possess any of the essential and defining properties of the Father, since they are indivisible qualities (They have no quantity and therefore cannot suffer division) pertaining to his substance.[82] In a more or less conciliatory letter to Alexander of Alexandria, Arius and Eusebius of Nicomedia had used this as an argument. They said: "As to such phrases as 'from Him,' . . . the consubstantial, and a *probole* (offspring), then the Father will be of a compound nature, and divisible, and changeable, and corporeal; and thus, as far as their words go, the incorporeal God will be subjected to the properties of matter."[83]

Arius's view derived from Origen. In Origen's Trinitarian theology, the Son was of a different *ousia* from the Father. (*Ousia,* for Origen, meant the individual member of a class.) Thomas A. Kopecek notes that the term and concept of *ungenerated* came from Greek philosophy and originally meant "what always is." It was equated with being as opposed to becoming. Used by Platonists and later by the Christian apologists and early theologians, it played a significant role in both early Arian thought and Neo-Arianism.[84]

Using the Middle Platonic view that means reveal essences, Arians attempted to establish an objective theological epistemology. Language, they argued, is not a human convention. Both the use of things and their names are given to men by the Creator as a natural capacity. The very essence of anything is, therefore, directly linked to its name, and a difference in name indicates a difference in essence. Eunomius, in his *Apologia Apologiae,* also manifested the Arian tendency to equate essence and nature. On this basis they argued that Father and Son must have different essence since they have different names.[85]

They insisted that a subject must designate either a substance or an accident, that in God there is nothing accidental (mutable), and that, therefore, every attribute of God must be a substantial one. If the personal attributes "begotten" and "unbegotten" cannot designate anything accidental, then they must designate essential differences.[86] God's ingeneracy must then pertain to his essence. Thus, the term *God* is not properly applicable to the Son, but only to the one Absolute. They therefore viewed the rejection of the term *creature* for the Son as illogical. According to the Neo-Arians, the Son is a unique and generated being who by definition cannot be the God. For example, in the first part of the *Syntagmation,* Aetius defended the expression "ungenerated God" in terms of causation.[87] The Arian trinity, therefore, consisted of absolutely simple, discreetly independent essences arranged in a rigid hierarchy of causation. All branches of Arianism stressed subordination of Son to Father and Spirit to Son, and used a whole array of Scriptures to fortify this position.[88]

Like the early Arians, the Neo-Arians rejected essentialist concepts in favor of voluntarist ones. But they promoted a creationist voluntarism of God and not the earlier ethical voluntarism of the Son. They designated *Father* as a term to describe God's will, not his essence, as in Arius. Thus they could say: the Father and Son are "like" while God and the Son are "unlike."[89]

God's role as Father is tied like the Son to his activity and will. The Father causes the positive attributes possessed by the Son, while they are the uncaused nature of God. Although the essence of God is without beginning, his activity in creation, as Father, is not. Therefore the Son can be generated, or rather created, once and for all rather than continually.[90]

The Ulfilan trinity is also a hierarchical one, in which a difference in nature implies a difference in degree. Like other Arians, Ulfilans believed that the essential error of the Nicenes and Homoiousians was a failure to distinguish between the Father, Son, and Spirit. They accused them of not acknowledging the distinct and characteristic qualities of the persons. Although they were less critical of the Ho-

moiousians, they still believed that their affirmation of a total likeness between the three persons overlooked their essential differences
(Max. Scol. 11, 21; Pal. Scol. 56, 65, 66, 84, 91; Aux. Scol. 26–28).[91]
Like the Neo-Arians, the Ulfilan system was based on the essential
opposition of "begotten" and "unbegotten."[92]

The Ulfilans, like the early Arians, emphasized that only the Father is truly God, since he alone is self-existent and unbegotten. His
transcendence, in their view, excludes any concept of limitation,
division, change, suffering, or corporality. The centerpiece of Gothic
Homoianism, the credo of Ulfila, recorded in the letter of Auxentius
in the *Scolia,* perhaps best expressed their views. When pressed by
Augustine to state his faith, the bishop Maximinus himself reverted
to this credo (Coll. 4; cf. Ulf. Scol. 24, 40). "Unbegotten" becomes,
for them, another name for God.[93] Some of the synonyms that Ulfila
used (and which also occur throughout Arian writings) for *unbegotten*
are "innate," "uncreated," and "unmade" (Scol. 24).

Unlike the Neo-Arians, the Ulfilans expressly rejected the term
*unlike.* They favored, instead, the term *different* and opposed it not
to *like,* as did the Neo-Arians, but to what they assumed was a
confusion of the persons by the Homoousians (Ulf. Scol. 40; Pal.
Scol. 54, 90, 91). The chief and most important teaching of this
category of Arians was their insistence on the Son's inferiority to
the Father and the Spirit's inferiority to the Son, a view they backed
with extensive scriptural references. In their view, the three divine
persons are three different beings. As J. N. D. Kelly notes, "Their
teaching thus ammounted to tritheism, and their Catholic opponents
never wearied of upbraiding them with reverting to the polytheism
of their barbarian background."[94]

There is no unique nature common to Father, Son, and Holy
Spirit, like the human nature common to men. Each possesses his
own appropriate *ousia.* Each of the persons possesses a specific existence, a *singularis natura,* which is appropriate to him.[95] In no way
can the persons be equal because their natures and operations are
different (Pal. Scol. 91). In their estimation, only the Father is the
true, unbegotten, and incomparable God. The Son is not unbegotten
like the Father and, therefore, does not possess any of the transcendent attributes of the Father, such as immutability, or any of the
positive attributes, such as goodness, except by participation (Max.
Scol. 22; Pal. Scol. 67–72). It is by this participation that the Son
partakes of the Father's character and attributes. Their unity, the
binding force that holds the Trinity together, is love. The Ulfilans

compared this unity of agreement and love to the unity the Spirit brings to believers (Scol. 24, 25, 40).[96]

## The Son of God

According to the early Arians, the Son was to be called God only in a lower and improper sense. He can not be God by nature, since by definition he can not share his Father's most crucial attribute: ingeneracy. Created from nothing by a definite and external act of the Father's will, he is therefore inferior in rank and authority and not strictly eternal.[97]

Because, like men, the Son is created from nothing, he has a contingent will and is capable of moral change, of good or evil. His holiness, therefore, is not essential, but acquired.[98] The Son's dignity and share in the divine prerogatives were granted because God foresaw his fidelity to the Father's will. Because his own efforts kept him sinless, he was adopted by God.[99] He is, therefore, a creature, or work of God, who has been promoted to the rank of divine Son and Redeemer.[100]

When the Arians said the Son is changeable, they primarily meant improvable. He advanced to virtue by desiring to advance. It is the advance to virtue along a modified Stoic view of virtue and advance, and thus Stoic ethics are an important key to understanding early Arianism. This changeability in the Son is yoked to advance and adoption. His likeness to the Father is one in the process of virtuous advance. He proleptically exists in God's foreknowledge. He advanced internally in virtue and knowledge so that at the resurrection God could grant him a promotion. Thus, he is made God by participation in God via obedience. But no matter how exalted the Son becomes, the central Arian model was that of a perfected creature whose nature remains always creaturely and whose position is always subordinate to and dependent upon the Father's will. The Son will always be merely an obedient servant or a favored creature.[101]

In one important respect, however, he greatly differs from other creatures. He alone was made directly by the Father, without any intermediary. All others were created through him. He even preceded time. The Arians believed that the biblical term *only-begotten* expresses the Son's unique relationship with the Father and his uniqueness in relation to other creatures.[102]

Some of the modern readers may bridle at the use of "only-begotten" as a translation of *monogenes*. But, in this study, such a translation is appropriate. By the time of the Arian controversy the term was clearly understood in that light. The turning point of the dispute lay in the relation between the Father and Son. Many Arians believed that one of the Father's chief distinguishing characteristics is that, in contrast to the Son, he was "unbegotten." During the period of the Arian controversy, the Latin word used to translate *monogenes* began to change from *unicus,* "unique", to *unigenitus,* "only-begotten." By the late fourth century, Western orthodoxy seemed to be in substantial agreement on this understanding of the term.

Although Arius and his colleagues did not materialize the divine generation by introducing the idea of time, they did tend to assert that there was when the Son was not. In their view, the Son seems to have preexisted only potentially in the counsel of the Father, in which all things are eternal.[103]

For the Arians, Christ, the Son, had only derivative and dependent authority. He is not an extension of divine nature but a creation of divine will. Like all other creatures, he is radically dependent upon God, whose sole method of relating to his creation is his will. Even his functions as Son were received. The mediator also has only limited knowledge. Like other creatures, he has no immediate and natural access to the structures of being.[104] According to the Arians, there is no direct *analogia entis* between his creatures and the God whose only *modus operandi* for relations with his creatures is through his will.

The early Arians proclaimed a degree Christology, in which the difference between Christ and any other man becomes quantitative rather than qualitative. Christ was viewed more in the role of creature than as Creator. He was as other men, only more obedient, more loving, and so on. Christ's unity with the Father derives from harmony, not identity. He is a representative Son and by no means the only possible Son. Robert C. Gregg and Dennis E. Groh have admirably summarized this Arian viewpoint. They state: "Servanthood by a creaturely nature freely electing such and divine fatherhood by grace are the twin foundations of early Arian Christology."[105] The union between Father and Son is one of will or agreement. The Son is the Father's student and apprentice, his created assistant, called Word *(Logos)* by grace and participation.[106]

The Neo-Arians also believed that the Father and the Son lack a common, or even a similar, *ousia* (substance) and that the sole relationship between them lays in the divine will.[107] But whereas Arius had held that the Son was promoted to the divine status and name as a reward for his virtue, Eunomius, the Neo-Arian, was prepared to agree that the Son enjoys these from the very beginning of his existence. This, however, does not obviate his absolute dependence upon God. In his view, the Son is every bit as subservient to God's will as his disciples were.[108]

For Eunomius, it was not the humanity of the Son that suffered for man's salvation but the divinity which "emptied itself" to become man. God did not become man, but the Son, the Word in the form of God, became man.[109] The Neo-Arians contended that to believe that the Son and God share a common essence would prevent belief in a true incarnation of a divine essence.

For the Ulfilans, the Son is the God of all creation, ontically anterior to the incarnation (Pal. Scol. 67; Max. Scol. 13).[110] Although he preceded all others, he was "created and begotten, made and established" by the Father (Aux. Scol. 22). They found the idea of the Son being coeternal with the Father unacceptable. They also rejected the idea of his omnipotence and any idea of personal equality that even hinted at a unity of substance.[111]

The Son is a creature who owes his existence to the Father. But his relation to the Father is unique. He received his being directly from the Father, along with unique powers and prerogatives which pertain to him alone (Ulf. Scol. 20). Palladius had refused to sign the condemnation of Arius's letter at Aquileia because this view, common to most subordinationists of the time, was expressed in it. Whole councils, like the one at Rimini, had accentuated this qualitative difference.[112] The Son was the "only begotten" *(unigenitus),* found in John 1; 14:18 and 3:16, and the "true" Son, in contrast to those who are sons of God by adoption (Pal. Scol. 66). The fact of his generation, they argued, does not imply any division or diminution of the Father's divinity (Aux. Scol. 25). It had nothing in common with human or animal generation. It was a spiritual process which God alone understood.[113]

The Son was generated before time itself, before everything but the Father, but he is not coeternal with the Father (Pal. Scol. 55). The Maximinus of the *Scolia* notes that his titles "begotten," "Son," and "Christ" imply that he had before him a begetter, a Father, and one who conferred on him the anointing (Scol. 13). The Arian authors of the *Scolia,* however, made little distinction between *beginning* in an ontological sense and the same word in a chronological sense and, for them, the term *sempiternus* practically became a synonym for "unbegotten" (Max. Scol. 21).

The Son functioned as the artisan of creation. He is the one through whom the Father executed all his works, as in John 1:3 and Colossians 1:15–17 (Pal. Scol. 84). But in the final analysis, it is the Father who was the genuine author of all things. The Son, by the will of the Father, served as his agent in creation, but is totally

dependent upon the Father. The Son is "the author of all things by
the Father, after the Father, on account of the Father and to the glory
of the Father" (Aux. Scol. 26).

Christ, the Son, was the beginning of all God's works in whom
he "made the heavens and the earth" (Max. Scol. 13). As such a
creature, he is the natural intermediary between God and the world.
Through him, God's gifts reach mankind (Max. Scol. 22; Pal. Scol.
94). Through him, men can have access to the Father (Max. Scol. 11;
Aux. Scol. 32; Pal. Scol. 55). The Son is unceasingly attentive to
the work of representing the Father to men (Aux. Scol. 26).

In this role, he is legitimately called mankind's God because men
directly owe their existence to his active obedience as Creator. The
authors of the *Scolia* never refused to call him God (Ulf. Scol. 40;
Aux. Scol. 33; Pal. Scol. 66, 94; Max. Scol. 11). Ulfilans went so
far as to affirm his eternality *(sempiternus)*.[114] They stressed that while
he has a beginning, he has no end. Like Arius, and indeed all earlier
subordinationists, they explicitly affirmed that the Son deserved to
be adored, celebrated, honored, and glorified in all things. He was
to receive the same honor as the Father because the Scriptures commanded that he be worshipped and adored. But he must not be
ranked as equal to *the* God (Aux. Scol. 32).[115] In their view, he
receives this worship and passes it on to the Father. His is a lesser
divinity, a divinity for mankind's sake. He has the image of God
but not his essence.[116] The Father is, thus, the God and creator of
mankind's God, and Christ is God to every creature (Aux. Scol. 29,
30; Ulf. Scol. 40; Max. Scol. 11). The Son himself, they claimed,
had proclaimed this openly both before and after the resurrection,
when he had quitted the form of a servant. The Son thus becomes
a sort of "God in second," who recognizes that the one above him
is really God. Ulfilans claimed that Christ himself stipulated this
when he stated in John 14:28, "The Father is greater than I." This
text, they insisted, must not be heard uniquely "according to his
flesh" as the Homousians claimed (Aux. Scol. 28; Pal. Scol. 73).

The Ulfilans claimed that the superiority of the Father to the Son
is also revealed in the fact that he sent the Son, thus disposing of
him according to his own will (Pal. Scol. 90; Max. Scol. 11). His
absolute obedience and submission to the Father were demonstrated
in the testimony he gave, in repeating what he had heard from the
Father, and in agreeing to atone for the Church through his own
blood. His inferiority manifested itself also in the fact that the Son
adored, praised, honored, venerated, glorified, gave thanks to, and
prayed to the Father, not only when he was in the "condition of a
servant," but also while abiding in heaven (Pal. Scol. 56, 88, 89).

Unlike the early Arians, they saw no special merit in his obedience and humility. It is the only possible proper relation of the only-begotten to the unbegotten.[117]

The Son possesses all the positive attributes of the Father; like him, he is good, wise, and powerful, but with one essential difference. The Son has these attributes because he has received them from the Father. Within these limits the Son is similar to the Father, whose perfection he reflects (Pal. Scol. 54). Ulfila's followers, however, continued to reject the Homoiousian insistence that the Son is like the Father "in substance and in everything" (Aux. Scol. 28). In another divergence from early Arianism, the Ulfilans believed that God has placed judgment in the hands of the Son.[118]

### Arianism: Logos/Sarx Christology

The Arian view of the incarnation was crucial to the Arian understanding of Trinitarian relations. A *Logos/sarx* (Word/flesh) Christology was quite natural to their system. Their clearest formulas portray a Christ who has a single, but composite nature. In the incarnation, the Son assumed only the body of a man and not a human soul. Christ was, therefore, a *systasis,* or *constitutio,* a single entity arising from the physical conjunction of the two—composite, yet unified.[119] This Christological conception was inherited to some degree from early Apologists, whose discussions sometimes seem to portray Christ as a being in whom the divine is imminent in a superlative degree, but who is essentially less than God.[120]

Since no human soul was present in Christ, the Son—as Word—provided all his psychical vitality and spiritual awareness. Therefore, the emotions and mental activities reported in the Gospels had to be attributed to the Son. If a human soul and not the Son had borne all these limitations and "imperfections" (grief, despair, and so on), then the Word had not really become man. A translation of an Arian fragment attributed to Eudoxius of Constantinople, the fourth-century Homoian bishop, states: "We believe in one single Lord Jesus Christ . . . made flesh, not made man; for he did not take a human soul . . . not two natures, since he was not a perfect man but God was in place of the soul in the flesh, the entirety one nature through articulation."[121]

The repeated charge that the Arians taught two "Wisdoms" or two "Words" is invalid. In Arian literature, *Logos* can refer either to God's own *Logos* or to the Son who may be called *Logos* by grace. The truly divine *Logos,* numbered among the attributes of God, could not exist apart from the Father. It was distinct from and anterior to the Son.[122] This distinction originated in the teaching of Paul of Samosata, who was linked to Arius through Lucian of Antioch.[123] Therefore, to claim the Son as the "Wisdom" or "Word" *(Logos)* of God in any but a participatory sense would reduce him to an impersonal quality rather than establish him as a divine person.[124] Arians rejected any role for the Son which implied a unity of nature with God the Father, since in their view this would destroy God's singularity.[125]

The *Logos,* or Son, can not be fully God, in the Ulfilan's view, since he, unlike the Father, had been able to participate in the contagion of human mutability (Max. Coll. 13). They abhorred the Nicene tendency to ascribe some of the words, actions, and emotions to Christ's divinity and some to his humanity. Palladius, for example, insisted that the "Lord of glory" himself, not just his human flesh, was crucified, suffered, and died (Scol. 71, 72).[126] His ability to suffer and his emotional and mental limitations, gleaned from the Bible, made it obvious to them that he can not be the same in essence as God the Father. By their definition of true divinity, the *Logos/sarx* Christ can only be a sort of secondary divine, yet created, being, intermediate between God and the world, and therefore inferior to God. Their Christ is a mutable Word who assumed a human body and, thus, was neither truly God nor man.[127]

Although others in the third and fourth centuries, notably Athanasius, may have ascribed to Christ a less than complete humanity, the general tendency of the orthodox party was to strive for an understanding of Christ that took seriously both his divinity and his humanity. Some of their attempted formulations can face the same accusations as the Arians'. However, the orthodox party did not end up with a Christ who is neither God nor man, or who is only man and not God.

## The Holy Spirit

From the very beginning, the Arians seemed to relegate the Holy Spirit to a lower plane than the Son.[128] Eunomius, the Neo-Arian, went beyond Arius's lack of an explicit doctrine of the Spirit. He affirmed that the Spirit is a creature, the work of the Son. The Holy Spirit is not to be ranked with God or the Son, but with other generated things. He is the first and most excellent work of the Son.[129]

The Ulfilans also placed him in third rank after the Father and the Son. They viewed him as the Son's servant (Ulf. Scol. 40; Aux. Scol. 34; Pal. Scol. 90).[130] Indeed, the Son inaugurated his creative work by calling the Spirit into existence, and then through him the Son worked to create everything else (Aux. Scol. 29; Pal. Scol. 92). Created by the Father, through the Son, the Spirit is neither God, nor Lord, nor King. He is not enthroned with the Father and Son and does not deserve human adoration (Ulf. Scol. 40; Aux. Scol. 30, 31; Pal. Scol. 88, 89, 92).[131] As the Son showed himself submissive and obedient to the Father, so the Spirit serves the Son, even to the point of regarding the Son as his God and Lord (Ulf. Scol. 40; Pal. Scol. 89). As the Son was given his mission by the Father, so the Spirit was sent to be the illuminating and sanctifying agent of divine grace by the will of the Son (Ulf. Scol. 40; Aux. Scol. 31).

The Spirit serves as the illuminator of mankind. He inspired the Old Testament prophets and leads men to the recognition and adoration of Jesus as their Lord (Aux. Scol. 31, 32; Pal. Scol. 88, 91).[132] He was empowered and given to the Church by the Son to guide, assist, and sanctify the elect, transmitting to them all he has heard from the Son. It is he who watches over the Church, organizes its ministries, establishes its bishops, and bestows spiritual gifts (Aux. Scol. 31; Pal. Scol. 90, 92). It is through him that all creatures sanctified by spiritual life gain access to the Son and then through him to the Father.[133]

## Arian Salvation

The early Arian system, like Pelagianism, stressed human choice and virtuous effort.[134] The Son is the pioneer of men's salvation. The Christ of early Arianism is a "saved" Savior, saved by dependence on the Father in faith and sanctified by suffering. He became the paradigm, or exemplar, for salvation and sanctification by ethical and moral advance. Adoption is the instrument of salvation for both the Son and for men.[135] The early Arian scheme pivoted on the idea of Sonship by adoption, both for Christ and for believers. If men will imitate the first adopted Son's persistent choice of virtuous obedience, they too may become the adopted sons of God. On the basis of Psalms 45:7, Arius tried to show that the Son of God, although not a son by nature, was chosen for the honor because he did not turn away from God as the others had. Sacred titles belong to the Son only as the representative of God to man. In his view, all believers become the sons of God, like Jesus is the Son of God.[136]

No properties of the Savior, nothing in his character or works, are beyond the reach of his fellow creatures. He is the perfect paradigm of the behavior which leads to a salvation. Men see redemption in his life as a creature and thereby behold the shape of their own redemption. Obedience to God is the true discipleship, and obedience in imitation of his obedience results in salvation. Christ becomes the captain of salvation because he shows man that he must participate in what the Father wills, through obedience, in order to attain salvation.[137]

While for early Arianism salvation came as a result of one's ethical activity in imitation of the changeable Son, for the Neo-Arian it came as the result of one's knowledge of God provided by him through his first creature, the Son. The understanding of propositional doctrine was the sole way to attain redemption. Late in his career Eunomius affirmed that only correct knowledge begets acceptable faith.[138]

The Ulfilians, on the other hand, struck a balance between the two positions. They rejected the view that Christ is God's Son only by adoption. Like the Neo-Arians, they saw Christ as the divine teacher, sent to reveal the truth about God. They retained the early Arian emphasis on the imitation of Christ as the way of salvation. But they saw, in his obedient death and resurrection, a conquest over the supernatural forces of evil and a gracious metaphysical "opening" that permitted an active faith leading to salvation.[139]

## Arian Hermeneutics

Arians, like their opponents, exegeted the Scriptures by a careful and self-conscious hermeneutic. They tended to emphasize only those passages which seemed to conform to their extrabiblical presuppositions. These prooftexts, usually metaphors which implied the subordination and dependence of the Son and the Spirit on the Father or the human frailties of Jesus, were then interpreted literally and without regard to immediate or general context. The Arians seem to have taken great delight in chronicling the creaturely limitations, apparent fear, and uncertainty of the Redeemer. They seized every opportunity to show that the Jesus of Scripture had to be a creature. Two of their favorite prooftexts were 2 Corinthians 2:9 and Philippians 2:5–11.[140] On this basis, they would conclude that the persons, called divine, evidently do not have the same essence, that they do not enjoy an equality, and that, therefore, they are not each God deserving of one identical title.[141] The most important example of this is the Arians' interpretation of the biblical term *begotten,* with reference to the Son. Origen himself had interpreted the generation of the Son as an eternal and continuous act. The Arians, however, though deriving many of their concepts from Origen, took the biological analogy behind the word *begotten* to impose a distinction between the ingeneracy of the Father and the generation of the Son. This, of course, excluded the ascription of full divinity to the Son.[142]

When the Arians encountered a text that seemed to teach a unity of Father and Son, they usually argued that any such unity had to be moral, or of the will, or in love, or an agreement in thought and teaching. They would then interpret that passage in the light of their preselected prooftexts. An example of how this worked in practice is their approach to John 10:30, which was certainly not one of their favorite passages. They said that it must be interpreted in light of John 17:11, 20–23; 10:38; and 14:10. A Homoousian interpretation of John 10:30, they argued, would force one to the ridiculous conclusion that all Christians are of the same essence as God the Father.[143]

Neo-Arianism tended toward a rationalist and purely formal philosophical approach, removed from the control of revealed truth and traditional approaches to interpretation. According to Theodoret, the Neo-Arians had turned theology into a barren exercise in the manipulation of logical categories.[144] Their method was polemical, arguing for Neo-Arian doctrine by attempting to demonstrate the logical inconsistencies of other ways.[145] Aetius's *Syntagmation,* for example, is a collection of terse syllogistic arguments on the "problem over the ungenerated God, that is, if it is possible for the ungenerated God to make the generated ungenerated."[146] While Aetius claimed to be conveying the meaning of Scripture in the *Syntagmation,* nowhere was he very eager to appeal to Scripture in his syllogisms. His basic dependence was on logic.[147]

Not until their final days did the Neo-Arians begin to deal seriously with questions of scriptural interpretation. Eunomius tied essence to name as in Middle Platonism. Language was not a human convention; both the use of things and their names were given to men by the Creator as a natural capacity. Essence and nature were equated.[148]

It is in the area of biblical interpretation that Ulfilan, or Gothic, Arianism developed many of its most distinctive and ultimately debilitating characteristics. By providing a Gothic Bible and liturgy, Ulfila may have cut off the Germanic Arians from the wells of Greek and Latin theology, as well as from the great theological movements of their day. As E. A. Thompson notes, "No characteristic of Germanic Arian theology is more marked than its aridity, its refusal to speculate, its pedestrian earthbound barrenness and lack of originality."[149]

The Germanic laity recognized the need for educated religious leadership and were themselves cut off from Greco-Roman scholarship by a barrier of language and their own lack of education. The Ulfilan community, therefore, tended to depend on religious leaders who were Roman, or romanized, and who immersed themselves in the subject matter, traditions, and techniques of Roman scholarship. These leaders showed a great but pedantic interest in both classical and early Christian authors and were able to capture the imaginations of their congregations with some carefully winnowed Roman ideas. Most of the barbarians retained their old social customs and language. But, like their Catholic counterparts, they gained their understanding of the Bible and its teachings from their leaders.[150] But, unlike the Catholics, they received their instruction from a very narrow circle of religious leaders. As Thompson notes, they became dependent on their leaders "to an extent that was not paralleled among the catholic Roman population."[151]

The Ulfilan theologians seem to have incorporated much of the worst of Roman scholarship into their study of the Bible. They also showed a marked inability to draw any practical lessons from scriptural texts. Their preserved sermons are arid, lack originality, and try to maintain what Thompson refers to as a "ponderous earthbound reliance on the Bible." He also notes that they found in it "no lessons bearing on daily conduct and no conclusions of practical value."[152] Instead, as Thompson discovered, they propounded a "succession of mystical interpretations and fantastic developments" that aimed at winning the favor of rulers and the wealthy among the barbarians and Romans.[153] And so, it seems, the Gothic Arians were addicted to a particularly unhealthy form of biblical literalism mixed with pulpit pyrotechnics aimed more at elevating the pulpiteer than at educating the congregation.

Ulfila's school "never produced a philosophic theologian."[154] These men claimed to base their views exclusively on the Scriptures and sought to fortify almost every assertion by citing prooftexts (See Aux. Scol. 25; Pal. Scol. 90)[155] Sometimes their arguments are merely long chains of Scripture texts strung together. As Michel Meslin has demonstrated, they are much more scriptural in their approach than were the Arians in the Eastern portion of the empire.[156] In a theological conflict, their favorite tactic was to inundate the opposition with a plethora of scriptural quotations.[157] This may have been developed as a weapon for maintaining the authority of the teacher-pastor by overawing any questioner which might arise from the barbarians or proselytized Romans.

The Scriptures were the "divine wisdom" and, therefore, a legitimate object for veneration.[158] Nothing was to be approved as true by Christians "except the divine Scripture," as properly interpreted by Ulfilans.[159] The Ulfilan leaders, therefore stressed a mechanical exactness in the translation of texts. As Thompson notes, they followed a "verbatim method of Biblical translation at the expense not only of idiomatic usage but even of grammar" that often resulted in "false and misleading renderings of an exegetical and misleading nature."[160] This textual mishandling appears to have been quite common among the Ulfilans. It probably began shortly after the death of Ulfila and was well established when Alaric sacked Rome in 410.[161]

Ulfilan Arians tended to get so involved in the details of a text as to miss its meaning. They were very argumentative over matters which seem, at best, academic and thrived on extreme detail. Writing to a group of Visigoths in the West, a frustrated Jerome begged them "not to raise such tiny matters as make no difference to the sense of the text."[162]

As Michel Meslin discovered, if the Ulfilans had any true originality it was to be found in their employment of scriptural argument, rationally pursued.[163] Proverbs, chapter 8, for example, was the foundation for their view that the Son, anterior to all other creatures, was himself "created at the beginning." They believed it to be an adequate refutation of the orthodox habit of ascribing subordination to Christ's human nature, or flesh (Pal. Scol. 74). And one of their number, probably Maximinus, gave a profoundly original interpretation of the figure of Job, seeing in him a type of Christ prefiguring the *kenosis* of the Son of man.[164] While these examples of creativity come from the Old Testament, the Ulfilans had a clear predilection for the Gospel of John. Their other favorites, in order of apparent popularity, were the epistles of Paul, the Old Testament, and the Synoptics.[165]

For the Ulfilans, tradition had an important role in the interpretation of Scripture. Its purpose was to transmit, in conformity to the "true meaning" of the Scriptures, the faith revealed in the Scriptures (Aux. Scol. 26, 28). Any authority, ascribed to a universal council reuniting the bishops of all churches and the church leaders of the past had to flow from their confirmation of the truth of the Scriptures as understood by the Ulfilans. The religious leaders of the Visigoths and other Germanic Arians considered themselves bound by the interpretations of earlier Ulfilan scholars. In their writings, as E. A. Thompson notes, one finds "an absence of speculation and originality, a hidebound traditionalism."[166] They did, however, urge the calling of a general council to solve the problems of controversy.

Firmly convinced of the truth of their position, they seemed genuinely surprised when others failed to agree with them. They believed that the truth would be victorious in a general council and that only a general council had the competence to decide conflicts which arise in matters of faith (see Aux. Scol. 27; Pal. Scol. 61, 78).

### Arianism: Theophanies

The Arians found support for their views in earlier Christian exegesis of the Old Testament theophanies. The Apologists and early theologians referred the theophanies to the Son, thinking of the *Logos* as the mediator between the one and the many.[167] The Arians pressed the Apologists' conviction that only the Word and the Spirit can appear in physical form to its logical conclusion. They argued that this inferred that the Son is both inferior to the Father and visible by nature.[168] This is a line of reasoning that fits well with their concept of subordination.

The Gothic Homoians of Ulfila's school saw many appearances of the Son in the Old Testament. It was he, for example, who walked in the garden with Adam, visited Abraham at the oak of Mamre, wrestled Jacob, and encountered Joshua before the conquest of Jericho (Pal. Scol. 71, 88). Like the early Arians, they refused to see any appearance of the Father in these theophanies, contrasting the invisible Father with the visible Son. From the visible Son, mankind had received the Old Testament law, and he alone appeared in the New Testament and took on a human body in order to be man's Redeemer and Savior (Aux. Scol. 26).

Many of the earlier church fathers, claimed by orthodoxy, such eminent men as Justin, Irenaeus, and Tertullian, had also argued that it was the *Logos* that represented God in the Old Testament theophanies. There is more than a hint of evidence that some of them both identified this *Logos* with the Son and felt him to be somewhat "less" than the Father.[169] But, within their approaches also lay the seed of further orthodox clarification of the relationship between Father and Son.

# 3

# AUGUSTINE AND ARIANISM TO THE TIME OF HIS DEBATE WITH MAXIMINUS

## Augustine in His Roman African Context

*Africa*

The wealth and importance of Roman Africa were measured in agricultural production. The landscape was covered with small agricultural towns whose chief crops were grain and olive oil. Only a few of the coastal cities like Carthage, Utica, and Hadrumetum were not primarily agricultural settlements.[1] Nothing like it existed in the northern part of the Western empire, where there were only a few large cities (usually administrative centers) and some tiny villages.

It was agriculture that gave the province its military and political importance. During the demands of the fifth-century crisis, African grain fed the Roman army. Roman Africa also supplied excellent cavalry recruits and horses. As province after province was lost to the central authority, Africa became ever more important to the Western government's survival. Command of its military forces was considered a prestigious position, given only to the most trustworthy.[2] A *comes Africae* could, under the right circumstances, play a powerful role as a kingmaker. Possibly due to this danger, the garrison of the province was almost always kept at the absolute minimum needed to guard its frontiers and maintain order in the province.[3]

The general social problems, prevalent throughout the empire, were also common in Africa. There was serious corruption in the imperial civil service and a general crisis in authority. A well-educated and wealthy upper class, spoiled by privilege, took little interest in public affairs and retreated to their huge private estates, while the condition of the common laborer came to approximate that of the serfs during the height of the Middle Ages. The power of the landlords over their tenants became so great that landlords were expected to "redeem" their *coloni* (tenants) from Donatism. The African aristocracy was also intellectually elitist. Carthage was second only to Rome in the study of Latin literature and, at a time when Greek was rarely taught in the Western empire, even the little town of Thagaste included the study of Greek in grammar school. The tradition of the African grammarians was so strong that it survived the Vandal invasions.[4]

Guarding this decadent society was a military establishment that was dangerously small, scattered, and universally unpopular. Some were notorious for bullying local farmers. They were also the region's only effective police force. A group of less than twenty-three thousand men was charged with the defense and policing of seven large provinces, in the face of continual Moorish raids. The *Notitia Dignitatum* assigns the region only three *legiones palatinae* (3,000 elite medium heavy infantry), eight *legiones comitatenses* (8,000 regular medium heavy infantry), one *auxilium palatinum* (500 elite light infantry), and nineteen *vexillationes comitatenses* (9,500 cavalry). They were also almost hopelessly scattered throughout Roman Africa because the whole fortification system was based on the defense and promotion of agriculture. Even the border guards were expected to farm. It was because of this scattering and because of the vast area they had to defend that such a high proportion of these troops, by Roman standards, were cavalry.[5] Despite these horrible disadvantages, they were relatively effective in maintaining the peace of Roman Africa. But they were already stretched to their limit before the civil war and the coinciding barbarian invasion of the late 420s.[6]

The one exception to general decline was the Catholic Church. After an earlier period of decline and a long warfare with Donatism, the African Church was surging ahead. It was becoming the driving force of Western Christianity. Catholicism had also finally begun to advance among the Moors and the less romanized elements of provincial society.[7] It was an advance that would survive the Vandalic invasion. By 484, for example, there were more than 120 orthodox Mauretanian bishops, and about half of those were from outside the provinces.[8]

## Augustine

Integral to the advancing fortunes of the African Church was one man, Augustine. As the new bishop of Hippo Regius, Augustine had resisted those who would have made of him just another aristocratic bishop, more interested in the classics than the Scriptures and more concerned with material comfort than spiritual duty. Instead, the bishop demanded of his clergy a monastic way of life. Like him, they had to don the *birrus* (a very simple black robe), subsist on a simple vegetarian diet, give all they had to the treasury of the church or to the poor, remain celibate, and devote time to the study of the Scriptures. From this "monastery" a new, capable, dedicated, and confident leadership for the African Church had emerged.[9] As Augustine, the brilliant and able controversialist, won debate after debate against Catholicism's rivals, men trained under his influence strained every nerve to advance the cause of the Catholic Church.

The spiritual empire, the empire of Christ, meant much more to such men than the Roman empire. While Jerome was deeply shaken by the plundering of Rome, Augustine's response was a reflective study, comparing the mortality of this world's institutions with the eternity of God's kingdom, his *De Civitate Dei*. In contrast, Jerome wept, his voice failed him, and he became so depressed that he temporarily abandoned his study of Ezekiel.[10] Augustine and his colleagues, unlike many others, refused to equate Christianity with the Roman empire. Also, unlike most well-educated Western bishops, Augustine strove to preach in a more popular and simpler style in order to draw the masses.[11]

Augustine, through his writings and his disciples, transformed the African Church. The bishop of Hippo became the central spiritual expert of Roman Africa, inundated with requests for books. He became the creator of African Christian culture.[12]

## Augustine and the Arians

*Early Contacts with Arianism*

The bulk of Augustine's Christian life lay between two great struggles against Arianism. Ambrose was just conquering the last great stronghold of Roman Arianism when Augustine's Christian life began. The invasions coming near the end of Augustine's life would mark the beginning of the Western church's struggle against a barbarian Arianism. The phantom, before encountered almost exclusively in the catechism and the writings of theologians, became a living fact. Augustine would die during a siege in which Arians, Visigothic soldiers of the emperor, were defending the walls of Hippo Regius from Arian tribesmen, the Vandal invaders of Roman Africa.[13] Refutations of the heresy, therefore, are found in relatively few of Augustine's works because Arianism was not a serious problem in Roman Africa until rather late in Augustine's life.[14]

Augustine's knowledge of Arianism was probably rather academic before his reception of the *Sermo Arianorum* in A.D. 418.[15] His only known personal encounter with the heresy prior to that was before his conversion while he remained in Milan and sat under the preaching of Ambrose (Conf. 9.7).[16]

In the 380s, Ambrose, who read the Greek theology of the East and publically preached against Arianism, fought continuously against the Illyrian Arians of northern Italy. Augustine's mother, Monica, was among those who joined Ambrose in occupying a basilica to prevent its use by Arian soldiers. Although threatened with violence by Justina, mother of the emperor Valentinian II, Ambrose's obstinate congregation prevailed (Conf. 9.7).[17] Augustine himself, however, did not participate in the struggle since, at the time, he was not yet a Christian.

Augustine's first contact with the theological arguments of Arianism was, thus, probably filtered through the sermons of Ambrose. The bishop of Milan's attacks on the Arians stressed the philosophical, rather than the exegetical, side of the conflict. Once converted, Augustine seems to have been in complete agreement with Ambrose's positions. He certainly deemed the bishop of Milan the hero of the conflict, since, according to Augustine, Justina had been spiritually "seduced by the Arians" to persecute God's servant (Conf. 9.7.15).

Even though Ambrose was fighting against Illyrian (that is, Ulfilan) Arianism, one must not suppose that this fully prepared Augustine for his later encounters with it. One must remember that, at Aquileia, Ambrose had failed to distinguish between Ulfilan Arianism and that of Arius. Ambrose often attributed to the Ulfilans positions which they did not hold. When, soon after his conversion, Augustine left Milan and Italy behind, his chances of encountering Arianism dramatically dropped. There simply was no Arian influence in Africa at that time. His knowledge of the heresy appears to have remained primarily academic until about 418. For this reason, the number of his anti-Arian writings is relatively small.

But Augustine's anti-Arian writings, though meager in number, were extremely important for the development of Latin theology. The method of refuting Arianism found in Augustine and the Athanasian Creed is not found prior to Ambrose and, as J. N. D. Kelly notes, first "reached its mature flowering in Augustine."[18] Through

Augustine's influence, this method would become a mainstay of Western theological polemics.

## Contributions of the Anti-Arian Writings

The Cappadocians had seen the Father's uniqueness in His "ingenerateness," but only rarely would that kind of approach appear in Augustine. Instead, Augustine argued that the Father's uniqueness lay in generating the Son. The key to Augustine's approach to the Trinity was in his conception of the divine nature preceding the persons.[19] It was this insight which made possible Augustine's concept of *filioque*, first found in *De Trinitate*. The bishop stressed that the Holy Spirit is the spirit of both Father and Son, the mutual love that proceeds from both (De Trin. 5.15).[20] This became a commonplace in the writings of Augustine, which was passed on to the whole of the Western Church. It was also Ambrose's pupil, Augustine, who effectively distinguished between texts referring to the Son acting as God and those which represented him as man. J. N. D. Kelly believes that even the influential Athanasian Creed "can be fairly and accurately described as codified and condensed Augustinianism."[21] All of these fruits, and others, derive from Augustine's efforts to deal with Arianism. But their final development is to be found only in the Arian conflict at the end of the bishop's life.

## Arianism in Africa

The date of Arianism's first penetration of Africa is uncertain. Since it was very popular with the army, especially its barbarian elements, Arians could have entered Africa as early as the late fourth century. There is, however, no evidence for their presence before the sack of Rome in 410.[22] Augustine indicates the presence of Arians among the Italian refugees of 410 but seems unsure of their identities (Tract. in Joan. 40.7).[23] Perhaps to be identified would have exposed them to retaliatory violence, since Arians had recently sacked Rome. From the context of his comments, however, it is obvious that the bishop was not concerned with combatting them. They posed no threat to his Church. He merely offered them an invitation to the true faith.

The first definite evidence for Gothic Arians in North Africa comes from a letter which Augustine himself wrote in A.D. 417. The tribune Boniface had written the bishop about an attempt by the Donatists to win the support of some of his Gothic troops. He wanted to know if Donatism and Arianism were theologically compatible. Augustine quickly assured the military man that in most doctrines Donatism was more like the Catholic faith than Arianism. Augustine stipulated that the Donatists do not deny that the Son is of the same substance as the Father, nor do they, like the Arians, Eunomians, and Macedonians, fight against the Holy Spirit's divinity (Ep. 185.1,48).[24] The bishop's encouragement seems to have been taken to heart by Boniface. In later correspondence, Augustine praised him for his valiant efforts. Boniface appears to have attempted to convert either his own Arian troops, the Donatists influencing them, or both (Ep. 185A).

The bishop's comments in that first letter to Boniface reveal no awareness of the subtle differences of belief between those he terms the "Arians" and the Eunomians. Indeed, he seems to have been only vaguely, if at all, aware of those differences. Nor is it clear whether the term *Arians* refers to Homoians or early Arians. But it is interesting that he makes a distinction between the two groups. In his works, before he began writing the *De Trinitate*, he did not make this distinction.

The Arianism that Augustine wrote against before he began his *De Trinitate* was neither Eunomian nor Homoian in character. In most of his discussions of it, it seems indistinguishable from Early Arianism. Indeed, in *De fide et symbolo,* written in October 393, he seems to be fighting against the Early Arian concept of salvation, its *Logos/sarx* Christology, and its view of the Son as a creature.[25]

In the *De Trinitate,* on the other hand, one finds an attempt to refute Eunomian Arianism. Augustine's knowledge of its theological arguments, however, seems to be rather limited. He had understood that the primary Eunomian presupposition was that "unbegotten" constituted an essential attribute of God and he encountered their idea that the Son is the son of the will of God. Against this philosophical Arianism, which depended heavily upon the method of dialectical logic, he also used logic and philosophical dialectic as his primary polemical tools. Augustine placed special emphasis on refuting the Eunomian argument for "unbegotten" as the definition of divinity (De Trin. 5.4; 15.38). He characterized this form of the heresy as *"maxime callidissimum machinamentum"* (De Trin. 1.5.4).

Some scholars, such as Alois Goldbacher, believed, on the basis of external evidence, that the *De Trinitate* was completed by about 416.[26] But today, there is a common tendency to assume that the Arianism of *De Trinitate* is the same as that encountered by Augustine in the *Sermo Arianorum,* his debate with Pascentius, and the *Collatio cum Maximino Arianorum episcopo.* Augustine's desire to discuss Arianism and his knowledge of Arian prooftexts and interpretations, found in the *De Trinitate,* are assumed to derive from his reception of the *Sermo Arianorum* in 418.

The most influential of those making this argument is the French scholar Anne-Marie La Bonnardière.[27] Her influence is especially apparent in the works of Eugene Teselle and Robert J. O'Connell.[28] La Bonnardière's assumption seems to be that Augustine's understanding of basic Arian concepts and prooftexts derives almost exclusively from the period of 418 to 421, when, according to O'Connell, the Arian challenge reached its most acute stage.[29]

La Bonnardière has used this assumption as part of her rationale for a rather detailed dating of significant portions of *De Trinitate.*[30] She appears to suppose that Augustine's understanding of basic Arian concepts and prooftexts in the *De Trinitate* came primarily from his reading of the *Sermo Arianorum.*[31] Much on the same basis, she believes that all of the *Tractatus in Joannis evangelium* past number 17 dates from after the appearance of the *Contra Sermonem Arianorum* in 418.[32] She, therefore, seems to assume Augustine's relative ignorance of all varieties of Arian thought prior to his reception of the *Sermo Arianorum.* But, as noted earlier, Augustine had sat under the skilled oratory of Ambrose, who read Greek theology and publically preached against Arianism (Conf. 9.7).[33] It seems reasonable, therefore, that Augustine's basic, academic knowledge of Arianism long preceded his reception of the *Sermo Arianorum.* And, as previously noted, Augustine had displayed a great deal of knowledge about some basic Arian positions in his *De symbolo ad catechumenos,* written in about 393 (De symb. 2). There is little reason to assume Augustine was basically ignorant of Arianism or its key doctrines prior to 418.

The real difference within the works of Augustine, with regard to Arianism, seems to be the type of Arianism which he was combatting. In *De symbolo,* he wrote against early, or classic, Arianism. In *De Trinitate,* he opposed Eunomian Arianism. But Augustine faced Ulfilan Arianism in the *Sermo Arianorum* and in his debates with Pascentius and Maximinus, not the Eunomianism found in the *De Trinitate.*

The Arianism of the *Sermo Arianorum* is Ulfilan. Teselle acknowledges that it is "a long statement of the Arian faith coming from the old and distant tradition of Ulfila."[34] The doctrines of the *Sermo Arianorum* perfectly matched those of the *Scolia.* It has been attributed to each of the *Scolia*'s authors.[35] Palladius, however, seems to be the most likely source for the work since it appears to be a summary of his theology. Augustine faced in it, and in the conflicts with Maximinus, a theological methodology and attitude different from that of the Eunomians.[36] This was probably his first real encounter with Ulfilan, or Gothic, Arianism.[37] The first contact with Ulfilan Arianism for which a specific date can be given, then, is his reading of the *Sermon Arianorum* in 418. One must seek another source for the bishop's awareness of the peculiarly Eunomian thought combatted in the *De Trinitate*.

From where, then, came Augustine's knowledge of the Eunomianism which he combats in the *De Trinitate*? It probably came from his reading of the third theological oration by Gregory of Nazianzus. Although some argue that Augustine could not possibly have read this Greek work, it seems to be the only source from which Augustine could have drawn his knowledge and refutation of the Eunomian arguments on whether the Son is begotten willingly or unwillingly by the Father. Gregory's crucial insight for Trinitarian thought came in his effort to answer the Eunomian argument that whatever is said about God in the Scriptures or on the basis of reason is said according to substance, not accident. They argued that since the Father is ungenerated and the Son generated, they must be different in substance. Gregory's solution to this problem was to transcend the opposition between substance and accident by the concept of relation. He did not, however, fully work out this fledgling theory of relations.[38] That task was left for Augustine (see De Trin. 5.3.4; 15.20.38). Stumbling across these Eastern statements on the trinitarian problem in about 413 may have led the bishop to a drastic revision of his *De Trinitate*.[39] Teselle notes that, in *Epistula* 151, Augustine had already expressed a desire to read ecclesiastical writers on the topic of the Trinity, while in *Epistula* 148 he noted that he had already read *opuscula* by Ambrose, Jerome, Athanasius, and Gregory.[40]

The Arianism combatted in the *De Trinitate* is not that which began to threaten in 418, since it seems to have been called forth by the reading of a Greek text at least five years before that date. Therefore, some of the most serious barriers to a relatively early date for the completion of the *De Trinitate* have been removed.

In about 416, Augustine, in a letter to Aurelius, the bishop of Carthage, declared that he had finished his work on the Trinity and was sending his fellow bishop a complete copy of the work with this cover letter (Ep. 174). Some scholars, presumably influenced by the assumptions mentioned above, have misinterpreted one phrase in the letter. On its basis they concluded that only the first twelve books had been finished in 416.[41] They cite Augustine's lament that some incomplete copies were already circulating. The bishop notes that there are "some persons who have the first four or, rather, five books without their introductions, and the twelfth without most of the last part" (Ep. 174). This is very different from saying that there are only twelve books.

Further evidence for the 416 date is found in two other letters written by the bishop of Hippo at about the same time. The first was written to the deacons Deogratias and Theodore and their companion brother Titianus. After writing them a brief exposition on the divinity of the Spirit and his unity with the Father and Son, he urges them to "keep themselves in readiness to read the books on the Trinity which I am now preparing to publish in the name of the Lord; perhaps they can convince you where this brief letter cannot" (Ep. 173A). Obviously, Augustine expected to send the *De Trinitate* to them in its complete form in a short time.

At first glance the second of these corroborative letters seems to support the position of those who argue for a late date. For in this letter, written in the last part of 415, Augustine indicates that he has no desire to give any attention to the unfinished books on the Trinity, because they are too exacting a work, and comprehensible to few (Ep. 169). But a second and more careful reading of the letter brings one to consider his comment that he has had the books "on hand for a long time." Although he says they were "not yet finished," one must see this statement in light of his Trinitarian exposition found in the letter itself. All the major features of the completed work *De Trinitate,* which relate to the nature of the persons, are present in microcosm (Ep. 169).

What is probably the best remaining evidence for a late completion of *De Trinitate* is found in the writings of Robert J. O'Connell. In his *The Origin of the Soul in St. Augustine's Later Works,* he makes the interesting argument that what delayed the finishing of Augustine's great work was the bishop's uncertainty regarding the origin of the soul. What flaws this otherwise excellent study is the author's heavy and almost slavish dependence on the chronology of La Bonnardière. This chronology, as we have seen, is based on the assumption that *De Trinitate* is an effort to combat the threat imposed by Ulfilan Arianism. This seems highly unlikely since an investigation of the contents, as related to Arianism, reveals that his chief concern was with Eunomian Arianism.

One could argue that the *De Trinitate* might have been issued as an emergency measure by the bishop. The work, after all, they might argue is against a form of Arianism, even if it was not the kind of Arianism which threatened Roman Africa. Perhaps the release of this rather academic exercise was Augustine's first salvo in his conflict with the Ulfilan Arians. If it was, it was a shot very wide of the mark. Establishing an exact date for the bishop's master work on the Trinity is beyond the scope of this investigation. Many eminent scholars, for what appear to be very good reasons, have disagreed rather violently at times about the completion of *De Trinitate*. As O'Connell has admitted, "When it comes to Augustine's later works, nothing is clearer than that confusion reigns."[42] But even if La Bonnardière and O'Connell are correct about the date of completion, a detailed study of the bishop's masterwork on the Trinity would be inappropriate for this opus since *De Trinitate* deals with the objections of Eunomian Arians to Trinitarian orthodoxy, not with the objections of the Ulfilans.

## The Letter from Elpidius

The letter of Augustine to Elpidius is also difficult to date. Frederick Van der Meer considers this response to an unsolicited letter Augustine's first contact with Arianism.[43] Elpidius seems to have been unknown to Augustine prior to this correspondence. But the term *eximius,* which Augustine uses in his reply, suggests that this Elpidius was an important person, possibly with some official rank.[44]

In an effort to convert Augustine, Elpidius sent a work by an Arian bishop for his perusal. He also suggested that a journey to Italy for a personal interview with the Arian teachers Bonosus and Jason would answer all the bishop's questions. Augustine replied with mild irony about the difficulty such a journey would entail (Ep. 242).

Augustine mentioned briefly the generation of the Son and wrote of the unutterable mystery of the Trinity. He closed with an assurance that given the time and opportunity to answer each point of the treatise he could convince these Arians of their error.

Was his comment about answering each individual point in the treatise that Elpidius had sent to him more than a rhetorical device? Could this Arian work, sent to him by Elpidius, be the *Sermo Arianorum* sent to him by someone in the summer of 418?

His statement could be seen as a promise to work on such a project, when he found the time. Only in *Contra Sermonem Arianiorum* and the *Retractationes* does Augustine ever mention an Arian work being sent to him (CS 39; R 78).[45] In the *Retractationes,* Augustine was referring to the *Sermo Arianorum,* against which the *Contra Sermonem Arianorum* was written. Thus, it seems likely that *Epistula 242* was written sometime in the latter part of 418 as Augustine's first response to reception of the *Sermo Arianorum.*

There are, however, some difficulties with this scenario. One is that Augustine failed to mention in the *Retractationes* that Elpidius was the one who sent *Sermo Arianorum* to him. The second difficulty is that in the last chapter of the *Contra Sermonem Arianorum*, Augustine says it was sent to him "a quibusdam fratribus" (CS 39; R 78). Would Augustine really refer to Arians as brothers? And, if Elpidius sent the *Sermo Arianorum*, why is the plural used instead of the singular?

The use of the term *brother* was very common in the era. Even those in bitter disagreement used the term. Pascentius, for example, had absolutely no love for Augustine but still called him "dearest brother" (Ep. 240). Nor was Augustine scrupulous about its use. Immediately after the council at Carthage in which Augustine had led the African Church to condemn Pelagius, Augustine, writing to Pelagius, referred to him as "beloved lord" and "much desired brother" (Ep. 146).

Any objection based on the use of the plural is also easily met. Elpidius, it seems, did not act without support. He had sent one of Augustine's works to the Arian teachers Bonosus and Jason in northern Italy, and they had provided the ammunition for Elpidius's campaign (Ep. 242).

As for the omission of Elpidius's name, Augustine may have simply forgotten it for a time. The last question remains. Was his statement a mere rhetorical device? His mention of dealing with individual points of the treatise perfectly matches his actual practice in the *Sermo Arianorum* and *Contra Sermonem Arianorum*.

Another piece of evidence is Augustine's failure to name the bishop who wrote the work mentioned in *Epistula* 242 and the fact that the *Sermo Arianorum* was sent to him without the author's name. It seems then that one should, at least tentatively, identify the work sent by Elpidius as the *Sermo Arianorum*. If it was the *Sermo Arianorum*, then one also has a firm date for Elpidius's letter: the summer of 418.

### Augustine and the Sermo Arianorum

In his *Retractationes*, Augustine noted that the sermon which he had received was anonymous. He answered it, he said, at "the insistence of the person who had sent it," and replied as "briefly and quickly" as he could (R 78). Augustine also noted that he himself numbered portions of the text so that he could comment on its theology point by point in his *Contra Sermonem Arianorum*. Some scholars believe that it was being distributed among the people of Hippo Regius in an apparent attempt to convert them.[46] They probably make this assumption, in part, because Augustine's writing of the *Contra Sermonem Arianorum* seems so rushed. They assume that its apparent haste is the response to an emergency. However, Augustine's haste actually seems to have come from a rush to clear himself of an onerous promise that had been wasting his valuable time. The attitude of his comments in the *Retractationes* and the final chapter of the *Contra Sermonem Arianorum* bear this out. In that last chapter one almost breathes a sigh of relief with the author when he says, "I am freed, I have responded to all those things which the sermon of the Arians contains, the one which was sent by certain brothers so that we might respond to it" (CS 39). Augustine had fulfilled his responsibility and now he could go back to more important works. Those expressions do not sound like a bishop who fears for the safety of his flock.

The case for Elpidius, Jason, and Bonosus becomes even stronger when Augustine indicates that he has even attached the original document to his work so that anyone may see "whether we have given a response to everything they wished to explore" (CS 39). This is not the language of serious controversy. Augustine clearly is not responding to an imminent threat to his flock but only to an irritating letter.

Certainly in 418 Augustine had other and more pressing matters to attend. He had been absent from Hippo almost continually from the second half of April to October of that year. He had attended a conference in Caesarea of Mauretania and had followed that by preaching five sermons in Carthage.[47] On his return he found two letters containing charges against him by the Italian Pelagians. He immediately launched himself into a defense. It was in the midst of all this turmoil that he had to reply to one more demand on his precious time; he had to refute the *Sermo Arianorum*.[48]

There is almost no real disagreement about the date of Augustine's *Contra Sermonem Arianorum*. Othmar Perler believes Augustine composed it in the winter of 418–19 and associates it with sermons 19 and 341.[49] Most scholars seem to be in substantial agreement with this date although some, like La Bonnardière, favor late 418 and others, like S. M. Zarb, prefer the beginning of 419.[50]

The author, the place of composition, and the place of delivery for the *Sermo* are all unnamed, but the theology of the *Sermo Arianorum* is the Ulfilan Arianism of the *Scolia*. Michel Meslin attributes it to Palladius of Ratiara. He claims that at the very least the *Sermo Arianorum* was a "logical and conscientious" digest or a sort of "schematic summary" of the theology of Palladius of Ratiara. His conclusion is based, at least partly, on observations of theological coincidence of the positions espoused in the *Scolia* and those of the *Sermo Arianorum*.[51]

Just who summarized it is uncertain. Were the languge of *Epistula* 242 slightly different, one might opt for Jason and Bonosus. But "the rich fruits of their arguments" was not made the grammatical equivalent of "the clever and forceful writing by one of your bishops." Perhaps it was Palladius himself. Whoever wrote it, when Elpidius sent it to Hippo Regius, he did not receive the response for which he had hoped. Augustine expressed no interest in becoming an Arian.

The real Arian threat was still ten years away for Roman Africa. Over the horizon of that decade was the debate with Maximinus and the Vandals' invasion of Africa. Here, in that irritating correspondence with Elpidius and his friends, Augustine had been given an outline of the Arian doctrines which he would meet in the debate with Maximinus.

The *Sermo Arianorum* is not a complete argument. As was noted above, its character is more that of a compendium, a synopsis of major doctrinal points. The doctrine is clearly Ulfilan.

The writer of this summary began with the identity of Christ Jesus. He is portrayed as the Father's agent for the creation of all things. He is the one who "took on human flesh" in order to show that "man is not vile but precious" (S 5).[52] But even this coming of Christ in compassion was done in a slave-like obedience to the Father. The author fortified his text with subordinationist prooftexts lest his readers miss this point (S 6).

At the crucifixion Christ laid aside his body, for it was only the body that experienced death. Christ was only insulted by this tearing of his garment. The author's Christ was the *Logos* clothed in flesh, a *Logos/sarx* Christology. He stipulated: "Thus Mary gave birth to a body of mortality, but God begot the immortal Son of immortality" (S 7).

Even the resurrection was accomplished "by the will and command of the Father," as the Son and his body were "caught up into glory by the Father as shepherd with his sheep, a priest with his oblation, a king with his royal robes, and God with his temple" (S 8). With the Son now enthroned by the command of the Father, the Son's character and office is that of a righteous judge, whose authority derives from the imperial laws. He establishes, therefore, a triad: the Father as emperor, the Son as judge, and the Holy Spirit as "advocate and consolation" (S 9).

On the basis of his earlier arguments, the writer outlined his views on the roles, relations, and functions of Father, Son, and Holy Spirit.

His Trinity is hierarchical. The Father is portrayed as the true God, the one that the Son adores as his God. The Son is the only-begotten God. He functions as God for the Holy Spirit and for mankind. The Spirit was seen almost excusively in the office of consoler and advocate.

He stressed the role of the Son as the image of the Father and the Spirit as the manifestation of the wisdom and virtue of the Son. But he was most insistent that each "is neither a part nor portion" of the other (S 23). He preached an absolute "distinction of three substances" (S 27). Their likeness and union is one of imitation. The Son imitates the Father and the Spirit imitates the Son (S 32).

The writer of the *Sermo Arianorum* also rejected the common orthodox argument that Christ only humbled himself for the sake of men. He asked how it is that Christ now continues in that humility when the need for it has passed (S 34). He also cited a number of scriptural passages in an attempt to support his view that the subjection continues as before.

Augustine's reply to the *Sermo Arianorum* laid the groundwork for all of his subsequent argumentation with Ulfilan Arians. Augustine's first response was to charge the Ulfilans with ditheism. This was the fundamental underpinning of his arguments. These Arians, who claimed to follow the Scriptures, were holding a position diametrically opposed to God's Word. Augustine's key reference was Deuteronomy 6:4, 13. He openly rejected the possibility of a God "in second" or a God "for us" (CS 1).

The bishop of Hippo then moved to the question of the Son's origin. Christ cannot have been made *ex nihilo,* for if he had been, then all things were not made through the agency of the Son. If the Son was truly God from God, then Father and Son must share the same nature (CS 3).

The African also violently disagreed with Ulfilan Christology. He claimed that their *Logos/sarx* Christology denies the human soul of Christ and thus prevents any true unity of person. The Ulfilan view, he insisted, negates the possibility of the Christ's dual nature and therefore the very possibiity of salvation. God the Son assumed a man in order to become Christ. The man was "created by the assumption" so that there was a complete sharing, a sort of *communicatio idiomatum,* by which his humanity received the name of his divinity (CS 7–9). While Augustine was not quick to use the actual term *communicatio idiomatum,* those words best describe his understanding of the relationship between Christ's humanity and his divinity.[53]

Augustine also pointed out that obedience does not necessarily imply diverse natures. Indeed, he maintained that Father, Son, and Spirit share one nature and are so unified that in some fashion the whole Trinity is present in every action of each person: Father, Son, or Holy Spirit (CS 11–13). He countered their prooftexts that seemed to support an inferiority within the Trinity with passages that seemed to show the Father, Son, and Spirit in synergistic activity. He also reinterpreted their prooftexts in the light of other Scriptures.

In chapter 16, the bishop of Hippo used one of his famous analogies from *De Trinitate*. Since man is formed in the image of God, according to Genesis 1:26, in the soul of man one would expect to find an image of the Trinity. He notes how man's memory, understanding, and will are always at work together. Yet, he continues, they are not one but three. They are ineffably joined as the three persons of the Trinity are ineffably joined (CS 16–19).

In this work, the researcher notes two new developments in Augustine's Trinitarian thought. The concept of the humanity of Christ being created by the assumption would only appear in Augustine's later works. One of its clearest and fullest expressions is found here (CS 8). Certainly there were tendencies in this direction even before *De Trinitate*. But here for the first time the position is clearly proclaimed and adequately defended. Another interesting and new feature first unveiled in the *Contra Sermonem* is the expansion of the role of the Son in illumination. In his earlier view, Augustine was tempted to divide between the interior sign of Christ and the inspiration of the Spirit.[54] In 389 he wrote to Nebridius that while "our knowledge" of the Father comes "through the Son" yet "the inward charm" and "sweetness of remaining in that knowledge and of despising all mortal things" is properly "ascribed to the Holy Spirit" (Ep. 11). But in the *Contra Sermonem*, the Spirit no longer has as strong a claim to "warning the oblivious." Now the Son participates more fully with him in this activity. In fact, "the Spirit . . . does not teach or illumine anyone at all without Christ" (CS 32). What is probably Augustine's best discussion of the concept of the *communicatio idiomatum* is also found in this work (CS 8).

### Maximus, the Former Arian

In *Epistula* 170 Augustine and his colleague Alypius gave the physician Maximus a brief reminder of his duties. Alypius was the bishop of Thagaste and a longtime friend to Augustine.[55] Maximus, who had become a Catholic after hearing one of Augustine's sermons, was a recent convert from Arianism. As an Arian, Maximus had used his influence to lead a number of people into the heresy. Now the two bishops were urging him to use his authority to redeem his family and *coloni* (tenant farmers) from Arianism. They also wrote to him an exposition on the relationship of the Father and the Son and the worship due the Trinity. At about the same time, they wrote to Maximus's bishop and requested the latter to beg the doctor not to take offense at the cheap paper and the fact that it was dictated to *notarii*.[56] The custom was to write important letters with one's own hand on parchment. Augustine was worried that they had offended the physician.

A little later Augustine alone wrote to Maximus. He outlined for him seven stages of the spiritual life. In this letter, Augustine warned Maximus to be careful with his interpretation of Scriptures. He urged the doctor not to object to scriptural passages that seem to conflict or to be nonsensical. Neither was he to impose his own ideas on the meaning of the text. Instead, he was to submit his own mind to the text (Ep. 171A).

*Epistula* 170 was a work written sometime after 413, for Peregrinus, the physician's bishop, was ordained that year. Wilfred Parsons, translator of the letters for the *Fathers of the Church* series, assigned it to about 415, while La Bonnardiére assigns the date of about 419–20.[57] La Bonnardiére gives the more satisfying date, but her reasoning is somewhat suspect. O'Connell, while in substantial agreement with her, wonders if her discussion of *Epistula* 170 does not need to undergo further review.[58] The trustworthiness of her dates in this regard is also viewed with some suspicion by this author.[59] Determining the actual date of the texts by external evidence seems, at present, impossible.

Augustine made no specific statement about which type of Arianism Maximus had abandoned. But it may be possible to determine it, at least tentatively, by a careful reading of Augustine's arguments against it in his exposition on the relationship of the Father and the Son. The Arianism that Maximus abandoned and which his household still served does not appear to have been highly philosophical or dialectical in nature. Indeed, Augustine spent most of his time examining Arian prooftexts and refuting their subordinationist interpretation. One does not encounter here the tightly reasoned arguments which he employed against the Eunomians in other places. There is no hint, for example, of the Eunomian view of the Son as Son of God's will or of the equating of "Father" with the will of God. While Augustine does refute the doctrine of "unlikeness," the whole thrust of his argumentation is aimed at an Arianism that teaches a strict subordinationism dependent almost wholly upon the interpretation of preselected prooftexts. It seems to be Ulfilan Arianism, or, at least, the Danubian or Acacian Homoianism of the last half of the fourth century.

Augustine's key arguments in this work derived from a study of the Greek word *latreia* (worship). He noted that according to the Scriptures, only one God is to be worshipped and obeyed. How, he asked, can the Holy Spirit be less than God when Christians' bodies are his temple? Since he is to be worshipped, then not just the Father but the whole Trinity is worthy of worship. He recognized that the concept of Trinity is beyond human reason. Only by faith can one accept it. From that point on he defended the concept of Trinity on the basis of hermeneutics. He tried to show that only a fully trinitarian approach avoids serious scriptural contradictions.

## The Encounter with Pascentius

*Epistulae* 238–41 comprise Augustine's correspondence with Pascentius. Letters 238, 239, and 241 are all from Augustine to Pascentius, while letter 240 is a reply from Pascentius. None of these letters has a formal address. Their occasion was the confused outcome of a conference between Pascentius and the bishop of Hippo, probably held at Carthage (Vita 17).

Eugene Portalié did not consider these letters to be genuine. He attributed them to Vigilius Thapsus, who published his *Contra Feliciano* and *De Trinitate et unitate Dei* under Augustine's name when persecution by the Vandals prevented him from using his own.[60] Were it not for the testimony of Augustine's contemporary and biographer, Possidius, one might be tempted to consider the validity of Portalié's suggestion (Vita 17). Augustine failed to mention the debate in his correspondence with Pascentius in his *Retractationes* or any other text, besides the correspondence itself.

There is little solid evidence from which to date Augustine's debate and correspondence with Pascentius. The famous French scholar Tillemont believed that the conference occurred in 406. Tillemont, like many later scholars, bases this on Augustine's reference to age, "pro merito aetatis ac dignitatis tuae." Tillemont believed that to be old enough to warrant the comment, Pascentius had to be at least sixty. For Augustine's words to carry any weight, he felt that the African bishop had to be significantly younger, yet old enough to have gained great renown. In 406 Augustine had begun his twelfth year in the episcopate and was fifty-two years old. Therefore, Tillemont decided that 406 would be an appropriate date. As Othmar Perler states, however, such a date is at best hypothetical.

Perler places the encounter between 404 and 414. Unlike some scholars, he rejects the possibility of it taking place in 414, since during
that year Augustine does not seem to have been in Carthage.[61]

Some modern scholars have attempted to date the encounter on
the basis of two assumptions. The first is that Possidius placed his
discussion of Augustine's opposition to Arianism between the discussions on Donatism and Pelagianism for chronological reasons.
Those two controversies overlap; the first ended in about 418,
whereas the second began in about 411 and lasted to the end of the
bishop's life. Some scholars have placed the debate somewhat before
mid-point of the overlap. Like Tillemont, they try to back this up
with a rather doubtful interpretation of Augustine's oblique reference
to the honor due Pascentius, "pro merito aetatis ac dignitatis tuae."
They assume that it indicates that Augustine was younger than Pascentius. Since in 414 Augustine was already sixty, they are reluctant
to consider any later date.[62]

But Augustine's use of the phrase "pro merito aetatis ac dignitatis
tuae," when read in the context of their bitter debate and correspondence, could as easily be a reprimand more in the spirit of, "at your
age and position in society you should know better." There is no
compelling reason for interpreting the phrase as evidence of Pascentius's greater age. Neither is the argument based on the order of
Possidius's discussions unassailable. Tucked into chapter 17 with his
discussion of Augustine's conflict with Pascentius is a discussion of
his debate with Maximinus, which occurred in 428 and, thus, clearly
exceeds the 411–18 overlap. Also weighing against this early date is
the fact that no reference to the debate and correspondence appears
in the *Retractationes,* or any of his other later works. This might
indicate a rather late date, perhaps shortly before Augustine's debate
with Maximinus in 428. On the other hand, the circumstances surrounding the conference and the lack of any reference to the conflict
between Boniface and the empress regent indicate a time before that
conflict and one after the overthrow of the usurper John in 425. One
can, then, tentatively place these events as late as the period between
A.D. 425 and 427.

Pascentius was a *comes domus regiae,* belonging to the grade of
*spectabilis* (Vita 17). His title indicates that he was probably of the
*res privata* but his specific position within the government is difficult
to determine.[63] Gerald Bonner, presumably on the basis of Pascentius's title, assumes that he was a commander of troops.[64] This is
possible, but he was probably in the *officia.* As noted previously, the
*comites domesticorum* could be either military or administrative offi-
cers. Pascentius's age and the nature of his official role in Africa as

the emperor's chief tax collector are strong arguments against his having held a military position. In either case, he was acting as tax collector in Africa and was almost universally despised for his rigor in carrying out this duty. He was an elderly, moody, obdurate, and prideful man, with a weakness for public speaking. He was also a self-proclaimed theological expert. The failings of his character soon become obvious to any honest observer.[65] According to Possidius, Pascentius found special relish in harassing the Catholic clergy. It was in response to this provocation that the special conference was called (Vita 17).

When the tax gatherer praised Auxentius at the beginning of the conference, Augustine's colleague Alypius posed him a potentially perilous question. He asked whether Arius or Eunomius had the support of Auxentius. Pascentius, sensing his danger, immediately anathematized Arius and Eunomius. If he had said anything favorable about either of them, he would have faced prosecution under the heresy laws.[66]

Bonner believes that he was praising Auxentius, the former Arian bishop of Milan.[67] But Pascentius was probably praising the theology of Auxentius of Durostorum, one of the writers of the Scolia and Ulfila's devoted student. Auxentius of Milan had long been dead, and Pascentius and his questioners were obviously referring to a living person.

After condemning Arius and Eunomius, Pascentius demanded that the bishops, Augustine and Alypius, anathematize homoousios. When they objected, he demanded that they show him the word in the Scriptures. The bishops replied that the word is Greek and that their own language was Latin. The assured him that they could show him the meaning of the word homoousios in the Scriptures. Pascentius, however, demanded repeatedly that they show him the term itself in the Bible and ignored their continued protests that the correct interpretation was what must be sought. Pascentius then delivered his confession of faith. He said that he believed in "God the Father almighty, invisible, unbegotten, incomprehensible, and in Jesus Christ, his Son, God born before the ages, through whom all things were made, and in the Holy Spirit."

His comments, attitudes, and particularly his confession of faith marked Pascentius as an Ulfilan. A fan of Auxentius of Durostorum, he repeated the Ulfilan condemnation of the term homoousios and sought to emulate the Ulfilan insistence on a strictly biblical basis for theology. His confession of faith reveals that he could not be a Eunomian since, for him, the Father is "incomprehensible" and the Eunomians stressed the "comprehension" of God as the way of salvation. It also matches the basic style and emphasis of the Ulfilans.[68]

When Pascentius had delivered his confession, Augustine said that he could sign such a confession. Pascentius assumed that he had convinced and converted the famous bishop. He quickly snatched up a scrap of paper and hurriedly scrawled his confession and handed it to Augustine for the bishop to sign. He was soon bitterly disappointed. He believed afterward that Augustine had been almost persuaded but had turned away from the pure and simple waters of truth to the polluted stream of human error (Ep. 240).

Augustine, glancing over the written statement, noted that Pascentius had, in his haste, left out the word *Father* and had substituted "unborn" for "incomprehensible." The bishop said he could still sign it but he had a question first. He asked if the words "unbegotten Father" ever appear in the Scriptures. Pascentius hurriedly assured him that they did. Augustine then asked Pascentius to show him this phrase in the Scriptures. The bishop of Hippo had cleverly turned the tables on the Ulfilan.

In shocked surprise, a bystander, whom the bishop later suspected was also an Arian, interrupted. He demanded to know if Augustine believed that the Father was begotten. Augustine answered that, indeed, he did not. The man then replied that if the Father is not begotten, then, logically, he is unbegotten. The bishop agreed but also noted that this illustrated his point about *homoousios*. A word itself not in Scriptures can correctly summarize a truth found in the Scriptures.

Pascentius replied that there was good reason for the term *unbegotten* not to appear in the Scriptures, for if it did occur, it would dishonor God. Pascentius was probably thinking of its similarity to the common expletive "misbegotten." Augustine pressed harder. He asked if, in writing the term, Palladius himself had dishonored God. Palladius, wavering, decided his use of "unbegotten" had been unwise. Augustine insisted that if the term should not have been used, then perhaps the tax collector should erase it from his confession. Pascentius refused. He decided that it had been correct for him to use. Augustine retorted that it was then also proper to use *homoousios* in this way. The tax collector at that point tore up his confession of faith. The two then made arrangements to meet in the afternoon for further discussion. Augustine asked that they have *notarii* in attendance, so that a record of what was said could be kept and consulted. Pascentius agreed.

Augustine depended rather heavily upon these professional note-takers. He trusted them more than his own memory. Many of his works appear to have been dictated through them and then later revised. He even prepared most of his personal correspondence in this way (Ep. 171A; 238).

In the afternoon, Augustine returned with his stenographers (notarii) and awaited Pascentius. When Pascentius showed up, he had no notarii with him. They waited for them for a while and then finally started without them.

Pascentius repeated his creed but left out the phrase "unbegotten." He then demanded a confession of faith from Augustine. Augustine asked Pascentius to repeat what he had just said for the benefit of the record, as they had agreed that morning. The suspicious tax gatherer cried out angrily that they were preparing a malicious legal charge against him and that was the reason for their wanting him to repeat his words.

The government official's fears were not groundless. Arianism was illegal and could be harshly punished. Only barbarians, the military, and some of the very highest officials seemed to be immune, and this immunity was by no means absolutely certain. Pascentius was evidently frightened that he might make utterances that were not legal. A written record could be used in a heresy trial against him.[69]

Augustine wondered aloud why Pascentius would fear a written record when so many illustrious witnesses were present. It may be that, like the "bystander" mentioned earlier, many of these men were secretly sympathetic to the Arian cause. Possidius says that their names were omitted from this letter to Pascentius "due to fear" (Vita 17).

The argument turned bitter. Augustine asked sarcastically and in a low voice, "Do you mean that we are preparing a malicious charge against you?" Augustine was insinuating two things by this question. One, the bishop was hinting that this was the sort of thing Pascentius himself had done to others. Two, Augustine was implying that a powerful official like Pascentius had little to fear from provincials.

But Pascentius had every right to fear such an action. He may have had in mind the precedents set by Ambrose. He knew that bishops could have considerable political clout. Perhaps he had read an account of the events at the Council of Aquileia and saw too much similarity in this conference.

Embarrassed and flustered by this exchange, Pascentius repeated his creed in a louder tone, but left out "God the Son." Augustine pointed out the error and asked again that they keep a record, since with it one could avoid such mistakes. Besides, he argued, a written account could be studied and discussed by others. The tax gatherer's anger flared. He retorted that Augustine fell far short of the fame that had preceded him. The conference ended with Augustine reminding Pascentius that when they greeted before lunch, the bishop himself had admitted that his reputation bore him false witness. He claimed to be only a servant of God, truthful only "because he who is true speaks in his servants."

Sometime after the conference, Pascentius claimed to have vanquished the famous bishop. He boasted that Augustine had feared to give his confession of faith. Augustine wrote *Epistula* 238 to refresh Pascentius's memory of the conference and to set the record straight. He presented a confession of faith in the last half of it, in order to show that Pascentius's claims of his fear might be proven false.

Only after his second letter did Augustine receive a brief reply. Pascentius compared Augustine's Trinitarian position to a twisted tree, with nothing straight in it. He was distressed at Augustine's insistence on the equality of the Father, Son, and Holy Spirit. He responded rhetorically,

> How can there be one God from three? Is he, then, one triple person, called by this name? If you had been willing and had possessed confidence in your profession of the faith, you and your fellow bishops would have sat down with me, with a pure and peaceful spirit, and spoken about the things of God which have to do with glory and spiritual grace. What use is there writing to one another what does not edify us? (Ep. 240)

Augustine's last letter to Pascentius was a plea to continue the discussion. Since there are no further letters, one must assume that it fell on deaf ears.

Apart from the earlier arguments, one of the best reasons for dating these documents after the *Contra Sermonem* is the growth and development one finds in Augustine's anti-Arian polemic. His argumentation becomes more consciously dependent upon the Scriptures. This new emphasis would reach its climax in the *Contra Maximinum Arianorum Episcopum*. His approach to controversy with the Ulfilans was quickly becoming a bi-level weave of comparative exegesis with syllogism and analogy.

One of the clearest and most succinct statements of Augustine's Trinitarian faith came in response to Pascentius. In *Epistula* 238, one can view the state of his Trinitarian faith prior to the debate with Maximinus.

Augustine's basic position and his assumptions had not changed substantially from *De Trinitate*. The only effect of the Arian intrusions into his life seems to have been found in a greater dependence upon the Scriptures and a growing insistence on the absolute unity of the persons of the Trinity. He described the Trinity as the true, invisible, immortal, eternal God in his absolutely immutable substance. He allowed no diversity whatsoever. There is a coinherence of the persons. They are inseparably joined. The very names of the persons and the relations that those names imply are all that distinguish each person from another. All three are spirit, since every incorporeal nature is called spirit. Father, Son, and Holy Spirit are, therefore, all one spirit according to substance. The third person of the Trinity is called Spirit because of his relationship in proceeding from both Father and Son.

# 4

# AUGUSTINE AND MAXIMINUS

## Augustine, Boniface, and the African Crisis

The Roman Boniface came to Africa in 414. His career had taken him from the Danube to Marseilles. He had lived among barbarians for much of his life. In Africa he was probably first stationed at the head of a band of Gothic mercenaries near Vescera (modern Biskra) on the southern border.[1] His rank at this time was probably tribune, the equivalent of a modern colonel.[2] The young tribune's *foederati* had notable success against Moorish raiders along the borders of Roman Africa.[3] He was already famous throughout the empire for his heroism, extraordinary generosity, and remarkable military abilities.[4] Part of his fame, no doubt, derived from his successful defense of Marseilles against Ataulf's Gothic forces in 412. When the Visigoths, fresh from sacking Rome, had attacked Marseilles, Boniface had helped organize the city's successful defense and had personally wounded Ataulf, the leader of the barbarians.[5]

When Boniface wrote Augustine about the Donatists approaching his troops and began to interest himself in combating the schism, Augustine was very impressed. Such interest in the things of God and the welfare of the Church was unusual in a career officer (Ep. 185.1; 189.8).

Some modern scholars question Boniface's sincerity. Marie Aquinas MacNamara, for instance, says:

> Boniface would not have minimized the value of Augustine's public support. The question has long been debated by historians, whether he was sincere in his apparent zeal for Catholicism, or whether he was merely trying to appear virtuous in Augustine's eyes. Later developments suggest that Boniface was at heart an opportunist who was both clever and successful enough to fool the discerning Augustine. His true colors were soon to become tragically apparent.[6]

This seems a rather harsh judgment. When his wife died in 420, the grief-stricken Boniface felt himself ready to abandon public life and from then on led a monastic life, like that of Augustine's clergy. Augustine, just getting over an illness, and Alypius, his friend and fellow bishop, met the military officer at Tubunae (Ep. 220).

Perler tentatively dates this meeting in 421. He does so for several reasons. First, the place of the meeting indicates that Boniface was not yet *comes Africae* because in time of peace, the *comes* would have his headquarters in Carthage, not on the frontier. In 422 Boniface was away from Africa. When he returned in 423, he had received the dignity of *comes Africae*. In 421 Augustine had, indeed, consulted with Alypius and probably went to see Boniface either immediately before or right after the Council of Carthage on 13 June.[7]

Augustine and Alypius believed Boniface to be one of the ablest soldiers of the deeply troubled empire; they urged him to take only a private vow of chastity and to serve the Church by protecting the empire from the barbarians. Boniface agreed to this and became one of Augustine's regular visitors at his monastry in Hippo (Ep. 220).[8] In retrospect, this advice was probably among Augustine's most regretted actions, for it may have made him an unwitting instrument of Boniface's moral decline and the descent of the Vandals on Roman Africa.

In 422 Boniface was sent to Spain on an imperial commission. By 423 he was back as *comes Africae*. While away, he had broken his vow of chastity and married a Vandal princess named Pelagia (Ep. 220).[9] Perhaps he married her for the purpose of a military alliance, like the one that Aetius had with the Huns. Boniface had not consented to marry Pelagia until she became a Catholic. She, however, soon relapsed into Arianism and had her infant daughter baptized as an Arian. Augustine heard about all this along with some disturbing rumors that Boniface himself was being promiscuous. The old bishop was scandalized and overwhelmed with sorrow but was afraid to write to the *comes* lest the letter fall into the wrong hands (Ep. 220).

In his *Prosopography*, R. J. Martindale supposes that Boniface's second marriage took place in 426 on a trip to Italy. Such a date does not leave much time for the birth of the child, its baptism, the rift with Augustine, and their eventual reconciliation. Based on the evidence of *Epistula* 220, the trip to Spain, in about 423, is much to be preferred. Martindale also identifies Pelagia as being "probably Visigothic."[10] One must wonder if he does so because of his prior assumption that the marriage took place on the trip to Italy in 426. This assumption about Pelagia's identity surely flies in the face of the apparent linkage between Boniface's marriage to her and his appeal to the Vandals for help. Pelagia seems to have been held in high esteem by the Vandals. This would be very unusual if she were a Visigoth, since the two tribes had long been at war.

It was in 425, with the return of Galla Placidia, that Boniface's rank was increased to *comes Africae et domesticorum*. When Galla Placidia was exiled in early 423, he had remained loyal to her, supplied her with money, and contributed to her return to power. He kept Africa loyal to her family during the time of John's usurpation and resisted his attempts to invade Africa. As a *comes domesticorum*, Boniface was not under the *magister militum*. *Domestici,* soldiers "of the household," were one of the three groups of imperial bodyguards. Unlike the other guards, they also served as a war college and academy for future generals. Officially, at least, he was on a level with the *magister militum* directly under the emperor. His troops were subject only to himself and the emperor.[11] This independence, given by Placidia to balance the ambitious Aetius, would later cause her to fear for his loyalty. It was this apprehension that would make her fall prey to Aetius's machinations.

Again Boniface's main task became the defense of the Roman provinces from African barbarians. His conduct in office was described by contemporaries as "just and incorruptible."[12] He appears to have been quite successful until disaster struck, in the form of Aetius's plots.

When Aetius's treachery came to fruition and Boniface was declared an enemy of the Roman people, the *comes Africae* gathered his scattered army and prepared to defend himself. African barbarians swept across the now unguarded borders and ravaged the countryside. Augustine was appalled (Ep. 220).

Boniface's concentration of forces is, from a military point of view, completely understandable. It was simply a problem of travel times and of maintaining sufficient force to defeat his enemies. Sea travel was much faster than the pace of footsoldier or horseman. The trip from Italy to Carthage, could take as little as two days.[13] Boniface could not afford to divide his meager forces between the two tasks, and he could never have gathered them quickly enough to avoid defeat in detail.

As Boniface prepared to defeat a Roman army under three generals, Augustine wrote to him. He rebuked Boniface for his love of the world, which according to Augustine had embroiled him in political troubles. What disturbed the bishop most was that Boniface had rallied his army to protect his personal power and safety, rather than giving all his efforts to protect the people from the African barbarians. He blamed the *comes* for all the ravages of war that afflicted Africa. He allowed Boniface no excuses. Even if he was falsely charged, it was his worldly passion for honor, power, pleasure, and so on, that had brought about this horrible situation. He should have imitated Christ and rendered good to those who had done him evil (Ep. 220).

Though disturbed by Boniface's actions, the bishop of Hippo worked for a reconciliation between Galla Placidia and Boniface. He also may even have sent his friend Alypius to the court at Ravenna to plead Boniface's case before Placidia (Ep. 224).[14] When Segisvultus came into Africa, Boniface, perhaps in response to Augustine's pleas for peace, retired to Sitifis.[15]

Distressed by the growing devastation of Africa, the bishop was heartened only by the coming of Darius, Placidia's representative for negotiations with Boniface. Augustine saw only good in Darius, for he was a man come to establish peace. Their exchange in letters is exuberant and filled with showy references that emphasize their knowledge of Latin literature. Augustine regretted that, in the winter of 428–29, his infirmities prevented his seeing Darius in person (Ep. 229–31).[16] The civil war ended, but there were still the Vandals.

The harried Boniface, perhaps on the basis of an alliance by marriage, had called for the aid of the Vandal king Gunderic in his struggle with the newly appointed *comes* Segisvultus. But Gunderic had died before the message arrived, and the ambitious and treacherous Gaiseric received it instead. It was the opportunity for which he had been waiting. In the spring of 429, the Vandals took ship and crossed from southern Hispania to the far western reaches of Roman Africa.[17]

The Vandals had now been in the empire for some twenty-three years. Their fortunes had varied. Together with the Suevi, they had plundered Gaul for three years and then crossed to Spain. At first they settled in Hispania as allies of the empire. Later the Visigothic allies of the emperor were sent to destroy them. The Siling branch of the Vandals was obliterated; the Asding Vandals and a few allied Alani and Suevi were driven into the mountains of Galicia.[18]

When Wallia and his Visigoths evacuated Spain and were given a home in southwest Gaul, a reward for a job well done, the Vandals turned on and fought the Suevi. They had them penned in the Nevasian Mountains of northern Spain, when Asterius, the Roman *comes Hispaniarum,* intervened on the Suevi's behalf. The Vandals immediately turned southward and invaded Baetica. In 421 Castinus, the *magister militum,* attacked them with a large force of Roman troops and Visigothic *foederati.* The Goths, however, betrayed Castinus. He was forced to retreat. The Vandals raided throughout the south and by 428 had captured the city of Hispalis and were besieging Nova Carthago.[19]

Weary of the constant pressure put on them by the Visigoths, the Vandals saw in Africa a more promising settlement. In its current political turmoil, they perceived an opportunity to seize the rich granary of the empire and make it their own.[20] Some eighty thousand of them made the crossing. When they landed, their military force of about twenty-five thousand faced no serious opposition until after they had passed through Mauretania.[21] Like the Visigoths, they were not the same tribe that had first entered the empire. Courcelle commented that the "Vandal tribe" which crossed over into Africa was really "the debris of diverse peoples or barbarian bands, who had lost their autonomy."[22]

As the Vandals plundered and burned town after town in Mauretania, Boniface soon realized that they had not come as allies but as conquerors (Vita 28).[23] The rough Visigothic soldiers "were lambs compared to the Vandal wolves."[24] In their search for treasure, all ages and both sexes were cruelly tortured. By their slow, inexorable, and devastating advance they inspired a terror unduplicated in the history of the invasions.[25] Children were cut in half, virgins had hot irons thrust into their breasts, huge numbers of women were raped, and local notables were impaled.[26]

But as horrible as these atrocities were, the Vandals reserved their worst tortures for the Catholic clergy—for two reasons. First, they sought the hidden silver and gold plate of the churches. Second, they recognized in the clergy a moral force for resistance.[27] They literally made war on the Catholic Church. They plundered and burned every church building in city after city (Vita 28). On one occasion, as a congregation celebrated Easter, Vandal soldiers shot them all to death with arrows.[28]

Augustine anchored the clergy in the midst of growing distress and terror. Though well aware of the brutalities, he emphasized the insignificance of physical suffering in comparison to spiritual suffering. Mortal peril was to be ignored. He stressed that the clergy must not abandon their people and flee. The priest, he argued, is never more needed than when his people are suffering. Also, if they should flee, how could the people have the spiritual will to resist the Arian clergy who accompanied the invaders? Those clergymen who remained would inspire the faith of their flocks.[29]

As the invaders advanced, Quodvultdeus (a deacon at Carthage), Honoratus (bishop of Tubunae), and an unnamed clergyman wrote Augustine about the clergy's right to flee from persecution, supporting their case with Matthew 10:23, 2:14, and 2 Corinthians 11:33. To these scriptural supports they added several practical reasons. They argued that their presence would not lessen and might indeed increase the suffering of the faithful and that, like the bishops of Spain who had fled before the barbarians and later returned after they had passed, they might live to serve Christ another day. Augustine soon wrote back: "Either, therefore, everyone should move to places of refuge, or those who have to stay should not be abandoned by those who should minister to their spiritual needs; so that all may equally live and suffer whatever the Lord of the household wishes for them to endure" (Ep. 228).

As only Augustine could, he drew moral lessons from the growing tragedy of the invasions. He noted how men gave up all their hard-won worldly goods in order to save their lives. Certainly, he insisted, they are worthless in comparison with the treasures that Christ offers. He noted that those who had mistreated their slaves out of greed for gain were betrayed by them to the Vandals, while those who had been generous were protected by them. He urged the people to strive to enter Christ's enduring kingdom.[30]

Once Boniface had made peace with Placidia, he hurried to meet Gaiseric in battle, only to be defeated. The Vandals then attempted to take Carthage but were repelled. Their force split. One group went east to Byzacena, where they martyred the bishops Vita and Urusita.[31] The other besieged Hippo, while Boniface himself defended the city. The siege began in late May or early June of 430 and lasted about eighteen months.

A number of bishops and refugees from all over the region crowded the city. As the siege began, Augustine continued to work on his refutations of Maximinus, the Arian bishop, and Julian of Eclanum, the Pelagian. He also treated with mercy and kindness those bishops who, through the weakness of the flesh, had fled to Hippo (Vita 17; 28). Augustine, who was already sick, sought to comfort his congregation with his presence among them. He constantly prayed and counseled. Finally, overcome with a fever, he retired to bed. It was about the third month of the siege. There, in seclusion, he read aloud the Psalms dealing with reprentance. On 28 August A.D. 430, the famous bishop of Hippo died.[33]

## Augustine and Maximinus: The Debate and After

Not until the very end of his life did Augustine face an Arian bishop. He would debate the man sometimes referred to as the "pope" of the Western Arians. This formidable opponent, an excellent public speaker, intellectually alert, with an unequaled scriptural knowledge, was an opinionated and stubborn logician with a courageous loyalty to his faith.[34] Augustine would debate Maximinus. But who was Maximinus?

Reconstructing his identity is not easy. The first problem is establishing his approximate date of birth. During the debate he indicated that he was younger than Augustine. This means he could not have been born earlier than the 360s. The fact that he was a bishop when he met Augustine in the debate probably means he was at least thirty years old. Thus, an upper limit of the 390s is established.[35]

Now, if he can be identified as the Maximinus of the *Scolia,* who was a disciple of Palladius of Ratiara, one of the defendants at the Council of Aquileia, the approximate date of his birth can be established. Another factor in this computation is whether he was an active disciple at the time of Aquileia. A number of factors combine. First, the indication in the *Collatio* is that he was only slightly younger than Augustine.[36] Secondly, his theology perfectly matches that of the Maximinus in the *Scolia.* Also, there is only one Arian bishop named Maximinus in the documents of this period.[37] Fourthly, as author of the *Scolia,* Maximinus had a reverence for Palladius and Secundianus, which combined with his apparent reliance on either memory or eyewitness verbal accounts, as well as written sources, indicates that he was an active disciple of Palladius at the time of the council in 381.[38] Finally, then, to be an active disciple he must have been at least in his teens. If one should establish his age as about sixteen in 381, then he must have been born in about 365 and been around sixty-two when he debated Augustine. This would allow the age differences to be noticeable but relatively close, since Augustine was about seventy-three at the time of the debate.

There is much controversy over the nationality of Maximinus. Michel Meslin provides the strongest arguments for a Roman origin. In fact, he believes he can identify the province and diocese. According to Meslin, Maximinus was of Roman Danubian descent, from the province of Valeria in Illyricum. Meslin argues that, first of all, his name is Latin, not latinized. Secondly, he notes a few scattered comments in works attributed to him showing scorn for the barbarians. Lastly, Meslin contends that Maximinus's eagerness to defend the honor and memory of Palladius affirms ties of spiritual affiliation, affection, and personal knowledge that is only present in people of the same background.[39] To these he adds an argument from silence. He notes that neither Augustine nor Possidius calls

Maximinus a Goth. They say only that he accompanied the Goths (Vita 17).[40]

German scholarship, however, often wants to view Maximinus as a Goth. Bardenhewer, for example, calls Maximinus a Goth who accompanied "his people" from the Balkans to Africa.[41] The Frenchman Pierre Paul Courcelle also believes that this is the correct view. He notes that the "anti-barbarian" references in Maximinus's works seem mainly to refer to the Vandals, who were usually the mortal enemies of the Goths.[42] However, Roger Gryson and Ernest A. Thompson disagree. They feel that the statements are typical of Roman, not Gothic, attitudes.[43]

While some of the leading scholars disagree on his nationality, however, even those who are the most insistent on his Roman identity note his extremely close association with the Visigoths. He preached to and wrote for the tribesmen, and his works were avidly read and cherished by them. This was only natural since, as disciples of Ulfila, they shared a common faith.[44]

Little else is known about Maximinus prior to his journey to Africa.[45] There are only guesses and speculations. Meslin, for example, sees him as the clandestine successor to Palladius in the persecuted Arian communities of Illyria after 381.[46]

When Segisvultus came to Africa, Maximinus accompanied him. Maximinus was probably sent along with Segisvultus to serve as chaplain to the large contingent of Homoian Goths. The newly appointed *comes* mandated the bishop to serve as his official counselor in religious affairs. Maximinus was to maintain peace in the Church, especially among the Arians, and to convince Catholics to accept the faith of Rimini (CM 2.14; Vita 17).[47] The attempt, in Meslin's view, was doomed from the very beginning.[48] How could the mere presence of a military force, in majority Homoian, suffice to establish in Africa a Homoianism condemned in the rest of the empire? The presence of an armed force would at least give the challenging faith a chance to be heard. The Ulfilans were sure that any reasonable person would see the truth of their position if it was once given a fair hearing.

Maximinus came on a visit to Hippo Regius. Augustine, distressed at having a heretical rival, attacked Maximinus in a sermon and called him a blasphemer. This understandably upset Maximinus. He speedily complained to Segisvultus that Augustine was meddling in his affairs, perhaps by spreading Catholic propaganda among the Gothic soldiers.[49] Concinnata indicates that fear of Segisvultus had greatly influenced Maximinus's favorable reception in Carthage and Hippo.[50]

Heraclius, Augustine's successor and colleague, challenged Maximinus to a debate.[51] The Arian worsted the deacon. But Augustine soon replaced his colleague as the advocate for the Catholic side. He insisted that *notarii* be present and that the debate be public.[52] The *Collatio cum Maximino Arianorum episcopo* is the official report by the *notarii* of this meeting. The following account of events is this writer's rather abbreviated interpretation of the official report.[53]

Maximinus began the conference by trying to establish some ground rules. He said that he would accept anything that was reasonable and any scriptural interpretation that was truly universal. But he wanted to ban "those expressions which are outside of Scripture." And he quoted Matthew 15:9 in support of this approach (Max. Coll. 1).

True to his Homoian principles, Maximinus wanted to exclude from the discussion terms such as *homoousios,* which the Catholics had used to define heresy. But Augustine had no intention of agreeing to that. Instead, he demanded that Maximinus tell of his beliefs concerning the Father, the Son, and the Holy Spirit. The Arian referred Augustine to the Council of Rimini. But the bishop of Hippo repeated his demand and went on to accuse Maximinus of failing to respond to his question. Maximinus protested that he had indeed responded. Augustine said that what he really wanted was Maximinus's personal views, not a reference to a council whose authority the African questioned.

While Augustine's demanding manner may seem harsh to modern sensibilities, the early Church was not troubled by demanding adherence to the entire Catholic faith, as they understood it. They often viewed this as a prerequisite to salvation. A regular feature of the creeds, from A.D. 300 to 700, was an appendix of anathemas, which threatened any deviation from the doctrines contained in them with eternal destruction.[54]

Maximinus rushed to explain that he had never meant to hide behind the authority of a council. He merely intended to indicate the authority on which his positions were based. Then the Arian noted that, though he was fully aware of the imperial laws, he must, nevertheless, confess his faith before men. He followed with a brief confession:

> I believe that God the Father is the one who received life from no one; and that the Son is the one who, because he is and because he lives, received from the Father so that he might be; and that the Holy Spirit is the one paraclete who is the illuminator and sanctifier of our souls. (Max. Coll. 4)

Maximinus claimed to base this confession on the "divine Scriptures." He also promised to respond fully to whatever questions Augustine might ask.

Maximinus had reason to fear persecution and even death. The imperial antiheresy laws specifically condemned Arianism and they were still officially in force, even if sometimes circumvented unofficially. His boldness here shows him to have been a man of conviction. The support of Segisvultus, newly appointed *comes Africae,* probably did nothing to detract from this boldness.

Since the Arian had promised to answer his questions, Augustine took the offensive. He asked why the Arian had attributed the role of illuminator to the Holy Spirit "as if Christ might not be our illuminator" (Aug. Coll. 5). Maximinus responded by advancing a hierarchy of illumination which proceeds from the Father, through the Son, and to the Holy Spirit who then may either provide the illumination directly or through the agency of other men. Augustine, then, wanted to know if Maximinus believed that the Father and Son could illumine only through the Holy Spirit.

Maximinus refused to give a simple yes or no answer. Instead, he quoted Titus 3:4–6, which indicates that Father, Son, and Spirit all play identifiable roles in the act of regeneration. As regeneration comes from the Father by the reception of the Spirit through the Son, so he believed does illumination. But he was also careful to attribute their unity in this act, as in all others, to their harmony of will rather than to a metaphysical unity.

The Arian had not taken the bishop of Hippo's carefully placed bait. Augustine wanted a simple answer of either yes or no. Either would have given him the base from which to build what he would consider an irrefutable argument for the orthodox Trinitarian view. He either misunderstood or pretended to misunderstand Maximinus's response. He accused the Arian of avoiding the issue and restated his demand.

Maximinus accused the orthodox bishop of misrepresenting the facts. He felt that he had given an adequate response. But Augustine accused the Arian of wasting precious time and not answering the question that he had asked. Maximinus felt that they had dealt with this question and that he had given an adequate answer. He proposed that they proceed with the discussion of some other point.

Augustine dredged up one of the Arian's earlier statements that, deprived of its context, could mean that the Holy Spirit illumines through Christ. Maximinus responded by accusing Augustine of being the one who now wanted to waste precious time. He briefly recapitulated his hierarchical view of illumination.

The bishop of Hippo then leapt to the attack. He argued that if both Christ and the Holy Spirit illumine through each other, then their power is equal *(par potestas est)*. How then, he wanted to know, is the Spirit subjected to Christ? He further explained that Christ was anointed by the Spirit with respect to his humanity, his form of the servant *(forma servi)*. He affirmed that the Son and the Spirit are of equal power *(par potestas)*, one substance *(una substantia)*, and the same divinity *(eadem divinitas)*. He continued: "Likewise, although we worship the Trinity, because the Father is not the Son, nor is the Son the Father, nor the Holy Spirit either Father or Son; we, nevertheless, worship one God because he revealed himself to be one God of ineffable Trinity and one Lord in lofty union" (Aug. Coll. 11). Augustine finished by accusing the Arians of ditheism and idolatry. It was common orthodox practice to accuse Arians of trying to divide the substance of God because they sought to rank the Spirit as inferior to the Son, and the Son as inferior to the Father.[55]

Maximinus registered shock at these malicious charges *(caluminiam)*. He affirmed the biblical basis of his own views concerning the singularity of the omnipotent God *(singularitatem omnipotentis Dei)*. The Arian demanded that Augustine show with scriptural testimony how the divine persons could be "three equals, three all powerfuls, three unoriginates, three invisibles, three incomprehensibles" (Max. Coll. 11). He ended by promising to produce however much evidence for his own position as Augustine might demand.

This attempt to accuse Augustine of tritheism must have shocked the African bishop. The orthodox often accused the Ulfilans of tritheism. They believed it was the logical outcome of Ulfilan Arianism because the Homoians worshipped Son and Spirit, while denying their "substantial identity with the Father."[56]

The bishop of Hippo denied the charges of tritheism. He stipulated that the Trinity itself is the one God *(ipsam Trinitatem unum esse Deum)* in whom each individual *(singulis)* is omnipotent and invisible. The power of divinity, he argues, exceeds the logic of number (Aug. Coll. 12). Augustine preferred *essentia* to *substantia* when talking about the Godhead.[57] So it is not surprising that the bishop repeatedly uses the various forms of *esse*, "to be," when speaking of the persons of the Trinity in the discussion with Maximinus.

The bishop of Hippo next attempted to use an analogical argument based on Acts 4:32. His point was that if men can be one through a union of love, why cannot God, who is infinitely greater, not be one in essence?

Maximinus quickly perceived the weakness of this argument. He pressed the analogy to its logical conclusion. Certainly the Father, Son, and Spirit are one: one in agreement *(in consensu)*, in harmony *(in convenientia)*, in love *(in charitate)*, and in unanimity *(in unanimitate)*. He rejected a unity of essence. If one should become the other, he would cease to be himself. Maximinus then launched into a brief exposition seeking to support this view with subordinationist passages from the Scriptures.

Augustine asked the Arian why he was trying to prove things to the orthodox that they already professed. He agreed that there must be no confusion of Father and Son. The Son indeed receives life from the Father, but the life he receives is equal to that of the Father. It is not a gift of grace. The Son always had this life. Augustine then shifted quickly to the attack. He took exception to Maximinus's use of Romans 8:26 as a proof of the Spirit's subjection. He saw insistence on this perpetual "groaning" as blasphemy against the immutable nature of God. The African claimed that, in light of Genesis 12:12, Romans 8:15, and Galatians 4:6, 19, the passage in Romans must be interpreted as God's causing the action of "groaning" in man. The groanings, he concluded, were human response to the Spirit's convicting power and, therefore, gave no proof of the Spirit's subjection.

Maximinus exploded. He castigated Augustine's position as extrascriptural. He spurned the orthodox view of a Trinity in which Father, Son, and Spirit are called one God. He sputtered, "By us one God is worshiped, the unborn, the unmade, the invisible, who did not descend to human contagions and to human flesh" (Max. Coll. 13). Certainly Christ is God, but, according to Titus 2: 13, he is "our God," "God for us." He is the true God's intermediary. How else could he truthfully call the Father "my God" (John 20: 17)? Maximinus clarified his position. He claimed that while there is only one who is fully God, Christ and the Spirit are God in the sense that they are his representatives to us.

According to Maximinus, the union of Father and Son is one achieved by imitation. The Father "by his example gave life in himself to the Son" (Max. Coll. 13). Their being is joined *(copulatos)* in love *(charitate)* and harmony *(concordia)*. His discussion of how Christ is great God and yet in subjection to the great God presents an interesting weave of Scripture texts alternately implying subordination and exaltation.

Maximinus claimed for himself a dogmatic literalism. His slogan was, "I profess what I read" (Max. Coll. 13). He insisted that his positions derived directly from the Scriptures and, therefore, even under torture he could not say otherwise.[58] Finally, with more than a touch of sarcasm, he offered to be Augustine's disciple if the bishop could prove an absolute equality of Father, Son, and Spirit.

Augustine realized the implications of Maximinus's comments on "human contagions." He pointed out that the Word made flesh was not susceptible to the human contagions. Christ "came to cleanse, not to be contaminated" and, "therefore, took upon himself a human soul and human flesh without any disease or contagion" (Aug. Coll. 14).

The English word *contagion* is a cognate of the Latin *contagium*. The major difference between their meanings is found in the Latin word's emphasis on moral contamination. It is very difficult, however, to express precisely what the word *contagium* meant. The word had a very negative semantic value. It indicated emotional and moral weakness as well as disease.

Then Augustine accepted Maximinus's challenge. He tried to prove to the Arian bishop the equality of Father, Son, and Spirit. He took John 10:30 to indicate a oneness in substance in Father and Son. The bishop of Hippo denied that the terms *unmade (infectus)* and *unborn (innatus)* are essential attributes of the Father. They are relational terms that indicate no diversity of substance. In fact, one must not apply the term *made* to the Son. How could the Son be the maker of all things if he himself was made?

Augustine then argued analogically. He observed that "true sons derive their substance from their parents," man from man, dog from dog, and, therefore, God from God. The Son, then, is "of the same substance" as the Father (Aug. Coll. 14). The Son was made a man by assuming the man. He assumed this form of a servant *(forma servi)* in order to intercede for men. It is only according to this form (Phil. 2:6, 7), therefore, that he could speak the words of John 20:17. The submission at the end of time (1 Cor. 15:28) is done on behalf of the redeemed since Christ will reign immortal in that form.

The argument that the Son equals the Father in divinity, while being inferior to him in his humanity, was a standard anti-Arian Christological formula.[59] It was designed to account for the human frailties in the scriptural Christ and to reconcile Jesus' biblical claims of unity and equality with the Father with his statements of subordination to the Father.

On the basis of 1 Corinthians 3:16 and 6:19, Augustine claimed that the Spirit must be true God since the redeemed are his temple. If he should not be the true God, then the redeemed are all guilty of sacrilege and idolatry. The Spirit cannot be inferior to the Son since, in contrast with the Son, he never assumed another into his unity. Nor are there any Scriptures whatsoever that stipulate the Father's superiority to the Spirit.

Augustine was confident of the validity of his arguments. He was convinced that unless Maximinus was incredibly stubborn, he would yield. He stated that if Maximinus would not now become a disciple, Augustine would waste no further discussion (Aug. Coll. 14).

At this point Maximinus launched into a long exposition that was to fill the rest of the day. He began by contrasting Augustine's failure to show proper reverence with his own patient exposition. Unlike Augustine, he promised that he would not abandon discussion. He had waited patiently through Augustine's long exposition and now asked him to be patient and not to interrupt while he responded to Augustine's observations, point by point.

The loquacious Maximinus launched into a long exposition of Ulfilan thought, and Augustine had to endure the unfamiliar and distasteful experience of being unable to interject a reply.

In his long exposition Maximinus claimed to reject all forms of philosophical speculation. He insisted, "Truth is not collected from argument, but is confirmed with trustworthy testimonies" (Max. Coll. 14.21). It is enough merely to read and believe. He claimed that, as a disciple of the Scriptures, he read and followed them "without any interpretation" (Max. Coll. 14.11).

Citing a plethora of subordinationist texts, primarily from John's Gospel, he gave them a decidedly Ulfilan exegesis. The Father, Son, and Spirit form a hierarchy in which each is distinct. The Father is to be adored as the author of all things. He alone is truly God and possesses all the attributes of divinity as an "ingenita simplex," a simple unbegotten (Max. Coll. 14.10). His superiority to the Son and Spirit derives from his role as the source of all existence. He alone is uncaused.

The Son, however, is God, the image of the one true God. While he is Creator and Redeemer from the very beginning, he is less than his Father, who is "before the beginning" (Max. Coll. 14.17). Although the Son is wholly dependent upon the Father, men are to worship him. Maximinus went to great lengths to "prove" to Augustine that the Son is inferior to his Father. The Son is visible. It was he who appeared corporeally in the Old Testament theophanies. He also currently intercedes with the only true God for the redeemed. Maximinus was quick to point out, against Augustine's expectations, that the substance of his divinity is neither *ex nihilo* (out of nothing) nor *de creatura* (from a creature) but *ex Deo* (out of God) and *a Patre* (from the Father).

The Holy Spirit is in third place. Although the Spirit is to be honored as divine, Maximinus argued that he must not be worshiped because there is no scriptural command to do so. He is the teacher, illuminator, sanctifier, cleanser, and guide of the redeemed. In submission to Christ, he intercedes for believers everywhere. According to Maximinus, the Spirit is not the Son's equal, for then there would be no only-begotten Son but two Sons. He believed that there was absolutely no scriptural support for Augustine's notion that the Spirit and the Son are equal.

One of the most interesting views expressed by Maximinus was his concept of the one *(unus)* and the united *(unum)*. In his view all the redeemed are to be united in the imitation of Christ's subjection to the Father, made one by all willing what the Father wills. Therefore, the Christ with others participates in the goodness, life, and illumination of God. On the basis of Luke 2:52, Christ could grow and indeed had grown in wisdom. Christ, then, is in every respect a creature who became good by participation in the divine. All except the Father are the "unum," while he alone is the "unus." The many are, thus, united to the one (Max. Coll. 14.20, 23).

When Maximinus finished speaking, he signed the official record of the debate. He knew that Augustine would not have time to make anything like an adequate rebuttal. The wily Arian had taken most of the day with that one exposition. It takes up well over half the space in the official record.

Augustine rose to speak with the time almost gone. He remarked bitterly that Maximinus's "diatribe" had occupied the time allotted for his response. Now there was not even enough time left for an overview of what the Arian had said.

The bishop of Hippo repeated his earlier accusation of ditheism and idolatry. He called into question the Arian's motives and his willingness to accept the clear teachings of the Scriptures. He urged Maximinus to accept the Trinitarian faith. Believing that faith precedes reason, he pleaded with the Arian first to believe so that later he might understand. Augustine then promised that if circumstances permitted, he would write a response to Maximinus's comments. Augustine then signed the official record. After this Maximinus wrote: "When you have completed this pamphlet and sent it to me, if I do not give a response to everything, then I will be blameworthy" (Max. Coll. 26).

Maximinus had to return to Carthage the next day. When he arrived, he claimed that he had triumphed over Augustine (Vita 17).[60] The bishop of Hippo immediately began work on a refutation. His contemporary and biographer, Possidius, said that this long work occupied the whole span of days that remained to Augustine

(Vita 17).[61] The work, when completed, was made up of two books. In the first book, Augustine attacked Maximinus's methods of controversial sabotage and attempted to demonstrate that it was Maximinus who had failed to meet his objections, not vice versa.[62] The second volume of *Contra Maximinum Arianorum episcopum* was a refutation of the Arian's doctrines. Although Maximinus had promised a reply, none is known to exist. Neither is there any evidence that such a work was ever written.[63]

What happened to Maximinus after the debate is something of a mystery. Segisvultus was recalled to court in Ravenna when Boniface was officially reinstated as *comes Africae* in A.D. 429. Maximinus dropped from sight. Did he remain in Africa or return to Italy with Segisvultus? No trace of him has been found among the Vandal Arian clergy.[64]

An Arian by the name of Maximinus surfaces in 440 during Gaiseric's conquest of Sicily. When the Vandal was besieging Panorma (Palermo), he was aided from the inside by an Arian fifth column led by this Maximinus. Previously condemned by the local Catholic bishops, Maximinus, after the fall of the city, persuaded the inhabitants to convert to Arianism. Evidence about this man is so scanty that it is impossible to determine if this is the same Maximinus who had debated Augustine.[65] In the *Scolia,* the writer usually identified as Maximinus expressed the desire to turn the tables on the Catholics. He seemed to expect to be in the position to do just that. The Catholics were to be considered non-Christians, their churches confiscated, and they themselves made to suffer the fate of Haman in the book of Esther (Max. Scol. 47). For this reason some identify the Maximinus who incited Gaiseric to persecute Catholics on Sicily with the Maximinus who debated Augustine. Bammel thinks that such a connection would fit well with the inclusion in the *Scolia* of two laws from the *Codex Theodosianus,* first published in 438. In his view, "Such a setting would readily explain how one of Maximinus' followers came into possession of this beautifully produced Catholic collection of Anti-Arian works."[66] Indeed, could Maximinus have found any protection after Segisvultus left except with the Vandals?[67]

Forty years later Cerealis, bishop of Castellum Ripense in Mauretania, was challenged by an Arian named Maximinus. To have been in conflict with Cerealis in the 480s, the Maximinus who opposed Augustine would have had to have been at the very least an octogenerian. There were several Arian polemicists who survived beyond this age. So it could just barely be possible that this was the same man.[68]

## *The* Contra Maximinum Arianorum Episcopum

This polemic against Maximinus is one of the very last theological offerings from the mind of Augustine (Vita 17). The first book is a detailed demolition of positions held by Maximinus in the *Collatio*.[69] Book 2 is Augustine's *tour de force* against Ulfilan Arianism. In it he makes his final effort to clarify and defend his Trinitarian views. At the very beginning of the work, Augustine pointed out that he was fulfilling his obligation to refute the arguments of Maximinus. The bishop expressed the hope that, when the Arian read this work, he would have a genuine conversion to the true faith. What follows below is an abbreviated summary of Augustine's arguments in the *Contra Maximinum*.

In book 1, Augustine pointed out that failure to recognize the substantial oneness of the Trinity violates the commands of both Old and New Testaments. The African bishop points out that in Deuteronomy 6:4, 13 and in 1 Corinthians 8:4 the command is given to worship and serve only one God (CM 1.1).

Augustine's standard answer to those scriptural passages that seem to indicate a subordination of the Son to the Father was to ascribe the subordination to the "form of a servant," the man assumed by the Son in the incarnation. The Father is greater than the "form of a servant." He is, in fact, God to the assumed man (CM 1.5, 7).

The Son, on the other hand, is only visible in the "form of a servant" and can be called "made" only according to the man. Only in this form can the Son be said to have been subject to Joseph and Mary and to his Father in heaven (CM 1.3, 8, 15, 17).

In Augustine's view, the Father and the Son are one, and each is beloved in the other. Certainly their primary distinction lies in the fact that the Father is unbegotten. But though he is unbegotten, the Son is still his equal because he is brought forth as an equal, much as men and animals bring forth after their own kinds. In fact, Augustine saw these as shadows of the relationship between Father and Son (CM 1.4, 6, 18, 20).

According to Augustine, Maximinus was wrong in assuming that the Father's testifying of the Son implied any inferiority in the Son. Even the prophets testified of the Father. He was also wrong in attributing the title "the only wise God" (Rom. 16:27) to the Father. How can he be "the only wise God" when the Son is the "wisdom of God" (1 Corinthians 1:24)? The answer which Augustine offered was that "the only wise God" is the Trinity (CM 1.13, 16).

Augustine could not understand how Maximinus could assume that the Holy Spirit is less than God. No scriptural passage claims that the Father is greater. Nor does the Holy Spirit adore the Father. Certainly, Romans 8:26 must not be construed as evidence for this. According to Augustine, the "groanings" are those which the Holy Spirit inspires in the souls of men. In fact, on the basis of 1 Corinthians 3:16 and 6:19, he must be fully God since only God is allowed to dwell in the temple (CM 1.9, 11, 19).

Augustine also had to combat the Gothic Arian's tendency to equate the mission of the Spirit as dove or fire with that of the Son as man. He pointed out that the Spirit and the dove or the Spirit and fire never became and remained one person, while the Son did through the assumption of a man (CM 1.19).

Augustine also set the record straight on the issue of the *"contagia humana."* Christ was "made sin" (2 Corinthians 5:20, 21) not by participation but as a sacrifice and symbol of redemption (CM 1.2). According to Augustine, the one God is, then, Father, Son, and Holy Spirit. They are not one only in their will. They are one through an ineffable joining, an *"ineffabilem copulationem"* (CM 1.10).

In book 2 of the *Contra Maximinum,* Augustine based his argumentation solely on the exegesis and comparison of scriptural texts. He did this because he was anxious to refute Maximinus's claim that he was drawing his theology from the simple and unbiased reading of Scripture. The African also wanted to demolish the Arian's bizarre and, what he felt were, unreasonable interpretations of the Scriptures.

For the most part, then, the value of this second book against Maximinus lies not in new conceptualizations, but in the biblical underpinnings of Augustine's Trinitarian views.[70] There are, however, a few exceptions to this characterization.

For a time Augustine had dropped his emphasis on the inward character of Old Testament revelation.[71] Now he moved to reassert it. Where Maximinus had stressed outward and corporeal appearances of the Word in the Old Testament, Augustine had striven to show the inwardness and the spiritual character of the appearances of God. It was, he insisted, the eyes of faith that revealed the Son of God to the patriarchs (CM 2.26.8).

In one respect, Augustine faced one of his greatest challenges in this work. He was finally forced to give his interpretation of Luke 2:52. In all his vast body of works, he only cites this passage six times. Even in those places, where one would logically expect the bishop to give an explicit commentary on the passage, it does not occur. He never even used this passage as an evidence of the reality of Christ's humanity.[72]

Now forced to give his interpretation of Luke 2:52, he contended that it was only Christ's humanity that progressed in wisdom. It was the "form of a servant" who participated in that growth process (CM 2.23.7). Augustine thus refuted the concept of moral progress in Christ. He did not pass from unrighteousness to righteousness. He never became wise after having been in moral ignorance. There was no moment when the Christ did not possess divine wisdom, according to Augustine.

The arguments on the Trinitarian relations, found in *De Trinitate*, are totally absent here. Yet this would seem a good place to use at least some of them. Perhaps they would have been too philosophical for the almost purely exegetical approach taken here.

All through book 2, Augustine strove to prove a consubstantial equality of persons expressed in Trinity. He gave almost no attention to the issue of their independent subsistences. This seems only natural since Maximinus had already granted that there are three persons but denied their unity of substance. Augustine gave here what is probably his strongest argument ever for the three persons having, *ad extra,* only one will and operation. In that context he discussed for what was probably the last time his understanding of the procession of the Spirit from both Father and Son. Below is a brief running summary of the contents of book 2, along with some commentary. Much has, of necessity, been left out. But, enough has been included to give the reader the flavor of this rather long refutation. A full accounting of the Scriptures used is available in the appendices.

In the Preface to book 2 Augustine gave a summary of what he believed is the Catholic understanding of the Trinity. Augustine argued that in the Catholic view, Father, Son, and Holy Spirit "are of one and the same substance, and that the one God is the Trinity itself" even though the persons are distinct (CM prefatio).

In the first chapter of book 2, Augustine answered Maximinus's charge that he had spoken without reverence for God. Augustine argued that, in fact, his reverence for God was greater than the Arian's since he believed God the Father was able to bring forth his equal, while Maximinus denied this was possible.

Turning to discuss Philippians 2, the bishop noted that Maximinus never asked whether "the name which is above every name" will have been given "to the man or to God" (CM 2.2). Augustine pointed out that, if only on account of obedience the Son was given this "name," before this happened "there was not God, the high Son

of God, the Word of God, God with God," and that there was a
point in time when "he began to have the name which is above
every name" (CM 2.2). Augustine could not believe anyone would
say something so incredibly foolish *(insipientissimus)*. The bishop of
Hippo contended that the only way out of this difficulty is to ascribe
the gift of this "name" to Christ's humanity.

In chapter 3, Augustine argued for the equality of the Holy Spirit
and the Son. He approached Maximinus's demand that he show
him in the Scriptures where the Spirit is adored. Augustine, then,
wondered aloud if this receiving of adoration is the proof of equality.
He professed not to understand how the Ulfilans could, as Maximinus had, confess to adore Christ as they did the Father, and then
refuse to admit his equality to the Father. Augustine also pondered
2 Corinthians 3:6. Surely, he argued, the Spirit who "makes alive"
deserves adoration. He asked where Maximinus ever read "that God
the Father is unbegotten or unborn" (CM 2.3). As he did in his
discussion with Pascentius, Augustine made the point that one must
go beyond the literal words of the text to their meaning. Certainly,
the bishop continued, this proposition is true. If Maximinus was
going to be so literal in his understanding of the text, then how
could he argue that "the Father is incomparable to the Son." Augustine pointed out that this is something which "you do not read,
nor is it true" (CM 2.3). The bishop then swung back to the "temple
argument," which he used in the *Collatio*. Surely, he contended, if
the Holy Spirit has us as his temple, "a temple not made with
hands," then he is truly God and truly deserves to be worshipped
in his own right.

In chapter 4, as he had at the end of book 1, Augustine complained
that Maximinus had wasted a lot of time by trying to prove to the
Catholics things they already believed. He affirmed that the orthodox do, indeed, believe that Christ is "seated at the right hand of
God, interceding for us."

The Arian had continuously erected "straw men" in the debate.
He seemed at times incapable of admitting the real positions held
by his opponents. Augustine seems to have suffered from the same
problem, as is apparent from his repeated inferences that the Ulfilans
were secretly polytheists. These misunderstandings are extremely
interesting to the researcher and could help anyone who wishes to
reconstruct what each side thought of its opponent's views. In the
future, perhaps, a detailed analysis of these preconceptions will give
current scholarship a more accurate picture of what each side thought
was at stake in the conflict.

Augustine, in the first part of chapter 5, explained his view of the

Spirit's procession. He said that the Father is the author of all things through the Son, and "that from Him and from the Son, the Holy Spirit so proceeds" (CM 2.5). Augustine expressed perplexity at how the Ulfilans could ascribe the title of "creator" to both the Son and the Spirit if they truly rejected a substantial unity. The bishop renewed the charge that the Ulfilans were really idolators since they, as Maximinus had argued, had a hierarchy of divinity, with the Father the greatest and the Holy Spirit the least. Augustine claimed they had separated the Trinity into "one, another, and a third one." As far as Augustine could see, their "faith" was paganism.

Next, Augustine questioned Maximinus's motives when he expressed horror at the African bishop's use of creatures for his analogies about the relation of the Father to the Son. Certainly, God can bring forth his own kind if the creatures can (CM 2.6). He also questioned why Maximinus used no comparatives about the relations of Father and Son in his confession of faith. If Maximinus really believed, as he confessed, that "Lord begat Lord, God begat God, . . . wisdom begat wisdom, . . . power begat power," how could he deny their equality (CM 2.7). If God cannot bring forth one equal to himself, Augustine asked, how can he be considered omnipotent? The bishop of Hippo then tried to justify his own use of earthly analogies, in discussing the divine, by an appeal to Romans 1:20. Augustine believed that the creatures were intended to be analogies pointing men to the knowledge of the truth about God.

Augustine thought that he and Maximinus were basically in agreement about the invisibility of the Son. At first, he remembered, Maximinus had attributed invisibility only to the Father on the basis of 1 Timothy 1:17, but later himself mentioned invisible creatures (Colossians 1:16) and, therefore, had retracted that earlier claim. Augustine believed the whole Trinity is invisible. He expounded on the passage in Timothy. Augustine stressed that the proper interpretation of the passage is "to the only God, who is the invisible God, not who is alone invisible" (CM 2.9.1). The African bishop then used this same line of argumentation on John 1:18 and 1 Timothy 6:16, in which Maximinus had found his justification for claiming that no one has seen God the Father. Augustine insisted, however, that these passages must be understood in the light of Matthew 18:10, John 3:13, and John 6:46. He feels this should make it clear that when these passages indicate that "no one" has seen the Father, they are referring to men on earth. Indeed, Augustine noted, according to 1 John 3:2, all the redeemed will someday see him. The African worked to destroy Maximinus's rule that "the lesser beings are seen by the greater, but the greater beings are not seen by the lesser ones" (CM 2.9.1).

Augustine established a pattern of interpretation here, in which, as he had elsewhere argued, Scripture interprets Scripture. The Scriptures are not for him what they seem to be for Maximinus, isolated nuggets of truth. For Augustine, they are a web of understanding in which no single passage gives its full meaning without reference to some other passage or group of passages. He understood them as having a complete coherence with what he called the Catholic faith. Scripture's complex web of meaning, in Augustine's schema, is directly equivalent to "the Catholic faith." Its fundamental truth is theological in nature.

Using the method he had thus introduced, Augustine moved against Maximinus's view that "the Father is incomprehensible (incapibilem) to the Son," while "the Son is fully comprehensible (capibilem) to the Father" (CM 2.9.2). According to Maximinus, the Father, therefore, "may contain" (contineat) the lesser Son. Augustine mocked this view by claiming that it makes the Son as dependent on the Father as an infant on the breast. He pointed out that such a view flies in the face of John 16:15, where Christ said, "All things which the Father has, are mine" (CM 2.9.2).

Augustine saw that Maximinus had a real fear. He was afraid that to admit the Catholic Trinity would be to make the Father a mere "part of the one God, who is made out of three" (CM 2.10.1). The African bishop contended that this fear was unfounded. He tried to show that the biblical claims about Father, Son, and Holy Spirit can only be reconciled with the claims about the oneness of God, found in 1 Corinthians 8:4 and Deuteronomy 6:4, 13, by accepting the orthodox conception of the Trinity. He claimed that Maximinus, while fearing to make the Father a part of the Deity, had fallen into the trap of worshiping three gods.

Augustine affirmed that in the Catholic conception of the Trinity there is no difference of natures and no diversity of wills; there is, instead, a oneness of substance. "These three therefore, who are one on account of the ineffable joining together of Deity, by which ineffably it is joined, is one God" (CM 2.10.2). In Christ himself, however, "the one person is of twin substance because he is both God and man" (CM 2.10.2). But, even in Christ himself, God is not a mere "part of his person" for God the Son "took on the form of a servant" (CM 2.10.2). According to Augustine, each to the Trinity is God, and yet the Trinity is one God. There are none greater or lesser within the Trinity, each is God and the Trinity is God. The Catholic bishop pleaded with Maximinus to accept and believe this doctrine even if he did not yet understand it, since, on the basis of Isaiah 7:9, belief precedes understanding.

Maximinus had asserted that the Father "is simple unbegotten power" *(virtus est ingenita simplex)*. Yet, Augustine noted, Maximinus had listed for the Father a rather extensive array of attributes. Augustine asked an interesting rhetorical question: "If, therefore, in the one person of the Father you both find plurality, and you do not find parts; how much more then is Father, Son, and Holy Spirit, both by reason of their undivided Deity, a single God; and on account of their unique properties, three persons; yet are not, by reason of the perfection of each separate one, parts of one God" (CM 2.10.3). He insisted that each of the persons of the Trinity is all powerful and each has "the same nature," *eamdem naturam*.

The Catholic bishop argued that unless Maximinus recognized the Son as all powerful, just as the Father is, then he was claiming that the Son was mistaken when he said, "All things, which the Father has, are mine." The idea that the Son is just as powerful as the Father, the African vowed, is also supported by John 5:19. In this passage, the Son claims to do whatever the Father does. Augustine explained the phrase "the Son can do nothing of himself" as referring to the origins of the Son. The Son is brought forth from the substance of the Father, and not from his own substance (CM 2.12.1). That is why, ultimately, he "does nothing of himself."

Here, Augustine was attacking one of Arianism's favorite prooftexts. In the following passages of *Contra Maximinum,* he would attempt to demolish, one by one, the Ulfilan interpretations of some of the key subordinationist texts and replace them with a "Catholic" understanding by considering each Scripture in conjunction with other Scriptures. One of his key assumptions was that the Christian Scriptures are a unified whole and do not contradict each other. The Bible, as divine revelation, reflects the unity and truth of God himself. Augustine's methodology was to show that the Ulfilan interpretations of those Scriptures, which they use as prooftexts, seem to make them contradict others in the Bible and, thus, destroy its unity. The African bishop appeared to believe that this was sufficient to prove the unacceptablity of the Ulfilan interpretation. He then demonstrated that the orthodox, or Catholic, interpretation of the same passages eliminates the apparent contradictions and confirms the unitary nature of Biblical revelation. This unity Augustine seemed to have considered sufficient evidence for the acceptance of the "orthodox" interpretation.

There is, of course, more than a hint of Aristotelian logic in this approach. Augustine was actually using Aristotle's law of noncontradiction. Two contradictory statements cannot both be true. The Catholic bishop tried to show that the orthodox schema of theological interpretation eliminates the contradictions. Since his preliminary assumption was that the Bible is true, then, as stated above, the orthodox scheme of interpretation must be true since it eliminates the apparent contradictions which occur in any Arian scheme of interpretation.

Augustine continued his demolition of this fundamentalistic form of Arianism by noting that there is, in fact, one thing that the Father could not do which the Son accomplished. The Son, because of his humanity, could suffer "under Pontius Pilate in the form of a servant" (CM 2.12.2).

Augustine moved immediately to those passages which contrast with the servant passages, those which speak of Christ as Lord and King. If the Arian's interpretation of the servant passages were correct, how could the Son also be the King of Kings and Lord of Lords written of in Revelation 17:14 and 19:15, 16? Augustine stressed that without the orthodox view of the Trinity these passages cannot be reconciled with the oneness of God. He noted that these passages also attribute immortality to the Son, even though God alone is said to be immutable and, therefore, to have immortality (CM 2.12.2).

Here, Augustine was reflecting the accepted Greek notion that mutability denoted deterioration and eventual death. Only something, or someone, that could not be changed could be truly immortal in this view. The bishop went beyond Greek thought to point out that even the so-called immortal soul can die. He did this on the basis of the Christian belief that the universe was created by God *ex nihilo*. All things depend completely, for their very existence, on the sustaining presence of God, which Augustine referred to as grace. Only God does not depend on another for his existence. If God removed his support from even the so-called immortal soul, it would cease to exist. God cannot be changed. Since he begins in perfection, God cannot sin and, therefore, cannot die (CM 2.12.2).

Augustine next met an Ulfilan objection to the omnipotence of the Son, based on the fact that the Son, unlike the Father, has not begotten a creator. The African argued that, while the Son could have begotten such a person, this would not have been appropriate. If, to prove their equality, each creator begotten by a creator had to beget another creator, then what would have resulted was an "uncontrolled . . . divine generation" (CM 2.12.3). One would have an unending series of divine begettings. Nothing is to be proven by pointing out that the Son, unlike the Father, did not beget a creator. The bishop, forthrightly, rejected the Ulfilan inference that this perceived inability to beget a creator proves that the Son was a creature. For Augustine, the meaning of the term *begotten* itself should dispell such a conception. The Son can do what he sees the Father doing because he is not a creature, but is truly God. As his long rebuke of the Arian interpretation of John 5:19 ends, Augustine included a quotation from it, as he exclaims,

> The omnipotent therefore begot the omnipotent Son, since "whatever the Father does, this also the Son does in like manner." Without a doubt, the Son was begotten from the nature of the Father, not made. (CM 2.12.3)

In the thirteenth chapter of the *Contra Maximinum,* the bishop of Hippo turned to the interpretation placed on the phrase "to the only wise God," found in Romans 16:27. The Ulfilans believed that this refers only to God the Father. Augustine maintained that the passage pertained to the whole Trinity. He carefully explained how his interpretation avoids many otherwise insurmountable problems in reconciling the Scriptures to one another. Here, he also repeated an earlier argument based on his interpretation of Deuteronomy 6:13. According to the bishop, both passages ultimately must be understood as referring to the whole Trinity.

In chapter 14, Augustine set out to delineate how the procession of the Spirit differs from the begetting of the Son. The Ulfilans had asserted that if Son and Spirit were both of the Father's substance, then they were actually both sons. In their view, this would be enough to refute the Catholic interpretation of "only-begotten" and establish the impossibility of a substantial union. Augustine's answer, of course, was that the Son is "begotten" *(genitus)* but that the Spirit "proceeds" *(procedens).* A key point in his exposition was the assertion that the Spirit proceeds "from both" *(de utroque)* Father and Son. To support his opinion of the Son's role in the procession of the Spirit, Augustine cited John 20:22, where Jesus commanded the disciples to receive the Spirit and then breathed him into them. He rejects the idea of the Spirit being born of both because

> . . . it would not have been fitting for him to have been born from both. He is, therefore, the Spirit proceeding from both. (CM 2.14.1)

The African bishop felt the necessity for a definition of the difference between being born and proceeding, but he felt inadequate to the task. He said he could get no further than the fact that "Every one which proceeds is not born, although each one which is born proceeds; just as every biped is not a human, although each one who is human is a biped" (CM 2.14.1). The exact nature of both the begetting and the procession were ineffable. Human speech, Augustine claimed, was incapable of expressing the reality of either divine generation or of divine procession. The African believed that the prophet Isaiah's encounter with this same difficulty was reflected in Isaiah 53:8.

Augustine was prepared, however, to support his view of double procession. He noted that the Holy Spirit is sometimes referred to in the Scriptures as the Spirit of the Father and at other times as the Spirit of Christ. Yet, there are also passages, like 1 Corinthians 12:13 and Ephesians 4:4, which show that he is a single Spirit. The only possible way to reconcile all these passages, according to the Bishop of Hippo, is to assume a double procession.

Maximinus had wanted to reject the substantial sameness of the Spirit, the Son, and the Father. Augustine pointed out that this conflicts with the Arian's repudiation of the ideas that the Son was born either *ex nihilo* or out of some already existing matter *(ex aliqua materia)*. Maximinus had spurned all of the logical possibilities. If the Son was "from the Father" *(ex Patre)* as Maximinus professed, then he must share the substance of the Father. The only other possible choices for Son's origins are either a creation from nothing or being made out of some other created thing which already existed. Augustine believed that Maximinus may have fallen into this error because he saw the suffering and corruption which take place in the begetting of humans, and rejected divine generation in order to preserve the Father's honor. The Catholic bishop warned the Ulfilan that he was in danger of accepting an adoption model, in which Jesus "was already the son of man" and later "was made the Son of God . . . by grace and not by nature" (CM 2.14.2). Augustine again recalled the Arian's refusal of the idea that Christ was created *ex nihilo,* and pointed out that an adoptionist stance would require one to assume this very point.

The bishop of Hippo next equated his own view of the relationship of Father and Son with the term *homoousios* and the decisions of the Council of Nicaea. He contrasted the truth and universality of this council with the Council of Rimini, where, he alleged, a few heretics, under the leadership of a heretical emperor, deceived many people. Augustine commented that *homoousios* means "of one and the same substance." He then discussed the meaning of John 10:30. He asked rhetorically, "What is, I say, *homoousios* except, 'I and the Father are one'" (CM 2.14.3)?

Augustine, however, refused to depend on the authority of councils. He declared that debate must be based on the authority of Scripture, and that the participants should avoid the use of "prooftexts" *(propriis)*. Instead, they must depend on "common witnesses" *(communibus testibus)*. The African bishop expressed his belief that the dispute must be fought out only with the comparison of texts and the use of reason. He then made appeals to both the Scriptures and to the Fathers, his predecessors, in order to support his view of substantial unity. Augustine also repeated his analogy of creaturely reproduction with the divine generation, but requested Maximinus to remember that suffering and corruption are to be excluded from the picture. The bishop moved from physical reproduction to the concept of living soul begetting living soul. He extended this concept even to the "new birth" in Christ. Augustine believed that this extension of the analogy is warranted by 1 Corinthians 4:15, but admitted its weakness, since the soul already exists before regeneration. Augustine thought he had made an airtight case for the Father and Son being one and the same substance because, logically, the Son could in no other way be the true Son of God (CM 2.14.4). In this section of the *Contra Maximinum*, Augustine repeated some of the analogies used in *De Trinitate*. He also tried to give each analogy some Scriptural support.

While attempting to explain that the Son is "begotten coeternal" *(gignenti coaeternus)* with the Father, Augustine compared him to the splendor of a fire that appears as soon as the fire does. The bishop also said that he could accept Maximinus's designation of the Father as "author" of the Son, if by that he merely was indicating that the Son derives from the Father, not the Father from the Son. The African, however, refused any notion that the "name of author" *(nomen auctoris)* implies that the Father is, by nature, greater than the Son, or is of some different substance than the Son. He also repudiated any concept of temporal precedence since "where eternity is, there is no age" (CM 2.14.6).

To the African's view, the son "was born equal" *(equalis est natus)*. He also "was born immutable" *(est immutabilis natus)* because, being eternal, he "was always born" *(semper est natus)*. In fact, according to Augustine, the Son has everything which the Father has. It is in this context that Augustine discussed John 5:26. He believed this Scripture teaches that the Son, like the Father, is self-existent and, therefore, completely equal to the Father. Indeed, the only distinctions which Augustine seemed willing to allow are the difference in name and that the Father gave and the Son received all things. Even during the incarnation, the Son remained completely equal to the

Father. It was only in his humanity, the "form of a servant" found in Philippians 2:7, 8, that the Son was less than the Father.

The Catholic bishop returned to his project of refuting Arian prooftexts with an attack on their interpretation of passages like Matthew 26:26; Mark 8:6; John 6:11; 8:29; 9:4; and 11:41, 42. These passages and others were used by the Ulfilans to support their view that the Son was inferior to the Father by pointing to his human limitations, during the time of the incarnation and before the ascension. Augustine tried to show that none of these passages really prove the Son to be less than one substance with the Father. Each can be met by an orthodox rule of interpretation in which any seeming inferiority of the Son must be ascribed to the "form of a servant" and any indication of equality with the Father ascribed to "the form of God." Augustine here used the "Catholic" conception of Christ's twofold nature as a way of resolving the difficulties posed by the Arian stress on Christ's humanity. Only in the "form of a servant" is the Son subject to the will of the Father, since in the "form of God" there is a complete identity of will between Father and Son. All that Arian prooftexts, like John 10:18, did is prove the servility of the "form of a servant." In the following discussion Augustine continued to use the orthodox interpretation which he felt he had established for John 16:15, John 5:19, and John 5:26 as a weapon against the Arian understanding of other Scriptural passages. This equality of the Son argument, along with the "form of a servant" scheme for interpreting those passages implying the Son's inferiority, were used repeatedly to refute Arian interpretations.

In chapter 15, Augustine repeated the charge of ditheism against Maximinus. He pointed him to the *shema* (Deuteronomy 6:4). The African bishop insisted that one cannot have a God, the greater, and a god, the lesser, since that denies the unity of God expounded in the *shema*. The bishop also repeated his charge that Maximinus was inconsistent in saying that the Son is the Son of God by nature and not by grace, and yet denying that Father and Son are of the same substance. The Arian was in danger of returning to pagan idolatry. Augustine applied Paul's warning, found in Galatians 4:8, 9 to the Arian bishop. The African bishop pleaded with his counterpart to cling with him to the decision at Nicaea, if he really wishes to say that Christ is the true Son of God. Though Maximinus claimed that he did not teach diverse natures *(diversa naturas),* that is the practical result of his denial that Father, Son, and Spirit have one and the same nature.

Augustine next attacked the problem of John 17:3. This was one of the Arian's strongest prooftexts. In it Jesus seems to be saying that the Father is "the only true God." Augustine used his "form of the servant" argument again. He said one must look at the rest of the passage. Jesus said in this Scripture that eternal life comes from knowing the only true God, "and Jesus Christ whom thou hast sent." It is only in his being sent forth, in "the form of a servant," that the Son can be separated here from "the only true God."

The African bishop then turned to the issue of the Holy Spirit. The Spirit's true union with the other persons is the only possible basis of his knowledge of "the deep things of God." This, Augustine claimed, should be apparent to anyone studying 1 Corinthians 2:10, 11.

Augustine commented that Maximinus's own logical inconsistencies caused him to provide arguments against himself (CM 2.15.5). Indeed, this does appear to have been true. The African bishop often used the Arian's own words against him. Perhaps the problem was not so much in Maximinus as in the immature hermeneutic which he felt called upon to defend. In this respect, the Arian bishop can be compared to the modern Christian cultist, whose uncritical acceptance of prooftexts is coupled with an unbalanced view of authority. For Maximinus human reason did not seem to be part of the equation. The Bible appeared to be, for him, a book of prooftexts used to directly undergird his tradition. Human reason, even that reason enlightened by the Holy Spirit, and the academic study of the Scriptures was automatically suspect. Augustine, on the other hand, appeared willing to put his tradition's understanding of the passages through tests devised by human reason. For Augustine, Scripture and reason worked together to reveal the truth and together form the basis for confirming an interpretation's truth.

In chapter 16, Augustine defended his position on the humility of Christ. Although this humility is to be referred to as the "form of a servant," it is, nonetheless, real. Even after the resurrection and ascension, Christ retains his humility. He keeps the humility because of his role as intercessor between humans and God. This, however, does not imply inferiority. The risen Christ, indeed, claimed that all power in heaven and earth had been given to him (Matthew 28:18). Augustine claimed that the reason the Scriptures did not say the Father had given this is that it was given by the Trinity. The bishop also focused on the command to baptize (Matt. 28:19). He noted that it is baptism "in the name," singular, not in the names "of Father, Son, and Holy Spirit." To Augustine, this was an irrefutable evidence of their unity of essence.

He also answered the Arian objection that before the incarnation the Father was called the God of Christ. Augustine saw all these scriptural references as prophecies pointing to the incarnation. The Arians made a particular issue out of the anointing of the Son in Psalm 45:7, 8; Luke 4:1; and Acts 10:38. Augustine used again his "form of the servant" argument. Christ's humanity needed the anointing, not his divinity.

On the basis of John 1:3, Maximinus had tried to deny that the Spirit is creator. He thereby implied the creaturliness of the Spirit. Augustine declared that John 1:3 must be interpreted in the light of 1 Corinthians 2:11 and Acts 2:38. Just because one of the Trinity is not mentioned in a specific text, Augustine asserted, one must not automatically assume that the Scripture excludes that person. The African bishop also saw in Psalm 33:6 a support for the equality of the Son and the Holy Spirit. To his understanding, the passage also supports the role of the Spirit in creation, as does Psalm 104:30. Augustine was well aware that the word for *spirit* and the word for *breath* in the Old Testament were the same. In fact, the bishop noted, the Holy Spirit was actually the creator of the human flesh of the Son. According to Augustine, this view can be supported by Matthew 1:18 and Luke 1:34, 35. He continued his defense of the Spirit's equality by emphasizing that the Spirit does things in the Church that Christ also does. His key text in this argument was 1 Corinthians 12:11 (CM 2.17.3).

Augustine next launched an attack on Maximinus's statement that, "The Son was in the beginning before there was any thing; the Father, in truth, was before the beginning" (CM 2.17.4). The orthodox bishop was quick to point out the extrabiblical character of that statement and offered his own interpretation of John 1:1 as a refutation of the Arian's claim. Augustine objected that Maximinus had made two "beginnings." This is a logical impossibility. There can only be one beginning. The Father, Son, and Spirit are all "in the beginning." Maximinus had tried to use Psalm 110:3 as a buttress to his position. Augustine saw in it, instead, a prophecy of the incarnation. The Son came as God, out of God, outside of time. He came as a human, out of Mary, "in the fullness of time." The Christ, therefore, has two natures. One is eternal. The other is temporal, in that it began in the realm of time. Christ only called his Father his God in relation to his human nature.

Maximinus had also tried to argue the Father's superiority on the basis of the Son's obedience *(obsequium)*. After insisting that the Son is in no manner *(nullo modo)* the true Son if his and the Father's natures are not identical, Augustine noted that a man is no less a man by being obedient to his Father. Augustine also responded to the Arian's use of Luke 2:51. The bishop of Hippo contended that the reason the Christ submitted to Mary and Joseph was on account of his "human" childhood. Christ, as the perfect Son, would do what was fitting in every situation. Augustine stipulated, "If he was submissive to his parents on account of his childhood, how much greater should be his submission to God on account of his human form" (CM 2.18.4)?

According to the bishop of Hippo, Christ came in human form and died so that, in the flesh, he might be the righteous judge of humankind. But, even though it is the Son who judges, the Father is "with him" in that judgment. In this, as in all of his other activities as a man, the Father is invisibly and inseparably joined with him. Augustine offered scriptural support for this view from Zechariah 12:10; Matthew 25:34; Luke 4:1; John 5:19–23; 8:50; 16:32; and Hebrews 2:8, 9 (CM 2.18.6).

After a brief recapitulation of his observations about the proper interpretation of Romans 8:26, Augustine returned to a discussion of John 10:30. Maximinus had declared that the oneness spoken of in this passage is a oneness of adherence. As in 1 Corinthians 6:17, whoever adheres to God is one in attitude and will with him. Augustine affirmed that the text in first Corinthians actually says they "are one spirit," while that in John says that they "are one" *(unum sunt)*. He, thus, accused the Arian of improperly relating these two passages, when attention to their grammar and immediate context reveals that they are about two very different things. The bishop went on to claim that Maximinus did not properly understand how to use Scriptures like Acts 4:32; 1 Corinthians 3:8; and 6:17 because he did not recognize their limitations as analogies to God's oneness. They are, Augustine insisted, less than the reality to which they point. The Father, Son, and Spirit do have an incomparable consent of will and an indivisible love, but there is more to their unity than this. Augustine tried to make it clear that their absolute unity of will and their unchangeable love are due to their unity of "nature and substance" (CM 2.20.2).

The bishop of Hippo insisted that the prayer at Gethsemane, which Maximinus used as evidence of the Son's inferiority, must be ascribed to the Christ's humanity. Jesus' statement that he was "sorrowful even unto death" was for Augustine, clear evidence that the prayer was a struggle only within the Christ's humanity. Maximinus had also assumed that John 6:38 revealed the distinctness of Son and Father, because the Son said he was sent "not so that I might do my own will, but the will of him who sent me." Augustine agreed that the Son's will came from the Father. He believed that, in connection with John 7:16, the true meaning of John 6:38 becomes apparent. Certainly, Christ must do the will of the Father "because he is the doctrine of the Father, which is the Word of the Father, and, anyhow, he is not from himself but from the Father" (CM 2.20.3). Augustine did not feel, however, that this, in any way, lessens the equality which exists within the Trinity.

In the last half of chapter 20, the bishop of Hippo contrasted the first and second Adam, mentioned by Paul in Romans 5. The first Adam did his own will and brought sin to humankind. The second Adam did his Father's will and provided redemption for humans. In this discussion, Augustine so stressed Christ's unity of person that one sees in it a very strong argument for a *communicatio idiomatum*. The African argued that, "If, therefore, you attend to the distinction of substances, the Son of God descended from heaven and the Son of man was crucified; if you attend to the unity of the person, the Son of man also descended from heaven and the Son of God also was crucified" (CM 2.20.3). The bishop felt this was the only proper understanding of the person of Christ because 1 Corinthians 2:8 says it was "the Lord of glory" who was crucified. This sets up his answer to those who might ask if there was a separation, or rift, in the Trinity when Christ was on earth. Augustine stated, "On account of this unity of person, not only is the son of Man said to have descended from heaven but is said to be in heaven, when he was speaking on earth" (CM 2.20.3).

In chapter 21, Augustine took up again a discussion of the Holy Spirit. As he looked at 1 Corinthians 3:16, the bishop insisted that not only does the Holy Spirit cleanse Christians so that they may be indwelled by God, the Holy Spirit *is* that indwelling. This is evident, Augustine claimed, not only from 1 Corinthians 3:16, but also from passages such as Acts 5:3, 4; 8:47, 48; Romans 9:5; 12:1; and 1 Corinthians 6:15–19. How could Jesus, he asked, be empowered by the Spirit, as he is in the New Testament, unless the Spirit is also God. The Spirit, Augustine argued, must be God since he is ubiquitous. Also, it is through his presence that human regeneration unto eternal life is accomplished. On every level of dignity and worship, Augustine equated the Spirit with the Son and the Father.

The African next looked at the difference between human unity and that of the Trinity. Humans are of one nature but not of one substance. Augustine used John 17:11–24 as a centerpiece for this argument. He accused Maximinus of confusing the unity of holy men with that of divinity. To Augustine's mind, these unities were so qualitatively different that to equate them was ludicrous. He abhorred Maximinus's distinction between the neuter form *unum* and the masculine form *unus*. Maximinus had claimed that the neuter form indicates a unity based on agreement, or harmony, while in its masculine form it signifies singularity of number. Augustine protested that in both its neuter form and in its masculine form the Latin word *one* always pertains to singularity of number. He challenged the Ulfilan: "Search, therefore the canonical Scriptures, Old and New, and find, if you can, where of any it is said that they are one which are of diverse nature and substance" (CM 2.22.2). Maximinus's claim that the "Spirit, water, and blood" of 1 John 5:8, although of different substances, were said to be one is explained by Augustine as "witnesses" used here to point to a sacramental reality beyond themselves. When one presses on to the realities which they signify, according to Augustine, he finds a true unity of substance. The African bishop then gave various examples of this principle of interpretation in operation.

The bishop of Hippo returned to his discussion of Deuteronomy 6:4. He also used Deuteronomy 32:39. Any unity which is less that substantial, he contended, would falsify these Scriptures. Therefore, anything less than a substantial union must be condemned as being against the Word of God. He then proceeded to attack Maximinus's interpretation of the greetings from Paul's letters and other passages which the Arian had, to Augustine's eyes, misrepresented. He differed strongly with the Ulfilan's renderings of 1 Corinthians 8:6 and Ephesians 11:5. But Augustine seemed particularly upset about the way Maximinus interpreted John 5:19. He said that the Arian's contrast of "out of whom," used of the Father, and "through whom," used of the Son, is a false and artificial one. He pointed out the horrible hermeneutical difficulties that would arise in other passages if the Arian's approach were used in them.

Augustine rejected Maximinus's understanding of Mark 10:17, 18. If the God referred to in this text is only the Father, then neither the Son nor the Spirit can be good. Augustine repeated his rule, that where *God* appears in the text it is not to be automatically ascribed to the Father only. The term *God* actually refers to the whole Trinity.

Chapter 26 deals with the issue of the Old Testament theophanies. Maximinus claimed that Christ, before the incarnation, was visible because he repeatedly appeared to people in Old Testament times. This led Augustine into a refutation of the Arian interpretations of the theophanies. Augustine wondered how Maximinus could have thought that Genesis 1:26, 27 had anything to do with the visibility of the Son. He asked why the Arian had wasted their precious time, especially with discussions on Genesis that seemed to have nothing to do with what Maximinus was trying to prove. When he reached the discussion of Genesis 3:10, Augustine wondered how the "heard" of the text became "saw" in Maximinus's account. Augustine admitted that Abraham saw God in Genesis 18, but noted that Abraham saw three men not one. He also pointed out that those three are spoken of in the singular as "the Lord." What Abraham saw was not the reality of God, but a mere appearance of the Trinity. As the story progressed, Augustine asserted that even Lot recognized that these men, standing in the place of God, were really angels. The bishop also noticed that all the things Abraham did for his guests he did equally to all. Augustine claimed that this means Abraham saw God in them all. He declared that both Abraham and Lot "saw with the eyes of the heart" (CM 2.26.7). That is why, when they saw God's representatives, they recognized the presence of God.

Augustine also rejected Maximinus's contention that Jacob literally saw the Son of God (Genesis 32:24–30). The African said this passage should be understood figuratively, as a prophecy of the Jews striving against Christ. It foreshadowed, he thought, the descendents of Jacob seeing the Christ face-to-face and overcoming him, temporarily, through crucifixion. The bishop believed he found support for this interpretation in Hosea 3:3–5. Augustine also thought God must have used an angel, as he had done with Abraham and Lot, for the wrestling match.

The African bishop contended that even the apostles never saw the Son of God, "as he is" *(sicut est)* in reality. For them to have seen the Son, "as he is," would have resulted in their immediate deaths according to Exodus 33:20. That stipulation never changed since God himself never changes. Augustine found support for this idea of God's unchangeableness in Exodus 3:14; Malachi 3:6; and Hebrews 1:10–12. That is why, he claimed, when the Son took unto himself the man, the Son was not changed in his essential character, only in a relationship (CM 2.26.10). The appearance to Moses in the burning bush should end the argument. Augustine believed that in this appearance even the Arians would have to see the presence of the Father. If the Son appeared to mortal eyes, so did the Father. The Old Testament theophanies are, according to Augustine, God—the Trinity—showing himself through a subjected creature.

As the bishop of Hippo began to close his arguments, he rebuked Maximinus, with glaring irony, for using nonbiblical categories when he described the Father as incomprehensible and immeasurable. Augustine declared that, according to the biblical evidence, each in the Trinity comprehends the other completely. He urged Maximinus to pray and seek after the truth, not emptiness. The bishop said he desired Maximinus's repentance so that he might become a disciple, along with Augustine. Augustine then quickly reviewed some of the key verses in his arguments. He ended the *Contra Maximinum* by pleading with the Ulfilan to turn to the truth of God and become a "disciple of the divine Scriptures, so that we may rejoice about your brotherhood" (CM 2.26.14).

# 5

# AUGUSTINE AGAINST THE GOTHIC ARIANS: A THEOLOGICAL REVIEW AND EVALUATION

## Introduction

The confrontation between the Ulfilans and Augustine was in one sense classic. In the early Church there were two starting points for discussion of the Trinity: the monist and the pluralist. The chief interest of the monists was the identity of Father and Son in revelation and redemption. The pluralists, on the other hand, began discussion with the full copresence of distinct entities within the Godhead and sought a bond of unity strong enough to support their convictions. Some suggested a unity of derivation from the Father, others a harmony of the will or even an identity of substance.

Augustine's starting point was clearly monist. For him, God by nature is absolute being, simple and indivisible. This assumption forms the ever-present background of Augustine's understanding of the Trinity. It then is no surprise that, according to Augustine, the divine nature itself is triune. This view was not particularly new. The monist viewpoint tended to predominate in the West. The Latin way of conceiving of the Trinity was to consider the nature of God before the persons, insist on attributing *ad extra* operations to the whole Trinity, and explain the processions or missions of the persons in a psychological fashion.[1]

Augustine accepted the Western Trinitarian doctrines as "a matter of faith beyond every doubt."[2] Certainly in Augustine's doctrine there was nothing strikingly original. It was merely "an unusually clear statement of the orthodox Christian faith concerning the nature of God."[3] Augustine also considered himself not as an original thinker in this regard but as a defender of the Catholic Trinitarianism which the Church had always taught (De Trin. 1.4.7).

The Ulfilans, like all Arians, began from the pluralist stance. They held to a substantial threeness in a psychological oneness, the precise opposite of Augustine's view. Like Augustine, they viewed their position as the traditional position of the Church.

Both Augustine and the Ulfilans claimed to find their views in the Scriptures. The Ulfilans were convinced that the fact of disparate substance was revealed through the relation of the Father and the Son recorded in the Scriptures. Augustine believed that the consubstantiality of Father, Son, and Spirit was supported by their relationships, as recorded in the Scriptures. The primary issue between them, then, was hermeneutic.

The basics of the Arian hermeneutic have been dealt with in a previous chapter. Let it suffice here to say that it was a method in which they mined the Scriptures for prooftexts to support their position and then interpreted other scriptural texts that seemed to oppose their views in light of the truths they claimed to have found in their prooftexts.

In the *Sermo Arianorum,* Augustine encountered only a compendium of an Arian leader's teaching. The debate with Pascentius had been a farce because of the latter's lack of theological training. Other samples of Augustine's anti-Arian writings are simply too brief to be considered responses in depth. Only the debate with Maximinus and the subsequent *Contra Maximinum* can possibly provide a broad enough scope for a thorough analysis of Augustine's theological polemic with respect to Ulfilan Arianism. The prospect is made even more fruitful by the fact that, at the time, Maximinus was the leading Arian theologian in the West. In the previous chapter, a sort of running account of the debates was provided. Here there will be an investigation arranged under headings representing the primary theological concerns of the debate.

## Scripture and Authority

The Arian bishop's views on the Scriptures, and on authority, were consistent with those of other Ulfilan Arians. Maximinus insisted that the debate between Augustine and himself be based upon the Scriptures. He went so far as to request a disallowance of extra-scriptural and philosophical terms. Because of scriptural injunctions, he was ready to defend his faith even under the threat of imperial law (Max. Coll. 1).

Maximinus claimed to abide by a strict adherence to the literal meaning of the Scriptures "sine alique interpretatione" (Coll. 14.11).

He claimed that his own views about Father, Son, and Spirit were based on the literal meaning of the Scriptures, while Augustine used "misrepresentations" which "come from the instruction of the philosophical art" (Max. Coll. 14.5). He actually seemed proud that he was not so trained yet asked "modestly" that his slips be excused and that the intent of his words, not their actual content, be the topic of discussion (Max. Coll. 14.7). He repeatedly demanded scriptural evidence for Augustine's statements.

Maximinus's concept of religious authority did not exclude church councils. He avowed a loyalty to the Council of Rimini, where "the fathers" had passed on "that faith which was according to the divine Scriptures" (Max. Coll. 4). Thus, though he believed the council was authoritative, its authority rested on the Scriptures.

In the debate, the Arian bishop refused to worship or even to reverence the Spirit because he had seen it commanded in no scriptural text. However, he reverenced the Father on the basis of Ephesians 3:14–15 and the Son on the basis of Philippians 2:5–11. Though he did not believe the Son to be true God as the Father is God, yet "by the authority of the Holy Scriptures themselves we worship Christ as God" (Max. Coll. 14.3).

When the Arian had mentioned Rimini, Augustine had been quick to point out that what he wanted to hear was what Maximinus personally believed (Coll. 2–4). Augustine believed that truth came to man in an inward fashion, by revelation. Augustine truly believed that if the Arian had possessed a genuine faith, he would have abandoned his ditheism and immediately accepted the Catholic Trinity (Coll. 14.26). At the very last of the debate with Maximinus, Augustine pleaded with him to believe in the three in one before he understood it. Since true knowledge springs from a true faith, Maximinus would then begin to understand the Catholic Trinity (Aug. Coll. 14.26).

The bishop also opposed Maximinus's interpretation of various prooftexts by comparing or applying other biblical passages to them. He accused the Arian of grossly misinterpreting Romans 8:26 and John 20:17. Romans 8:26, Augustine insisted, must be interpreted in the light of Galatians 4:6, 19; Romans 8:15; and Genesis 12:12. In each of those passages, Augustine perceived an attributing to God of an action which he caused man to carry out. Thus Augustine was convinced that the "groanings" of the Romans passage were those groanings of men which the Spirit caused. The John 20:17 passage he countered with Psalm 22:10 (Aug. Coll. 14).[4]

One must remember that the debate between the bishops ended in a filibuster by Maximinus, with only a few moments given to

Augustine for rebuttal. In the second half of the debate, the part dominated by Maximinus's filibuster, the Arian was particularly insulting to Augustine and extremely cavalier with his handling of the Scriptures. The *Contra Maximinum* was the bishop of Hippo's chance to refute Maximinus's concept of hermeneutics and his practical handling of the texts.

Augustine accused Maximinus of being a fraud, purposely deceitful in his handling of the Scriptures (CM 1.2). He repudiated, for example, the Arian's interpretation of 1 Timothy 1:18 as dishonest. The proper interpretation, he insisted, was "only God who is invisible," not "the God who is alone invisible" (CM 2.9.1). He pointed out that Maximinus's immature hermeneutic caused a number of self-contradictions and inconsistencies in the Arian bishop's arguments (CM 2.15.5). He asked why, if Maximinus were so concerned about the use of nonbiblical categories and terms, the Arian continued to use such phrases as "incomprehensible" and "immeasurable" (CM 2.26.13). He also chided the Arian bishop for misunderstanding the principle of analogy, whereby things point beyond themselves to a greater reality. In the case of their debate, he noted, it had been the reality of the Trinity's substantial oneness (CM 2.20.1).

The African insisted that Maximinus was also inconsistent in his reasoning. How could the Arian deny both *ex nihilo* and "of the same substance" and claim that the Christ is the Son of God and not of some creature? How could Maximinus claim that Christ is the Son of God by nature not by grace, and yet deny that he is of the same substance as the Father (CM 2.15.5)?

Augustine urged the Arian to accept the true faith, the Homoousian faith of Nicaea. He contrasted the chicanery, deceit, and obvious coercion of Rimini with the straightforward and exemplary conduct of the Council of Nicaea. But beyond conciliar authority, he urged the Arian to become the disciple of the Scriptures in truth, to avoid "prooftexts" and rely instead upon the "common witnesses," and to compare the texts and to use reason (CM 2.14.3).

Augustine insisted that Maximinus must come to apply all subordinationist texts to Christ's humanity, the "form of a servant," and all the texts teaching Christ's equality to Father and Spirit to the divinity, "form of God" (CM 2.14.8). Where the Scriptures say "God," Maximinus must not automatically say "Father." Instead he should say "Trinity" (CM 2.23.5–7). Augustine also explained that the Old Testament theophanies were not literal appearances of the Father, the Spirit, or even the Son. Rather God, the Trinity, used angels as his representatives (CM 2.26).

He pleaded with Maximinus to pray for the true enlightenment and urged on him a list of verses to be studied in honesty. He pleaded with the Arian bishop to become a true "disciple of the divine Scriptures so that we may rejoice in your brotherhood" (CM 2.26.14).

Augustine's method was more similar to that of the Arians than one would, at first, suppose. His system of interpretation brought to the text a *regula catholicae fidei* (rule of the Catholic faith) forged in the flames of earlier conflicts between the orthodox and the Arians. As early as 395 he had mentioned it in a discussion of 1 Corinthians 15:28.[5] This Catholic *regula* (rule) of interpretation consisted of two points. When the Son is spoken of as being less than the Father, it must be understood as referring to his humanity. When the reference is clearly made to his divinity, then a distinction between begetter and begotten must be what is meant. Augustine never strayed from this anti-Arian tradition in his exegesis.

It was perfectly logical, given Augustine's presuppositions, to use this method of special pleading. For Augustine, Scripture was best conceptualized as the primary authority "inseparably fused with its churchly context and its signifying function."[6] For Augustine, then, the real and ultimate authority lay not in the text itself but in the spiritual reality of God, whom he had already assumed was the Catholic Trinity. He seldom interpreted scriptural texts purely for the sake of exegesis. He always seemed to have some aim in mind. What Augustine did with biblical texts was not truly exegesis; it was theology.[7]

Augustine, as noted in a previous chapter, used the Aristotelian law of noncontradiction in conjunction with the presupposition of the truthfulness and unitary nature of the Scriptures and their message. His approach was obviously informed by his knowledge of logic. The bishop of Hippo used a dialectical approach which he believed was divinely ordained in its principles, forms, and structures. Augustine recognized the difference between valid argument and sound argument. He knew that logical validity alone does not prove an argument to be true. He understood that in a truly sound argument the premises must be true and the inference valid. If either premise or inference was faulty, then the proposition could not be proved true.[8]

Augustine saw in Ulfilan thought two common fallacies. The first was sophism, contrived ambiguities or equivocations. An example is quickly found in one of the syllogisms underlying much of their "exegesis": The Father is not the Son; since the Father is true God, the Son is not true God. The other common fallacy that Augustine perceived in their arguments is that of affirming the consequent and denying the antecedent of a conditional argument. An example lies in their argument: Since the Father is unbegotten, he is true God, the fountain of all existence; the Son, however, is not unbegotten and is, thus, not true God. On the negative side Augustine pointed out the fallacies in their arguments. His positive response was grounded in an epistemology influenced by Neo-Platonism. He assumed an ontological approach to knowledge, an acceptance, by faith, of a revelation which precedes human reason. Truth, for Augustine, seems to equal divine illumination and is mediated to the believer through his trust of the revelation given to him. Thus, the guarantee of genuine knowledge is centered in the actions of God.[9] Augustine's ultimate plea to Maximinus was to adhere to a simple faith which would later develop into an understanding of the ineffable mystery of the Catholic Trinity.

In his conflicts with the Ulfilans, Augustine's stress was more on the unity and full divinity of Father, Son, and Spirit than on the doctrine of Trinitarian relations so prevalent in earlier works like the *De Trinitate*. This prevailing silence on the Trinitarian relations resulted primarily from the circumstances of the conflict. Against Eunomians, one spoke and reasoned directly on metaphysics. Against the Ulfilans, one had to overcome an avalanche of prooftexts.

Metaphysical Arianism had died at the hands of the Cappadocians.[10] They had chased Arianism from the field by using the logical distinction between universals and particulars. They defined the universal of the Trinity as uncreatedness. Within the uncreated Godhead, they perceived three particular modes of being: generacy, generation, and procession. This approach challenged the Arian premise that the Father alone was truly God because he alone was ingenerate. It also destroyed the Arian quibble about a grandson or brothers in the Godhead. The Arians had spoken as if ingeneracy were self-evidently clear, but the Cappadocians had recognized that all three categories, if indispensable, were equally ineffable. They had destroyed the idea of the Son as *deutera ousia* with an Aristotelian concept of the *prote ousia*. They thus stressed that the *ousia* in the Godhead is identical in each person, while with men the manhood is generic. Their formula, three *hypostaseis* in one *ousia,* meant that the one divine essence expresses itself in three modes of being, differentiated in terms of causality. It was a view that basically coincided with the Latin tradition of the West.

Metaphysical Arianism had failed when Arians had learned that they could no longer overcome the orthodox in philosophical argument.[11] But under the cover of their antispeculative and literalist claims, the Ulfilans were still advancing many of the positions that had been proved untenable by the Cappadocians. The success of their survival lay in their claim to simplicity in the faith. Their theologians and scholars portrayed themselves as simple exegetes who only proclaimed what the Scriptures teach and did not concern themselves with this world's vain philosophy. This purposely unsophisticated approach was highly successful, particularly among the barbarians. Thus, despite their protests to the contrary, the Ulfilans had a hidden philosophical agenda—one that, like the anti-Arian tradition of Augustine, determined how they read the Scriptures.

The rhetoric used in the bishop of Hippo's arguments also deserves a brief overview. Augustine's rhetoric at times seems to follow the classical model. Augustine's longer passages in the *Collatio cum Maximino* and the *Contra Maximinum,* often follow the traditional pattern rather closely. The traditional argument, in classical rhetoric, included an *exordium* (to put the audience in a receptive mood), a *narratio* (containing a description of the issue and method of treatment), the main body of the speech, and the *conclusio* (a summation that often contained further attacks on the opponent and an attempt to arouse sympathy for one's own position).[12] The *narratio,* however, is usually missing in the passages found in these works.

Augustine's rhetoric in these works alternates between the plain, the middle (or mixed), and the grand style. When he instructs Maximinus, his style is very plain, abrupt, and almost gruff. When he critiques Maximinus's exegesis, he does so primarily in mixed style. But there is little praise because he can find little which he considers praiseworthy in the arguments of the Ulfilan. Seldom does he bring the grand style into play, but when he does, it is usually when trying to unveil the self-evidence of the Catholic Trinity to his hearers or readers.[13]

## Trinity

Augustine's Trinitarian views are presented in a number of works. Some of the most notable of these are his *Enchiridion ad Laurentium, De Fide et Symbolo, De Doctrina Christiana, Tractatus in Evangelium Johannis, Epistulae* 2 and 170, his anti-Arian writings, and in the fifteen books of his magnificent *De Trinitate.* Of these works, *De Trinitate* was the least concerned with controversy. It was a contemplative study, thoroughly traditional, and yet intensely personal. In books 1 through 7, he sought to establish the doctrine of the Trinity according to the Scriptures and the Fathers and to answer objections to it. Books 8 through 15 were his quest for analogies in man that would throw a new light on the mystery. The second section was, of course, "much more original and rich in the new avenues of speculation it opens up."[14]

Augustine's work in the *De Trinitate* was not primarily an attempt to offer proofs of the divinity of the Son and the Holy Spirit or to prove their equality with the Father. In *De Trinitate,* he was on a quest for an "understanding" of the revealed truths which are already possessed in faith, but after an inward fashion *(modo interiori).* Although the outline of Augustine's Trinitarian doctrine had already been worked out before his conflicts with the Gothic Arians, in the furnace of those encounters Augustine's polemical arguments for a Trinitarian faith would reach their final form.

While his doctrine of Trinitarian relations is not the primary concern of the anti–Arian works reviewed in this study, it does inform their arguments. The key to his theory of relations is also the key to his anti–Arian stance. This key is the difficult concept of nontemporal causation.

Each person of Augustine's Trinity individually possesses all of the divine perfections "in himself" *(in se)* and not through his relations to the others. Even in the *De Trinitate,* he had tried to stress this. The relations bring no further perfections to any of the persons. For Augustine it was one and the same thing to be Father, Son, or God (De Trin. 7.1,2,6,11).

So, in Augustine, a divine person in the Trinity is both *in se,* or self-existent, and *ad alium,* or essentially directed toward others. God is therefore the only perfect prototype of that which all love between persons strives to achieve. He is absolute unity with distinction, a genuine communion.[15]

Like all Ulfilans, Maximinus conceived the Trinity in terms of a hierarchy of being. The one true God was the Father. He was described as incomparable, unlimited, incomprehensible, invisible, immeasurable, unmade, and unbegotten. He was the one *(unus)* to whom each of the "unum" was united. Each of the Ulfilan Trinity was a distinct subsistent with his own distinct "virtus." The other two persons were united *(unum)* to the Father through a perfect obedience to his will and an imitation of his character. As with believers, their unity is not one of essence but a consent, a harmony, a love all directed toward the Father. This total distinction of essence rested on the grounds that each simply could not be the other and yet remain himself. Spirit and Son were shown to be the inferiors of the Father on the basis of subordinationist statements found in the Scriptures. Maximinus believed that this system avoided the danger of tritheism. He accused Augustine of worshiping "three equals, three all powerfuls, three unbegottens, three invisibles, and three incomprehensibles" (Max. Coll. 11).

Augustine was ready to admit a distinction of the persons but insisted that according to revelation one must worship only one God. Augustine insisted that only by worshipping the Trinity in his lofty and ineffable union *(ineffabilem copulationem)* of Father, Son, and Holy Spirit can one avoid ditheism (CM 1.10). He points out that since Deuteronomy 6:4, 13 enjoins God's people to worship only one God, the Trinity and each of its members must be equally and fully God (CM 1.1). Augustine admits that this might not sound logical, but the power of divinity exceeds the logic of numbers. He claims that there is no hierarchy in God for that would be an idolatry equal to the worst paganism (CM 2.5). The Trinity works all actions together at the same time. The Holy Spirit and Christ are of the same power as the Father and themselves equal in power, for each and all is one God. Each and all together as one is fully immortal, equally invisible, the only wise God (CM 1.4,15,16). The name of "author" does not make one superior to the others (CM 2.14.6). Indeed, there is a perfect coincidence of will, because there is only one will (CM 2.14.8). In Christ indeed one finds subjection, yet this is to be attributed to the humanity assumed by the Son in the incarnation.

Augustine chided Maximinus about his placing the Father "before the beginning." Then he himself offered a rather unique interpretation of John 1, when he equated, "In the beginning was the Word" with "in the Father was the Son." He then added the Holy Spirit to the equation. He decided, "The beginning is threefold, Father not beginning from the beginning, Son beginning from the beginning, Spirit the beginning proceeding from both" (CM 2.17.4). Augustine also spent a great deal of space in his *Contra Maximinum* showing by scriptural interpretation the presence of the whole Trinity in every act of each person, as, for example, at Gethsemane (CM 2.18.6–2.20.3).

While it is not Augustine's primary concern, the issue of Trinitarian relations is addressed. His approach is based in philosophy. Essential to his argumentation is the view that "the fourth Aristotelian category, that of relation, is *per se* neither substance nor accident, but can be either, as the subject matter allows."[16]

Perhaps Augustine limited his use of the analogies because he realized their inadequacy. He had no illusions about their limitations. Although he had laid the foundations for the psychological theory of the procession through them, he recognized how remote and imperfect they were.[17] Even within the imprints left by Deity on the creation, there were levels of remoteness. Images came the closest to picturing the Trinitarian reality. This is why Augustine preferred personal human analogies. Humankind was created in God's image. These were followed in order of preference by what the bishop called vestiges and shadows.[18]

## Father

Augustine and Maximinus's estimates of the Father both agree and disagree. While Augustine accepts his ingeneracy as determinative of the Father's identity within the Trinity, he, nevertheless, perceives it in a Cappadocian sense as the distinction which makes the Father, by definition, the Father. He centers the true grounds of Godhood in uncreatedness. Since in his view neither Son nor Spirit is created, the fact of the Father's ingeneracy has no bearing on the relative divinity of the persons. Augustine keeps separated the concepts of ingeneracy and uncreatedness.

Maximinus's characterizations of the Father are typical of the Ulfilan view. He stressed the singularity of the one omnipotent God who is called the Father. He alone is completely God, an "ingenita simplex" (simple unbegotten) who contained no parts and had no origin. He alone was incomparable in his power; he alone was deemed truly wise. In short, he alone was the real possessor of the attributes in which he empowered the Son and the Holy Spirit to participate. He was the only immutable one and the fountain of all goodness. Although his Son was in the beginning, this transcendent God was "before the beginning and without beginning" (Max. Coll. 14.17). The Ulfilan sees a precise correspondence between ingeneracy and uncreatedness. They are for him, in a sense, synonyms.

For Augustine, however, the Father was not in any sense exclusively God. He certainly was most of the things which Maximinus had called him. He was not, however, the only true God. Hence there was really only one issue concerning the Father that divided Maximinus and the other Ulfilans from Augustine. If they could only have agreed that Son and Spirit were also individually and together true God, then on that point, nothing important would have separated them.

## Christology

For Maximinus the Son is "the God of every creature" (Coll. 14.2). He is worshiped as God because of the command of the Scriptures. He is also the only one who had his being directly from the Father. The Son is God's intermediary for man. Since he is mutable, he could suffer the limitations for man's sake that the Father could not. The Son also intercedes for men with his Father. He is, thus, a lesser God, a God by participation and imitation.

Maximinus rejected with horror any attempt to equate the Son with the Father. To do so was tantamount to rejecting the existence of the Son. His whole character was derived from another. The Son himself expressed his inequality with the Father, even calling the Father his God in John 20:17 (Max. Coll. 13). Truly he was unequal to the Father, for he was visible while the Father was not. Maximinus ascribed the Old Testament theophanies to the Son. The Son's ultimate superiority to mankind rests in his complete adherence to the Father's will (Max. Coll. 14.20). Maximinus, thus, has laid himself open to the charge that he supported a "degree Christology."

Augustine stressed that the Son is as fully God as the Father is. Indeed, as the Father has life in himself, so he begat the Son to have life in himself. The fact that he is the Father's only begotten Son indicates to Augustine a substantial bond between them. If, as Maximinus insisted, the Son comes not *ex nihilo* but *ex Patre,* then he must be of the same substance as the Father (CM 2.14.2). Augustine saw the begetting of each creature after his kind as an analogy of the Father's begetting a Son of the same substance as himself. Certainly the Son is distinct from the Father. He is distinct by having been begotten by him (CM 1.16,18). As God's Word, the Son is immutable. As God's wisdom, the Son shares the Father's immortality. Indeed, if Christ is confessed by the Scriptures to be the wisdom of God, how can the phrase "the only wise God" be applied exclusively to the Father? The phrase must refer to the "whole Trinity" (Aug. Coll. 13,14; CM 1.16; 2.13.1).

This immortal and invisible Son, however, according to Augustine, voluntarily assumed a human nature into union with himself and became in that sense the visible "form of a servant," according to Philippians 2:5–11. He did not, therefore, in the incarnation relinquish the "form of God." Augustine insisted that the exaltation spoken of in this passage and elsewhere must also be applied to the "form of a servant" (Coll. 14; CM 1.5–6).

When, in John 20:17, Christ spoke of the Father as his God, it was said with reference to the "form of a servant" (Christ's humanity). This, Augustine argued, becomes clear when one views the statement in John 20:17 in the light of Psalms 22:10, which shows that "from the womb," that is, as a man, Christ called the Father his God. As a man also he will reign eternally, according to 1 Corinthians 15:28 (Aug. Coll. 14).[19]

Humility before God caused Christ to say those things in the Scriptures that the Arians have misinterpreted. This humility should be ascribed to the "form of a servant," not to the "form of God." But even the Son of God in one sense shares this humility, because Christ is a twin substance and yet one whole person. This is the mystery of the incarnation that "una persona est geminae substantia et Deus et homo est." Because he truly is one person, there is a veritable *communicatio idiomatum* through which the statements about the divinity must apply equally to the man (CM 2.10.2; 2.16.1).

Apart from a letter to Volusianus in about A.D. 412, Augustine wrote no special treatise on the incarnation, yet on no other point is his teaching more logically connected, lucid, or constant (Ep. 137).[20] Augustine's Christology, in distinction from earlier writers, derived from his doctrine of the Trinity. The whole Trinity was operative in the assumption of humanity and in the continuation of his union with God. This was certainly no new position for the elderly bishop since it appeared at least as early as A.D. 389 (Ep. 11).[21] The *Logos* achieved not only an *assumpta natura* but also an *assumptus homo,* assuming not human nature in general but a specific, concrete, individual man.[22] As Augustine is quick to point out, however, this humanity never had an existence independent of its union with the only begotten Son.[23]

It was the Origenist character of his Christology that allowed Augustine to effect so close a union of the Son of God and the Son of Man. In this Christology, "the soul of Christ is the medium of the union between the Word and the flesh and . . . is inseparably united to the Word with such an intensity of affection and immediacy of intuition that it becomes like the Word in every respect, as iron heated in fire becomes fiery itself."[24]

From such a base, the move to a communion of idioms was rather short. It follows from Christ's unity as person coupled with his diversity of natures. Although the Son of God was in heaven and the Son of Man on the earth, yet they were one. The Son of Man on earth, though in fleshly weakness, was also in heaven by participation in divinity.[25] So, according to this system, Christ can be freely acknowledged as divine yet remain radically subordinate to divine nature (Conf. 7.18–21).

Augustine was the inheritor of a Christological principle of exegesis that had been forged in the flames of earlier Arian conflicts. He referred to it as a "regula catholicae fidei" as early as 395. According to Augustine, this *regula* stipulated that when the Son is spoken of as being less than the Father, this must refer to his humanity except where it clearly makes reference to his divinity, and then it must signify only the distinction between begetter and begotten.[26]

In his very first observations concerning Arianism, Augustine also had recourse to this hermeneutical principle (De Trin. 1.7.4).[27] By writing De Trinitate, the African theologian had begun to express this principle in terms of the antithesis between the "form of God" and the "form of servant" found in Philippians 2:6 (De Trin. 1.11.22).

One sees no major developments in Augustine's Christology, but one does see further developments in the bishop of Hippo's apologetic in defense of his Christology. By the time of the Contra Maximinum, Augustine was very successful in presenting the case for Christ as God by nature (Deus natura) over against the Ulfilan "God for us" (Deus nostro) by the polemical use of hermeneutics.

## Pneumatology

Maximinus ascribed to the Spirit the role of "illuminator and sanctifier of our souls" (Coll. 4). But even in this, his principal office, the Ulfilians placed the Spirit at the bottom of a hierarchy. All illumination came to him from the Father and through the Son. His only genuine unity with them was one of submission, by agreeing to do as the Father had commanded in perfect obedience. His very role as intercessor was, for Maximinus, evidence of his inferiority since he served as an intermediary with the Father. Maximinus also had asked the embarrassing question about what difference there is between the procession of the Spirit and the begetting of the Son (Coll. 14.14–15). How are they not both sons if both equally came from the Father?

Augustine opposed this view of the Spirit on the grounds that Maximinus had misinterpreted the Scriptures to come to his conclusions. With one eye glued to the concept of God's immutability, Augustine insisted that Romans 8:26 must be interpreted in the light of 1 Corinthians 3:16 and 6:19. If believers were the temple of God and the Spirit indwelled them, then how could he not be God, since, according to Deuteronomy 6:4, 13, worship was forbidden to any but God alone. He countered the Arian's insistence that the Spirit is inferior to the Son by noting that the Spirit never assumed a creature as the Son had and that the Spirit had never said that the Father is greater than himself (Aug. Coll. 13,14).

Maximinus assured the bishop of Hippo that he agreed to the

Spirit's ubiquity and that he is, at least in some sense, divine. But to Augustine's claim that the Spirit is shown to be true God on the basis of 1 Corinthians 3:16 and 6:19, Maximinus responded that certainly the Spirit purges the temple so that the Father might take up residence (Coll. 14.21).

Augustine responded by claiming that Maximinus was continuing to misinterpret the Scriptures and he repeated his earlier arguments (CM 1.9,11,19; 2.3). Augustine attempted to answer the Arian bishop's question about the Spirit's relationship to the Son, but he seemed a bit frustrated with it. He asserted that the Spirit is not a son because he proceeds from both Father and Son and it "would not be fitting" for him to be born from both of them. But the bishop confessed that he felt inadequate to explain the difference between begetting and procession. He was only certain that the Spirit came from and was shared by both since he is spoken of in the Scriptures as both the "Spirit of the Father" and the "Spirit of Christ" (CM 2.14.1). Certainly, he insisted, the Spirit is as fully God as Father or Son. How could Christ have been empowered by one less than himself (CM 2.21.1)?

Augustine, despite his inability precisely to define procession, had nevertheless gone far in defending the Spirit as integral to his Trinitarian theology. He had in earlier writings made him an important member of his Trinity and not a mere afterthought as in most earlier theologies. In these, his final studies of the Spirit's divinity, Augustine was continuing to widen the horizons of his theology. His defense of the Spirit's divinity could well be the most important contribution of his anti-Arian works.


## Salvation

This issue was almost neglected in the debate. Perhaps it surprised Augustine that the Arian view of salvation differed but little from the Pelagian view. He may have gotten some inkling of this at the debate, but if he did, he did not choose to emphasize it in the debate or in his *Contra Maximinum*. Further debate on this issue could have proved very interesting simply because the views were so diametrically opposed.

For Augustine, redemption seems to be a mystical or spiritual action on God's part which results in man's yielding to God's will. The Ulfilan's view, on the other hand, saw redemption as the result of commitment and obedience on the part of the redeemed which came through yielding oneself to God's will and by following Christ's example.

According to Maximinus, the saints were made one with God by willing what he wills as the Son did. In imitation of Christ, one places himself into subjection to God and so experiences his indwelling of love. He is united with God through obedience (Max. Coll. 14.22). Thus, Maximinus sponsored a "works salation" in which the key role is played by the will of the individual instead of God's prevenient grace.

In Augustine's view, grace preceded human activity. Christ was "made sin for our sakes." The redemption, thus provided, came not in response to a free and humanly willful decision to "follow Christ." Redemption came directly from God as a result of Christ's sacrifice. Christ was made sin for the redeemed, but not so that he literally became sin. Christ was made sin in the sense that he became the sacrifice for man's sin (CM 1.2). His merit, gained for man on the cross, was applied by grace to the sin of man. Augustine, as in the Pelagian controversy, opted for a salvation wholly dependent upon grace.

For Augustine, the application of this redemptive grace to man is what takes place in salvation. While the grace was wholly from God, the bishop also stressed man's response to God's initiative. Grace is a mercy received. It was a gift of the power to do God's will.[28] God, through grace, chose to cooperate in the redemption of man. It is this cooperation of God and man that resulted in salvation. For Augustine, the first step in this cooperation was baptism. The grace found in baptism delivered the child from the guilt of original sin and took away the sinful character of the concupiscence of his flesh.[29] For the adult, penitent faith was also required because the act also effected the forgiveness of all actual transgressions committed before baptism. On the basis of John 3:5, Augustine, like many in the ancient church, believed that baptism was necessary for entrance into God's kingdom. Baptism then, as the sacrament of regeneration, was the first step in that application of redemption which resulted in salvation. Negatively, it was a means of forgiveness of original and actual sin. Positively, it was the foundation of a new spiritual life of faith, of a "gratia operans et co-operans" (grace working and co-operating). So, while the salvation of the Arians depended on a self-redemption, the salvation in which Augustine believed depended on the application of the redemption won by Christ through a grace active first in the willingness of the heart and only secondly in acts of obedience.

# CONCLUSION

## Context

One of the key questions that this book set out to answer was why Augustine encountered Arians in North Africa so long after Arianism had been officially banished from the Roman empire. The answer is rather complex. Chapters 1, 2, and parts of chapters 3 and 4 provide the data for answering this important question.

The context of the struggle determined its character. A number of factors coincided to insure the survival of Arianism after it had been officially eliminated. One of the chief reasons for its continued existence was the conversion of the barbarians to Arianism. There were, of course, several important steps and a number of important factors involved in their move into Arianism. Christianity had first been introduced, probably by Cappadocian captives, in the third century. Though Christians were few in number, their zeal was high.

When Arius and Eusebius of Nicomedia were banished to the borders of Gothia, these Danubian provinces suddenly became an Arian stronghold. This probably assured Arianism a hearing among the neighboring Goths. A talented young half-Goth named Ulfila soon headed the Arian church among the Goths. A great wave of persecution caused Ulfila to lead a number of his followers into Roman territory. This greatly enhanced the young bishop's authority and position. When persecution struck again, and more severely, a few years later, Catholic and Audean Christianity were obliterated from Gothia. Arianism proved more durable because its leadership was within the empire and, therefore, survived.

When threatened with domination by the Huns in the late fourth century, the Visigoths pleaded for entry as allies into the empire. They urged the respected Ulfila to head their embassy to the Eastern emperor. The emperor Valens, himself a Homoian Arian, seems to have demanded that they accept his religion as the price of admission. Ulfila, a loyal Homoian teacher, probably urged them to accept the emperor's offer. Under the tutelage of Ulfila, the Visigoths began to accept Homoian Arianism. Soon the Visigoths would evangelize the other barbarians. Almost all of them would enter the empire as Arians.

Mistreatment of the federated Visigoths led to a revolt and the disastrous Roman defeat at Edirne. As a result of Edirne, the Visigoths became a power to be reckoned with in a declining empire. Many troops were detribalized and served with distinction in the Roman army. Examples abound. Two are the forces under Boniface when he was a tribune in Africa and the army that Segisvultus, himself a Goth, brought to Africa.

The ambitions of a Gothic general and tribal leader named Alaric and the draconian measures taken to curb his assault on Italy led directly to the ravaging of Gallia and Hispania from 406 to 408 by the Vandals and their allies. Alaric himself sacked Rome in 410.

With the rise of barbarian power came the threat of barbarian Arianism. Though in retrospect its weaknesses are obvious, at the time it appeared to be a deadly rival for Catholicism. Arian teachers could expound their doctrine under the protection of barbarian swords, partly because of the barbarians' special relationship to Roman law. Within the empire, Roman law was enforced on Romans only. Arian chaplains, therefore, often accompanied military forces. Maximinus himself, for example, came to Africa in the entourage of Segisvultus as a chaplain for Gothic Arian troops.

Boniface, the Roman military man, first befriended the bishop when he wrote to Augustine with questions about differences between Donatism and Arianism. The bishop's friendship for the *comes Africae* and his concern for the defense of the African provinces were to involve Augustine firmly in one of the empire's most tragic political rivalries and may have contributed in some small way to his encounter with Maximinus, the Arian bishop.

Augustine's importance as a theologian, coupled with the coming of Arianism to North Africa and his friendship with Boniface, meant that it was inevitable that he confront the heresy. The misfortunes of the empire engulfed Augustine's closing days in a sea of Arianism. When the Vandals invaded, he sought to steel his clergy for the coming struggle with the heretical sect. Augustine's very last days were spent in a Hippo Regius guarded by Gothic troops, who were professing Arians, against Vandals, who were also professing Arians.

## Type of Arianism

Another important question posed at the beginning of this study was the type of Arianism that Augustine faced in his closing years.

In chapter 2, its origin, development, and theology were scrutinized. In chapter 3 it was determined that, indeed, the type of Arianism encountered in Augustine's later works is the Homoian Arianism of the Ulfilan school. It is an Arianism fully deserving of the title "Gothic": Ulfila was the first Arian Gothic bishop, the Goths were instrumental in spreading and protecting it, and the Goths continued for a long time to be its primary advocates.

## Arianism in Roman Africa

Another key question of this study was, When did Arianism come to Roman Africa? It may be impossible to establish an exact date because of the heresy's popularity with the army, particularly among troops of barbarian origins. It could have entered the provinces almost any time during the late fourth or early fifth centuries.

The first real evidence that Arianism was present came a short time after the sack of Rome. During a sermon, Augustine invited any Arians that might be in the audience to accept the "true faith." Later, in 417, Boniface wrote for advice about Donatists, who were claiming spiritual kinship with his Gothic Arian troopers. By the summer of 418 and the arrival of the *Sermo Arianorum,* it is fairly certain that Arianism had at least some adherents in Roman Africa. But the movement was obviously not yet felt to be a major threat by the bishop of Hippo.

## Encounters

In the summer of 418, Elpidius sent Augustine the *Sermo Arianorum* along with a cover letter. The Arian was probably writing from northern Italy, where Bonosus and Jason were defending the Arian cause. Elpidius was hoping to convert the bishop of Hippo. Augustine, however, had no intentions of becoming his coreligionist. Instead, the bishop prepared a careful point-by-point refutation of the *Sermo Arianorum,* known as the *Contra Sermonem Arianorum.*

This one encounter set the tone of Augustine's conflicts with Gothic Arianism. In it the bishop of Hippo began to develop further the exegetical basis from which to defeat the long *catenae* (chains) of Ulfilan prooftexts in the battle with Maximinus ten years later.

The encounter with Maximus is a comparatively minor incident. A wealthy physician and formerly an Ulfilan Arian was urged to use his authority to lead his household back into orthodoxy. Maximus, interestingly enough, had been converted from Arianism by the bishop's preaching (perhaps by one of Augustine's sermons on John's Gospel). Yet, even in this work, Augustine developed a bright little gem of an argument for Catholicism over Arianism. The bishop's chief theological concern in the letters was the development of Maximus's respect for the integrity of Scripture and its absolute authority. Already the issue of hermeneutics was emerging as the major battleground between Augustine and Ulfilan Arianism.

Although this correspondence occurred sometime after A.D. 413 there seems to be no external evidence that would further isolate a specific date for it. On the basis of internal evidence, some scholars have decided, however, that it most nearly fits the state of Augustine's theology in about A.D. 419. The researcher, on the basis of the bishop's theological views, must place it somewhere between A.D. 418 and 428.

The bishop's encounters with Ulfilan Arianism had been, thus far, exclusively literary. The debate with Pascentius was probably Augustine's first face-to-face meeting with an Ulfilan Arian. Unfortunately, Pascentius was an untrained, overconfident, even arrogant layman. The proceedings were a farce. Pascentius seems, in retrospect, a buffoon. The one really valuable exposition found in the documents is the confession of faith offered by Augustine. The confession is an interesting weave of comparative exegesis, syllogism, and analogy.

It is extremely hard to assign a date to Augustine's debate with Pascentius. The researcher believes that the debate and the subsequent correspondence must be placed in the period of relative calm between A.D. 425 and 427.

Augustine's last and most important encounter with Ulfilan Arianism was his debate with Maximinus. Maximinus was the leading Ulfilan theologian and much more representative of the best in Ulfilan thought than Pascentius. The recounting of this debate and the analysis of its theology should be the centerpiece of any future discussion of Augustine's conflicts with Arians. In future, no one should use the debate with Pascentius as the centerpiece of such a discussion.[1]

## Changes or Development

Careful analysis of the documents has shown that Augustine did not change any major elements of his doctrines of the Trinity, Christology, pneumatology, or soteriology. These doctrines remained as they had been expressed in the *De Trinitate*. The major development which one finds in the anti-Arian writings is the elaboration of more effective polemical, apologetic, and exegetical arguments in support of Augustine's basic positions.

Only on minor issues does one find any change at all. There is, for instance, a small development in the Son's role in illumination. He comes more fully to share both interior and exterior modes with the Holy Spirit. In his letter to Nebridius in A.D. 389, Augustine had tended to divide the operations of the Son and the Spirit (Ep. 11). One, of course, finds this more mature understanding of a joint role in all aspects of illumination in many of Augustine's later works. And, for Augustine, the content of illumination was always found in the Son, not in the Spirit.[2]

Another new development is that Augustine was finally forced to deal with Luke 2:52 and growth in the Lord's wisdom. He refuted the view of moral progress in the Christ. It was the "form of a servant" and he only who was able to progress, since there could be no time when the "form of God" did not possess all divine wisdom.

A major difference between the *De Trinitate* and the later anti-Arian writings is the lack of emphasis given to the use of analogies to the Trinity found in the latter. This indicates not so much a shift in the thought of Augustine as a difference in purpose in these works. In the anti-Arian writings, Augustine was primarily interested in proving the unity of substance for Father, Son, and Holy Spirit, not elaborating on how this one substance is yet three persons.

In the struggle with the Ulfilan Arians, the key issue became hermeneutics. Maximinus, for example, often tried to substantiate rampant eisegesis with the barest citation of Scripture. The Ulfilans were guilty of a "prooftext" method as bad as that of the modern cults or the worst in Fundamentalism. Their hidden philosophical and theological agendas dictated which scriptural texts the Ulfilans would emphasize and how they would explain those which did not seem to fit their interpretation. What is most appalling about the Ulfilans is the claim which they made to bare literalism, despite interpretations that are sometimes obviously artificial and contrived. For this reason they are to be most strongly condemned. The Ulfilans claimed to be doing exegesis, and exegesis only, when they were really doing a poorly conceived theology. Augustine also did theology rather than pure exegesis, but his theological presuppositions were clearly and repeatedly stated. Augustine was self-consciously, and admittedly, doing theology.

Whereas his opponents thought "Father" when they read "God," the African thought "Trinity." Augustine very clearly enunciated his presupposition that any scriptural reference implying the Son's inferiority must be referred to the humanity which Christ assumed. Augustine's system was consistent and logical. He tried to show that his method was the only valid way of interpreting the Scriptures because only a Trinitarian system could take seriously both the passages, like Deuteronomy 6:4, 13, that stressed the absolute oneness of God and forbade the worship any other and those various passages that proclaimed that one or the other, Father or Son or Holy Spirit, was to be worshiped or referred to as God. One must remember that underneath this methodology was an assumption that the Bible was a single divine message, which by its nature had to be self-consistent. Within his arguments against Maximinus, one also finds Augustine's final views on illumination and, of course, one of his most complete discussions on the Holy Spirit.

## Contributions of this Work

This study of Augustine and the Ulfilan Arians presents an all too rare analysis of Ulfilan theology and hermeneutics in the English language and establishes the probable identity of the sender of the *Sermo Arianorum*. The date of Augustine's letter to Elpidius and its connection with the *Sermo Arianorum* have been made relatively certain. What the author feels is a more logical date has been assigned to Augustine's correspondence with Pascentius. And, for the first time, a relatively complete discussion of the contents of the *Sermo Arianorum,* the *Contra Sermonem Arianorum,* the *Collatio cum Maximino,* and the *Contra Maximinum* has appeared in the English language. Hopefully, it can serve as a springboard to further investigation of these all too often neglected works.

# APPENDIX I: SCRIPTURE REFERENCES

The following is a listing of scriptural citations in the S = *Sermo Arianorum;*
CS = *Contra Sermonem;* C(M) = *Collatio cum Maximino* with Maximinus
speaking; C(A) = *Collatio cum Maximino* with Augustine speaking; and
CM = *Contra Maximinum.* The Psalms are numbered according to the
Protestant system, not acording to the Vulgate.

## Genesis

| | |
|---|---|
| 1:26,27 | CS.16.9; C14.26(M); CM2.26.2 |
| 1:31 | C14.16(M) |
| 2:18 | C14.26(M); CM2.26.2 |
| 2:21 | CM2.26.2 |
| 3:10,11 | C.14.26(M); CM2.26.4 |
| 3:19 | CM1.2 |
| 18–19 | C14.26(M); CM2.26.5–8 |
| 22:6–13 | CS25.21; C13(A); CM1.9; CM2.19; CM2.26.9 |
| 23:2–7 | CM2.3 |
| 32:23 – 030 | C14.26(M); CM2.26.9 |
| 49:11 | C14.26(M) |

## Exodus

| | |
|---|---|
| 3:2,6 | CM2.26.11 |
| 3:14,15 | C14.26(M); CM1.19; CM2.26.10; CM2.26.11; CM2.26.14 |
| 7:1 | CM2.15.3 |
| 8:19 | CM2.21.2 |
| 12:1 | CM2.21.2 |
| 13:21,22 | CM1.19 |
| 17:6 | CM2.26.9 |
| 31:13 | CS32.30 |
| 33:11,13 | C14(A); CM1.15; CM2.26.10; CM2.26.12 |
| 33:20 | C14.26(M) |

## Deuteronomy

| | |
|---|---|
| 4:2 | C14.13(M) |

## Job

## Psalms

145:18        C14.21(M)

## Proverbs

8:30,31       C14.16(M)
9:1           C14.8(M); CM2.17.2
10:19         C13(M)
20:6          (Vide LXX) S5; CS5.5

## Ecclesiastes

3:22          CM2.11

## Isaiah

7:9           C14.26(M); CM2.10.2
7:13          C14.9(M)
40:5          C11(A)
48:12–16      CS19.9; CM2.20.4
53:1          CS12.9
53:7,8        C14.14(M); CM2.14.1; CM2.26.9

## Daniel

3:87          CS19.9

## Hosea

12:3,4        CM2.26.9

## Zachariah

12:10         CS11.9; CM2.18.6

## Malachi

3:6           C14.26(M); CM1.19; CM2.26.10; CM2.26.14

## Matthew

1:18          CM2.17.2

## Mark

## Luke

| | |
|---|---|
| 2:51,52 | CS22.7; C14.18(M); CM1.8; CM2.18.4; CM2.23.7 |
| 3:21–23 | S6; CS6.6 |
| 4:1 | CS22.18; CM2.16.3; CM2.18.6; CM2.21.2 |
| 4:18,21 | CS22.18; C11(A) |
| 4:43 | S6; CS6.6 |
| 6:45 | C14.23(M) |
| 12:4 | C14(A) |
| 12:20 | C14.9(M) |
| 13:46 | CS9.7 |
| 15:4,7 | C14.9(M) |
| 16:10 | C14.19(M) |
| 18:19 | CM2.23.5 |
| 23:46 | S7 |
| 29:49 | C14.10(M) |

# John

| | |
|---|---|
| 1:1–4 | CS2.3; CS11.9; CS15.9; C10(M); C14(A); C14.17(M); C14.21(M); CM1.19; CM2.17.1; CM2.17.4; CM2.23.7 |
| 1:9 | CS32.30 |
| 1:14 | CS9.7; CS12.9; CS27.23; C11(A); C14(A); C14.8(M); C14.26(M); CM2.22.3 |
| 1:18 | C13(M); C14.9(M); C14.26(M); CM2.9.1 |
| 1:29 | C14.5(M) |
| 2:19 | CS15.9 |
| 3:13 | CS8.6; CM2.9.1; CM2.20.3 |
| 4:24 | C14.15(M); CM2.15.2; CM2.22.3 |
| 5:1 | CM2.12.1 |
| 5:19 | S20; CS15.9; CS22.18; CS23.20; CS29.27; CM2.14.8; CM2.20.4; CM2.23.4 |
| 5:21 | CS8.6; CM2.12.2; CM2.20.4; CM2.23.7 |
| 5:22 | S9; CS11.9; CS14.9; CS15.9; CS18.9; C14.18(M); CM2.18.6 |
| 5:23 | CS29.27; C14.8(M); C14.18(M); C14.21(M) |
| 5:26 | CS17.9; C13(A); C14(A); C14.14(M); CM2.14.7 |
| 5:27 | CS11.9 |
| 5:30 | S9; CS11.9; CS14.9; CS18.9 |
| 5:31 | C13(M) |
| 5:37 | C13(M) |
| 6:11 | CM2.14.8 |
| 6:38 | S6; CS6.6; CS7.6; CS8.6; C14.20(M); CM2.20.3 |
| 6:44 | CS30.28 |
| 6:45 | CM1.3 |
| 6:46 | C14.9(M); CM2.9.1 |
| 6:55 | CM2.17.2 |

## Acts

| | |
|---|---|
| 2:3 | C14(A); C14.26(M); CM1.19 |
| 2:31 | CS9.7 |
| 2:32,33 | C7(M) |
| 2:38 | CM2.17.1 |
| 4:32 | C12(A); CM2.20.1; CM2.22.2 |
| 5:3,4 | CM2.21.1 |
| 7:47,48 | CM2.21.1 |
| 9:4 | C14.9(M) |
| 10:38 | CM2.16.3 |
| 13:2 | C14.2(M) |
| 13:35 | CS9.7 |
| 13:47 | C5(M) |
| 17:24 | CM2.3 |
| 17:27,28 | CS30.28; CM1.12 |
| 20:35 | CM2.14.7 |

## Romans

| | |
|---|---|
| 1:7 | C14.23(M); CM2.23.3 |
| 1:10 | CM2.7 |
| 1:20 | C14(A); C14.7(M); CM2.14.3 |
| 3:20 | C11(A) |
| 5:5 | CS25.21 |
| 5:12 | CS7.6; CM2.20.3 |
| 5:19 | CS7.6 |
| 6:10 | CM1.2 |
| 8:3 | CM1.2 |
| 8:9,11 | CM2.14.1 |
| 8:15 | CS25.21; C13(A) |
| 8:26,27 | CS25.21; C12(M); C14.19(M); CM1.9 |
| 8:32–34 | S34; C12(M); C14(A); C14.4(M); CM1.19; CM2.4; CM2.20.4 |
| 9:5 | CS15.9; CM2.21.1 |
| 10:10 | CM1.1 |
| 10:17 | S34 |
| 11:33–36 | CS3.4; CS32.30; CM2.23.4 |
| 12:1 | CM2.21.1 |
| 12:10 | CS23.19 |
| 15:6 | C14.16(M) |
| 16:25–27 | C13(M); C14(A); C14.13(M); CM1.16; CM2.13.2 |

## 1 Corinthians

| | |
|---|---|
| 1:3 | C14.23(M); CM2.23.3 |
| 1:24 | CS26.22; C14(A); C14.13(M); CM1.16; CM2.17.2 |
| 2:8 | CS8.6; CM2.20.3 |

## 2 Corinthians

## Galatians

| 1:3 | C14.23(M); CM2.23.3 |
|-----|---------------------|
| 2:16 | CS9.7 |
| 2:20 | CM2.20.4 |
| 3:11 | CS9.7 |
| 3:13 | C14.5(M); CM1.2 |
| 3:28 | CM2.22.2 |
| 4:4 | S6; CS6.6 |
| 4:6 | CS25.21; C13(A) |
| 4:8,9 | CS25.21; C13(A); CM2.15.2 |

## Ephesians

| 1:2 | C14.23(M); CM2.23.3 |
|-----|---------------------|
| 1:17 | C14.16(M) |
| 2:5,6 | CM2.21.3 |
| 3:14,15 | C14.3(M) |
| 4:4 | CM2.14.1 |
| 4:5 | CM2.23.3 |
| 4:30 | CS25.21 |
| 5:8 | CM1.12 |

## Philippians

| 2:5–11 | S6; S34; CS6.6; CS8.6; CS11.9; CS38.34; C10(M); C11(A); C14(A); C14.2(M); C14.4(M); C14.15(M); CM1.5; CM2.2; CM2.14.7; CM2.15.1; CM2.15.5; CM2.23.7; CM2.25 |
|--------|---------------------|
| 3:21 | C14.8(M) |

## Colossians

| 1:15–18 | CS34.32; C13(M); C14.14(M); C14.17(M); CM2.9.1; CM2.18.5 |
|---------|---------------------|
| 2:14,15 | C14.8(M) |
| 3:1 | C14.4(M) |

## 2 Thessalonians

| 4:15 | S9; CS11.9; CS12.9 |
|------|---------------------|

## 1 Timothy

| 1:17 | CM2.11 |
|------|--------|

| | |
|---|---|
| 1:18 | CM2.9.1 |
| 2:5 | CS7.6; CS9.7 |
| 3:2 | C14.14(M) |
| 4:15 | C14.11(M) |
| 6:13–16 | C13(M); C14(A); C14.14(M); C14.26(M); CM1.4; CM2.9.1; CM2.12.2; CM2.26.1 |

## 2 Timothy

| | |
|---|---|
| 2:2,4 | CM2.1 |
| 3:16 | C14.16(M) |

## Titus

| | |
|---|---|
| 2:13 | C13(M) |
| 3:4–6 | C6(M) |

## Hebrews

| | |
|---|---|
| 1:3 | C14.4(M) |
| 1:10–12 | CM2.26.10 |
| 2:7 | CS5.5 |
| 2:8,9 | CM2.18.6; CM2.25 |
| 9:24 | C14.9(M) |
| 13:2 | C2.26.6 |

## James

| | |
|---|---|
| 1:18 | CS27.23 |

## 1 Peter

| | |
|---|---|
| 1:12 | C12(M); C14.21(M) |
| 2:21–23 | C14.5(M); C14.9(M) |

## 1 John

| | |
|---|---|
| 2:1 | CS19.9 |
| 2:16 | CS25.20 |
| 3:2 | CM2.9.1 |

| | |
|---|---|
| 3:20 | CS9.7; CM2.25 |
| 5:1 | C14.13(M) |
| 5:8 | CM2.22.3 |
| 5:20 | CS1.1; C14(A); CM1.5; CM2.14.2 |

## Revelation

| | |
|---|---|
| 17:14 | CM2.12.2 |
| 19:12 | CM2.13.1; CM2.15.4 |
| 19:15,16 | CM2.12.2 |

## Baruch

| | |
|---|---|
| 3:26,36–38 | CM2.26.13 |

## Wisdom

| | |
|---|---|
| 1:7 | CM2.21.2 |
| 8:1 | CS4.4 |

# APPENDIX II:
# A FEW NOTES ON IMPORTANT
# WESTERN TEXTS

One of the major problems in reconstructing a picture of the Arian Church and its theology is that many of the relevant documents have been destroyed. Relatively little heterodox literature of any kind survived to the modern era.[1] Most of the extant Arian works are incomplete fragments. They are usually preserved either as quotations in works written to refute them, as writings falsely ascribed to a famous orthodox writer, in palimpset form (when the parchment on which they were written was erased partially or completely by scraping in order to make room for another text), or as *marginalia* (marginal notes) in a text deemed too valuable to erase. An Arian commentary on Job, for example, has been slipped into the works of Origen. Labriolle describes this treatise as being of "tiresome mediocrity."[2] Some few, like the *Sermo Arianorum,* were preserved by their theological opponents for reference purposes. The Catholics did not see fit to preserve the bulk of them for posterity.[3] Many were consigned to the flames. The Visigothic king of Spain Reccared provides an example of what was all too common. He was converted from Arianism and in 589, at the Third Council of Toledo, ordered all Arian books burned. Many anti-Arian works were also burned. His actions alone did much to plunge us into darkness concerning Gothic Arian theology and, especially, their liturgy and practice.[4]

Little was done about analyzing the Homoian or Latin Arian texts until relatively recent times. Most of the attention was and still is given to the Arianism of the Eastern empire in the period between A.D. 318 and 381. Real analysis of Western texts began in the nineteenth century among German philologists. Unfortunately, many of them were ardent nationalists who tried to shape the evidence to give added racial prestige to the Germans.[5]

The *Collectio Veronensis* (ms. Verona, Bibl. Capit. IL[49]) contains a group of texts otherwise unknown, which are for the most part Arian. It includes an exposition of the names of the apostles, a series of twenty-four homilies on the Gospels, another fifteen sermons on the principal feasts of the year, a tract against the Jews, a tract against the pagans, a short polemic directed against the doctrine of the equality of the Father and the Son, some fragments of the *Liber locorum* by Jerome, a homily by Augustine of Hippo, and the last of an ancient Latin version of the *Constitutiones Apostolicae*.[6] Angelus Mai seems to have attributed the authorship of the nineteenth sermon and two other fragments to Palladius or Maximinus.[7]

Manuscript lat. 8907, in the Bibliothèque Nationale in Paris, is a collection of Nicene writings relative to the Trinitarian controversy, copied in the common uncial script of the first half of the fifth century. This manuscript contains the *De Trinitate,* the *Contra Auxentium,* and the *De synodis* all by Hilary, the first two books of the *De fide* by Ambrose, and the acts of the Council of Aquileia in A.D. 381. The Arian *Scholia in Concilium Aquileiense,* often referred to as the *Dissertatio Maximini contra Ambrosium,* is found in the margins of this work. It constitutes one of the most important and one of the most hotly debated of the Western Arian texts. These *marginalia* provide insights into the Arian view of Ambrose and the fortunes of Arianism in late fourth-century and early fifth-century Illyricum.[8]

They appear in the margin of *De fide* and in the margin of the acts of Aquileia.[9] One of the curious features of the account of the acts of Aquileia is that it ends abruptly in the middle of the interrogation of the second accused bishop, Secundianus. The marginal notes in both places concern the same subject: the controversy between the Arian bishop Palladius of Ratiaria and Ambrose, which culminated in the Council of Aquileia in 381, where Palladius was condemned with his colleague Secundianus. Some parts of the text are obviously missing.

The *marginalia* begin with a few illegible lines. When the writing becomes legible, the record is seen to be a copy of the proceedings of the Council of Aquileia, interspersed with Arian comments attributed to a bishop named Maximinus. These ten passages, the Arian comments, are directed against Ambrose. Shortly after the last of these interruptions, the copy of the council's acts breaks off less than halfway through, with the comment that the rest of the proceedings may be read in the main body of the manuscript. There immediately follows some further discussion of the council's proceedings, including a comparison of the faith of Ambrose's party with that of the letter of Arius, which had been read at the council. The second part of the first block of *marginalia* contains a letter by Auxentius, a profession of faith by Ulfila, and a few closing remarks. It is an account of the aftermath of the council illustrated from the letter of a certain Auxentius, probably Auxentius of Durostorum, and an explanation of why, when the Arian bishops at the council had addressed their opponents as fellow Christians, the latter are now regarded as heretics. The letter was written by a disciple of Ulfila, probably right after the Gothic bishop's death, as an exhortation to his fellow Arians to stand firm in their faith, and it includes a profession of faith by the famous Goth. Altaner believes that this was the work of Auxentius, the bishop of Durostorum.[10] Gryson also rejects Auxentius of Milan as a possible author of the letter found in the *marginalia*. Instead he opts for Auxentius of Durostorum, a bishop of lower Moesia. Gryson argues: "The author of the letter presents himself as the disciple and spiritual son of Ulfilas to whom he had been entrusted at a very young age, and from whom he had received his religious instruction. Well, it was precisely in Moesia that Ulfilas took up residence with his Goths."[11]

The second major block is separated from the first by a gap of twenty-four pages. It begins with two extracts from Ambrose's *De Fide,* each followed by a reply ascribed to someone called Palladius, probably Palladius of Ratiara (condemned at the council). The second reply of Palladius is followed by an Arian account of the council's proceedings, still addressing Ambrose directly in a tone of protest and ending with an appeal for a new hearing before the Senate at Rome. It portrays Palladius and Secundianus as confessors of the faith faced with a false bishop, Ambrose, and a band of ignorant conspirators. The apology itself was written by Palladius sometime between 3 September 381 (the date of the council) and the death of Pope Damasus, that is, 11 December 381, for a living Damasus is alluded to in the work. Finally, there is a concluding note by Maximinus. After the end of Palladius's work, there is a further historical notice about the visit of the Arian bishops to Constantinople, followed by the quotation of two laws of the years 388 and 386 taken from the Theodosian Code of 438.

Vigilius of Thapsa noted that an Arian bishop named Palladius had written against the Trinitarian doctrine of Ambrose. Gryson believes that these fragments, attributed to Palladius, are a work in which Palladius of Ratiara in 379 sought to refute the first two books of Ambrose's *De fide*.[12]

The first critical edition of the *Scolia* was only partial. In 1840 Georg Waitz published the letter of Auxentius concerning Ulfila, the so-called Apostle of the Goths. Wilhelm Bessell published a new edition in 1860 that included some other passages along with the letter. Not until the work of Frederich Kauffmann in 1899 was a complete text available.[13] It was Kauffmann who gave it the title by which it has popularly been known, *Dissertatio Maximini contra Ambrosium*.[14] Unhappy with the many flaws in Kauffmann's edition, Roger Gryson brought out a new edition in 1980, including a translation into French and an extensive introduction covering the historical and theological background of the texts.

Both George Waitz and Friedrich Kauffmann regarded the *marginalia* as a single work by a certain Maximinus whose name appears in the first part of them. They differed, however, in that Waitz assumed that the *marginalia* comprised an autograph whereas Kauffmann held that they were a copy. Kauffmann believed that the *marginalia* were an abbreviated form of a commentary by Maximinus on the council. Most scholars have now accepted the evidence that the *Scolia* is a collection of separate items but hold fast to the idea of a single work or compilation by Maximinus, perhaps in the form of a sort of anthology which incorporates them all.

Most of the major critics have held that the Maximinus who wrote the comments in the *Scolia* is the same as the one who debated Augustine.[15] Altaner believes that Maximinus wrote it in 383. Albert Hamman, the editor of the *Supplementum,* for example, assumed that Maximinus was responsible for the collection and that this Maximinus was the same as the one who debated Augustine in 427–428.[16] Gryson has no doubts that this Maximinus must be deemed the author/editor of this work because "we know precisely one Arian bishop of this name [Maximinus], living in the epoch which followed the council of Aquileia."[17] Based on a complicated argument over word usage in the *Collatio cum Maximino Arianorum episcopo,* Gryson concludes that the author/editor of this section of the scolia can be no other than Augustine's opponent in the *Collatio* in A.D. 428.[18] Gryson also rejects Kauffmann's contention that when these *Scolia* were first written, Maximinus was not yet a bishop. He does this on the basis of the phrase *episcopus disserens* in the formulas of introduction and because there is no real reason to suppose that Maximinus was not a bishop when he wrote his comments.

The *marginalia* are probably not an autograph. They do seem to be a copy of excerpts from other Arian works. Bammel suggests that the manuscript from which the Paris scribe (whoever it was who wrote in the margins of 8907) copied was one in which the *Acts of the Council of Aquileia,* the letter of Auxentius, and the work against Ambrose by Palladius formed the main text, and in which the comments of Maximinus appeared as *marginalia.*[19] Bammel ascribes the first section of these *marginalia* to the Maximinus mentioned therein, assuming that after a few marginal comments on details of the *Acts of the Council of Aquileia,* Maximinus changed to a more general attack. He suggests that "Maximinus may have written his attack as a continuous piece with reference to a letter of Auxentius which appeared as part of the main text of his own manuscript, and that it was the Paris scribe who inserted the complete quotation of the letter at the appropriate point."[20] Bammel's reconstruction of the assembly of the *marginalia* is as follows:

1. A group of Arian works directed against the Council of Aquileia was collected, including the *Acts of the Council,* the letter of Auxentius, and the work or works against Ambrose by Palladius of Ratiara. It would have been, but need not have been, formed by Maximinus. Palladius himself, for example, could have done it.
2. Maximinus annotated a copy of this collection with his own comments.
3. The collector of these *marginalia,* himself an Arian and perhaps a disciple of Maximinus, copied into the margins of 8907 his own selections from the main text together with all or some of Maximinus' annotations.[21]

Bammel cites Maximinus's comment, "ut et ego [nos?] ab ipsis patribus nostri Christi servis sedentes in memoratum urbem [Constantinople] saepius audivimus," as an indication of "some distance from the events described (the death of Ulfila)."[22] Like Bammel, Charles Perrat (the noted French scholar) and Meslin agree that "the *marginalia* in Paris 8907 could have been made in the middle of the fifth century by a cleric in the entourage of Maximinus."[23]

Bammel offers as an explanation for the confused state of the *marginalia* to 8907 the suggestion that the scribe started in the margins of the *Acts of the Council of Aquileia,* which was the obvious place for his material. After writing for a while, he realized that he would not have enough room and so turned to the beginning of Ambrose's *De Fide* and used its margins. He notes that the handwriting started out small and neat and gradually became larger and more careless. Bammel believes that section 2 was written before 384 since it mentions the Roman bishop Damasus as still alive. He notes that although Palladius, along with the other Arian bishops on whose behalf it was written, remains in the third person, it is usually regarded as Palladius's work. The author of the first section indeed refers to it under Palladius's name. Most scholars see in this material extracts from two separate works by Palladius: one in the year 379, attacking Ambrose's *De Fide* books 1 and 2, and the second in the year 382–83, written in protest of the Council of Aquileia. Palladius's accounts in section 2 appear to be on the basis of firsthand knowledge, while those of Maximinus in the first section display some uncertainty about the details of the event. The section's author seems to have written with Palladius's work and Auxentius's letter already before him. Bammel, because of the two laws from the *Codex Theodosianus,* believes that the final compilation could not have happened before 438.[24]

Labriolle, for the same reason, doubts that this brief appendix, which ends the *Scolia* and relates the failure of steps taken by Ulfila, Palladius, and Secundianus and their partisans before Theodosius, was really the work of Maximinus. He thinks that it was added sometime after the fifth century.[25]

The Ambrosian Library of Milan in Italy contains an exemplar of the *Excerpta ex Augustino* by Eugippius. In this eighth-century palimpsest, twenty-four leaves come from an Arian commentary on the Gospel of Luke, copied in the uncial script of the sixth century. Albert Hamman says that this *Tractatus in Lucan evangelium* is of unknown but ancient authorship.[26] Otto Bardenhewer believes that it was probably written by Ulfila in about 370.[27] It appears to be only a small portion of a much larger work, comparable in its fullness of exposition to the *Opus imperfectum in Matthaeum,* since the complete commentary of the Gospel would cover about sixteen hundred pages.[28] The *Opus imperfectum in Matthaeum* is an incomplete collection of homilies on the Gospel of Matthew. It, unlike the *Sermo Arianorum* and the commentary on Job, is far from mediocre. For a time it was considered the work of John Chrysostom, although it is not the least ambiguous in its Arianism. The author speaks in the authoritative tone of a bishop with extreme bitterness over the victory of the Nicene formulations. The author also claims to have written works on Luke and Mark. Some, such as Ernest A. Thompson, think Maximinus a likely choice.[29] In this palimpsest are found many statements characteristic of Homoian Arianism.[30]

Besides the commentary on Luke, often referred to as the *Tractatus in Lucam,* the Ambrosian Library in Milan contains other Arian palimpsest leaves in a famous manuscript on the acts of the Council of Chalcedon in A.D. 451, which is preserved in part at the Vatican Library in Rome (ms. lat. 5750) and, in part, at the Ambrosian Library (S.P. 9/ss., olim E 147 sup.). This manuscript originally comprised some 792 pages, of which 54 have been destroyed. In the seventh century it was bound with two secular works; one was the correspondence of Fronto with Marcus Aurelius and the other some *scolia* on the discourses of Cicero. A very short time after this was done, the document was found to be damaged or mutilated for some unknown reason, and it was necessary to verify and replace some 140 pages. At that time, some leaves from an Arian theological manuscript were used, along with others from a collection of discourses by Symmachus and Pliny on a manuscript containing the satires of Juvenal and Perseus, and from a Gothic commentary on John. The Arian text, written in two columns of a pure uncial script with abbreviations limited strictly to the *nomina sacra,* is certainly, from the paleographic point of view, anterior to the commentary on Luke. Gryson refers to these documents as the *Fragmenta Theologica Rescripta.*[31]

The materials in this palimpsest were collected by the monks of the Abbey of Bobbio, founded by Columban in 613. They had the responsibility of combating the Arianism perpetuated in Italy by the Gothic, and later the Lombard, domination. Nineteen of the twenty-one fragments preserved in this palimpsest refer to Arianism. Angelo Mai first edited them in 1828. There are among them works on homiletics, dogmatics, and polemics. There is no positive difficulty in ascribing them all to the same author. Maximinus, Auxentius of Durostorum, and Palladius have all been suggested since there are indications that the author was a bishop from the region of the Danube.[32] Michel Meslin attributes it to Palladius of Ratiara. Meslin believes that he can identify some of the authors of works usually listed as anonymous. For example, he attributes the *Sermo Arianorum* to Palladius of Ratiara. He claims that at the very least the *Sermo Arianorum* was a "logical and conscientious" digest or a sort of "schematic summary" of the theology of Palladius of Ratiara. His conclusion is based on observations of theological coincidence of the positions which he espoused in the *Scolia* and those of the *Sermo.* The *Opus imperfectum in Matthaeum,* the *Vetus interpretatio,* and the *Commentarius in Job* he assigns to Maximinus. He feels that due to a lack of evidence the *Tractatus in Lucam* must remain anonymous.[33]

The original manuscript contained two different tracts. The first was a polemic directed against those called "orthodox" and the Macedonians. The other was an "instruction on the true faith," destined for one who, though not Christian, sympathized with Christianity. It explained that faith in the Trinity had nothing in common with pagan polytheism. The same collection also contained fragments of a Latin version of *The Ascension of Isaiah.*[34]

# APPENDIX III:
# GOTHIC ARIAN WORSHIP

Most of the details about Gothic Arian worship practices and organization have been lost. Only the broad outlines of their hierarchical structure and a few of their practices are known.

Soon after the events related in this book, the Gothic Arians had pretty much abandoned Roman hierarchal control and had begun to Germanize their ecclesiastical organization.[1] At first, probably due to Ulfila's influence, they had accepted the supremacy of the Arian bishop of Constantinople. But after the death of Demophilus in 386, they, and their bishop Selenas, shifted their allegiance to Dorotheus of Antioch.[2] This was only the first in a series of shifts which ultimately led them out of the Roman system altogether. Their movement eventually became fully indigenous and independent of the Roman system. A proprietary church system was established, possibly under the influence of their old proprietary temple system.[3] Of all the Germanic Arians, only the Vandals ever established a regular patriarchate. The Arian fellowship became, for them, the only true church, the only church loyal to the teachings of Christ.[4]

Local organization of the Gothic, or Germanic, Arian Church was modeled on that of the Roman army, with the smaller units grouped in hundreds, five hundreds, and thousands. Those actually in the Roman army had their own portable buildings and their own regional prelates.[5] Unlike the Catholics, the Gothic Arians were not drawn to monasticism.

Gothic Arianism lacked any central organization. The point of unity for the various tribal churches and for affiliated Arian army chaplains was acceptance of the Homoian creed of the Council of Rimini.[6] The authority of Rimini was universal among the Gothic, or Germanic, Arians. Even the fierce and independent Vandals, who had only the most vague links to Latin and Greek culture, subscribed to it.[7] Hunneric, the Vandal king, finally issued the "Dated Creed" as official doctrine over a hundred years after the council. Rimini would remain the foundation of Gothic faith until condemned by the Gothic king Recarred at the Council of Toledo in 589.[8]

Arian Christianity modified the customs and values of the barbarians and helped to take the edge off their wild ferocity. Augustine attributed the moderation of the Visigothic sack of Rome to Arianism's influence. He, as well as the historian Orosius and Jerome, noted the reverence with which they treated Christian personages and religious objects. This estimate must, however, be tempered by a knowledge of the persecutions later inflicted by the Vandals, ostensibly in the cause of their faith. There were also a few persecutors among the Gothic kings. But only under Euric did the Visigoths systematically persecute Catholics.[9]

Sometimes their Arian convictions inspired violent fanaticism. At Eleusis, for example, chaplains in the Visigothic army beat the old hierophant and his assistants while their troops looted the treasure of the pagan sanctuary.[10] But they were usually fairly tolerant of the Catholics, whom they preferred to persuade rather than persecute.

For the most part, the Gothic Arians were content to follow Roman liturgical forms. They carried with them into the West an Eastern liturgy, somewhat modified to suit their practical and theological needs. It caused some variation. Offices practiced by Westerners in the morning were sometimes held at another time of day. There were also differences in the time of the Easter celebration. But the most important differences derived from the influence of Arian theology. There were key differences, for example, in the terminology surrounding the Eucharistic celebration. These differences often alerted an orthodox population to the heresy's presence.[11]

Their services incorporated an ethical system which stressed strength and heroism. Everything was calculated to appeal to and exalt the soul of the mystically minded warrior. Influenced by these modifications, the barbarians were shocked by what they considered the unbridled corruption of some African and Roman customs. To them may also be traced the Germanic laws against magic and divination.[12]

There was no specifically Arian ritual of baptism in the late fourth and early fifth century. Like the orthodox ceremony, their ritual included the renunciation of Satan, the laying on of hands for the reception of the Spirit, and triple immersion in honor of the Trinity.[13] But some Arians did change the traditional baptismal formula to stress the differences in the persons of the Trinity. They changed it to read, "In the name of the Father, through the Son, in the Holy Spirit."[14] In Hispania, some of the orthodox reacted to this by going to a single, rather than the more common, triple immersion. After the threat had subsided, probably because of the reaction of other Catholics accusing them of anti-Trinitarian Sabellianism, they returned to triple immersion.[15] Some of these later Arians, like Maximinus, also held the old third-century view that baptism by a heretic was invalid.[16]

# ABBREVIATIONS

## Names

| | |
|---|---|
| Aug. | Augustine of Hippo |
| Aux. | Auxentius |
| Max. | Maximinus |
| Pal. | Palladius of Ratiara |
| Ulf. | Ulfila |

## Ancient Works

| | |
|---|---|
| CM | Aug. *Contra Maximinum Arianorum episcopum.* |
| Coll. | Aug./Max. *Collatio cum Maximino Arianorum episcopo.* |
| Conf. | Aug. *Confessiones.* |
| CS | Aug. *Contra Sermonem Arianorum.* |
| De Trin. | Aug. *De Trinitate.* |
| Ep. | Aug. *Epistulae.* |
| Hist. Eccl. | The *Historiae Ecclesiae* of Socrates, Sozomen, and Theodoret. |
| R | Aug. *Retractationes.* |
| S | Pal? *Sermo Arianorum.* |
| Scol. | Aux., Max., Pal., Ulf. *Scolia Arriana in Concilium Aquileiense.* |
| Tract. in Joan. | Aug. *Tractatus in Joannis Evangelium.* |
| Vita | Possidius, *Vita Sancti Aurelii Augustini.* |

# NOTES

## Preface

1. Possidius, *Vita Sancti Aurelii Augustini* 17. Quotations from and observations based on this work will be cited in the text with the abbreviation "Vita."

2. Gerald Bonner, *St. Augustine of Hippo: Life and Controversies* (Philadelphia: Westminster Press, 1963); Frederick Van der Meer, *Augustine the Bishop: Religion and Society at the Dawn of the Middle Ages,* trans. Brian Buttershaw and G. R. Lamb (New York: Harper & Row, 1961).

## Introduction

1. William G. Rusch, "Series Forward," in *The Trinitarian Controversy,* Sources of Early Christian Thought (Philadelphia: Fortress Press, 1980), p. vii.

2. See Hans-Georg Gadamer on the dynamics of the hermeneutical problem and historical consciousness, *Truth and Method,* trans. Garrett Barden and John Cumming (New York: Seabury Press, 1975).

3. Two notable examples are Eugene Portalié, *A Guide to the Thought of Saint Augustine,* trans. Ralph J. Bastian (Chicago: Henry Regenery, 1960), and Alfred Schindler, *Wort und Analogie in Augustins Trinitätslehre* (Tübingen: J. C. B. Mohr, 1965).

4. Etienne Gilson, *Introduction à l'etude de saint Augustin* (Paris: J. Vrin, 1941), and Odilo Rottmanner, *Geistesfrüchte aus der Klosterzelle* (München, 1908).

5. See especially Emilien Lamirande, *Church, State and Toleration: An Intriguing Change of Mind in Augustine* (Villanova, PA: Villanova Press, 1975).

6. Andreas Derk Rietema Polman, *The Word of God according to St. Augustine,* trans. A. J. Pomerans (Grand Rapids, MI: Eerdmans, 1961), pp. 9–12.

7. Thomas Forsyth Torrance, *Reality and Evangelical Theology,* The 1981 Payton Lectures (Philadelphia: Westminster Press, 1982), p. 15.

8. Edmund J. Fortman, "Introduction," in *The Triune God: A Historical Study of the Doctrine of the Trinity* (Corpus Instrumentorum, Inc., 1972; reprint ed., Grand Rapids, MI: Baker Book House, 1982), p. xxiv.

## Chapter 1. Fifth-Century Context

1. Norman F. Cantor, *Medieval History: The Life and Death of a Civilization* (London: Collier-Macmillan, 1969), p. 109.

2. Ibid., p. 110.

3. Robert Latouche, *Les Grandes invasions et la crise de l'Occident au Ve siècle* (Paris, 1946).

4. Peter Brown, *Religion and Society in the Age of Saint Augustine* (London: Faber and Faber Ltd., 1972), p. 15.

5. A. H. M. Jones, *The Later Roman Empire 284–602: A Social, Economic and Administrative Survey*, 2 vols. (Norman: University of Oklahoma Press, 1964), 2:1038, 1039, 1044, 1045, 1048.

6. See Carl Stephenson, *Medieval History: Europe from the Second to the Sixteenth Century*, 3d ed. (New York: Harper & Brothers, 1951), pp. 34–35; H. Daniel-Rops, *The Church in the Dark Ages*, trans. Audrey Butler (New York: E. P. Dutton & Co., Inc., 1959), p. 70.

7. Jones, 2:1055–63.

8. See M. T. W. Arnheim, *The Senatorial Aristocracy in the Late Roman Empire* (Oxford: Clarendon Press, 1972), p. 168.

9. Jones, 2:1062.

10. Charles Jules Revillout, *De l'arianisme des peuples germaniques qui evahi l'empire Romain* (Paris: Madame Veuve Joubert, Libraire, 1850), p. 59.

11. Robert Latouche, *Caesar to Charlemagne*, trans. Jennifer Nicholson (New York: Barnes & Noble, 1968), pp. 199–200; W. H. C. Frend, *The Rise of Christianity* (Philadelphia: Fortress Press, 1984), p. 723.

12. Jones, 2:1038.

13. John Bagnell Bury, *History of the Later Roman Empire from the Death of Theodosius I to the Death of Justinian*, vol. 1 (London: Macmillan, 1923), pp. 42–43.

14. Revillout, p. 48.

15. Pierre Paul Courcelle, *Histoire Littéraire grandes invasion germaniques*, 3d ed. (Paris: Etudes Augustiniénnes, 1965), p. 253.

16. Jones, 1:199–201.

17. Daniel-Rops, p. 87.

18. Joseph Vogt, *The Decline of Rome*, trans. Janet Sondheimer (New York: New American Library, 1967), p. 202, Jones, 1:543.

19. Robert Austin Markus, *Christianity in the Roman World* (London: Thames and Hudson, 1974), p. 147.

20. Ibid., p. 144.

21. Ibid.

22. Frend, p. 722.

23. J. M. Wallace-Hadrill, *The Barbarian West 400–1000*, 3d rev. ed. (New York: Hutchinson & Co., 1967), pp. 22–23.

24. Markus, pp. 143, 149.

25. Wallace-Hadrill, p. 26.

26. Peter Brown, *Religion and Society*, pp. 152–53.

27. Jones, 2:1064.

28. Ibid., 2:1067–68.

29. Ibid.

30. Ibid., p. 1030–31.

31. A. Piganiol, *L'Empire chrétien* (Paris: Presses universitaires de France, 1947), p. 422; see Frend, p. 701.

32. John Bagnell Bury, *The Invasion of Europe by the Barbarians* (New York: Macmillan, 1928; reprint ed., New York: Russell & Russell, 1963), p. 123; *The Conversion of Western Europe, 350–750*, J. N. Hilgarth, ed. (Englewood Cliffs, NJ: Prentice-Hall, 1969), p. 63.

33. Jones, 1:2015, 2:1067; Bury, *Invasion*, p. 123.

34. Sidney Painter, *A History of the Middle Ages: 284–1500* (New York: Alfred A. Knopf, 1961), p. 26; Daniel-Rops, *Dark Ages*, pp. 61, 88–89.

35. Frend, pp. 723, 725.

36. Revillout, p. 42.

37. Ibid., p. 43.

38. *Studies of Arianism*, 2d ed. (Cambridge: Deighton Bell & Co., 1900), p. 261.

39. See Pierre Paul Courcelle, *Histoire littéraire grandes invasion germaniques*, 3d ed. (Paris: Etudes Augustiniennes, 1965), p. 253.

40. C. Warren Hollister, *Medieval Europe: A Short History*, 2d ed. (New York: John Wiley & Sons, 1968), p. 21.

41. Daniel-Rops, pp. 68–69.

42. Ibid.; *Conversion*, p. 63.

43. Cantor, p. 116.

44. Ibid., p. 118; Daniel-Rops, p. 54; Hollister, p. 21.

45. B. H. Warmington, *The North African Provinces from Diocletion to the Vandal Conquest* (Cambridge: University Press, 1954), p. 59.

46. David Bentley-Taylor, *Augustine, Wayward Genius: The Life of St. Augustine of Hippo* (Grand Rapids, MI: Baker Book House, 1980), p. 211.

47. Stewart Perowne, *The End of the Roman World* (New York: Thomas Y. Crowell Company, 1967), p. 47.

48. Bentley-Taylor, p. 213; Bury, *Invasion*, p. 117; Charles Christopher Mierow, *The Gothic History of Jordanes in English Version with an Introduction and Commentary* (New York: Barnes & Noble, 1966), p. 171.

49. Bury, *Invasion*, p. 117, 244–46; Prosperus Tyronis, *Epitoma Chronicon* in the *Chronica Minora*, cols. 1294–95. See Augustine, *Epistula* 220.

50. Jones, 1:177.

51. Bury, *Invasion*, p. 117, 244–46; Prosperus Tyronis, *Epitoma Chronicon* in the *Chronica Minora*, cols. 1294–95; R. J. Martindale, *The Prosopography of the Later Empire*, vol. 2 of *A.D. 395–527* (Cambridge University Press, 1980), pp. 239, 1010.

52. Bury, *Invasion*, p. 119; Martindale, p. 240.

53. Ibid., p. 120; Ferdinand Lot, *The End of the Ancient World and the Beginnings of the Middle Ages*, trans. Philip and Mariette Leon (New York: Harper Torchbooks, 1961), p. 206; Jones, 1:176.

54. Bury, *Invasion*, p. 124.

55. Cantor, pp. 119–20.

56. Jones, 1:190.

57. Sidonius Apollinaris, *Letters*, trans. O. M. Dalton, vol. 2 (Oxford: University Press, 1915), pp. 107–9.

58. Bonner, p. 140.

59. Gwatkin, p. 272.

60. J. N. D. Kelly, *The Athanasian Creed: The Paddock Lectures for 1962–3* (New York: Harper & Row, 1964), pp. 76–78.

61. Ibid., p. 78.

62. Ibid., p. 80.

63. Roger Gryson, *Scolies Ariennes sur le Concile d'Aquile: Introduction, Texte Latin, Traduction et Notes*, trans. and ed. Roger Gryson, Sources Chrétuiennes, no. 267 (Paris: Les Editions du Cerf, 1980), p. 144. While this could be considered a primary work, the writer's use of it has focused primarily on its introduction and

notes. Gryson's judgements about the Ulfilan Arians have proven to be extremely valuable in helping one to understand their theology.

64. Revillout, pp. 44–50.

65. Gwatkin, p. 271.

66. Revillout, pp. 48–49, 53, 59–60.

67. Bonner, p. 141.

68. Frend, p. 727.

69. Revillout, p. 75.

70. Karl Baus et al., *The Imperial Church from Constantine to the Early Middle Ages,* trans. Anselm Biggs, vol. 2 of *History of the Church,* 6 vols., gen eds. Hubert Jedin and John Dolan (New York: Seabury Press, 1980), p. 229; Revillout, p. 61.

71. See Daniel-Rops, p. 111.

72. Revillout, p. 117.

73. Ibid., pp. 51, 54, 55, 111.

74. Daniel-Rops, p. 113.

75. Revillout, pp. 106–7; Baus, p. 229.

76. Charles Revillout provides an interesting picture of their struggle. Revillout, pp. 107, 114–17.

77. Daniel-Rops, p. 113.

78. Revillout, pp. 23, 24.

79. From his *Abecedarium,* as quoted in *Conversion,* p. 70.

80. Revillout, pp. 125–27.

## Chapter 2.  The Rise of Ulfilan Arianism

1. *A Dictionary of Christian Biography,* 1887 ed., s.v. "Valens (4)" by G. T. Stokes.

2. *The Concise Oxford Dictionary of the Christian Church,* 2d ed. abridged, s.v. "Sirmium, Blasphemy of." The name comes from Hilary of Poitiers's description.

3. Thomas A. Kopecek, *A History of Neo-Arianism,* 2 vols. (Cambridge, MA.: Philadelphia Patristic Foundation, 1979), 1:136.

4. Michel Meslin, *Les Ariens d'Occident, 335–430,* Patristica Sorbonensia, tome 8. (Paris: Éditions du Seuil, 1967), p. 253–54, 264, 291.

5. Ibid., pp. 31–78.

6. J. D. Burkhard, "Les Ariens d'Occident," *Revue d'Histoire et de Philosophie Religieuse* 51, no. 2 (1971): 173.

7. Ibid.

8. Meslin, p. 270.

9. Burkhard, p. 172.

10. For a fuller discussion of the councils and their decisions, see *Concise Oxford Dictionary of the Christian Church,* 2d ed. abridged, s.v. "Ariminium and Seleucia, Synods of"; Kopecek, 1:214–15; Gwatkin, p. 182; Revillout, p. 97; Louis Duchesne, *Early History of the Christian Church from Its Foundation to the End of the Fifth Century,* vol. 3 of *The Fifth Century* (London: John Murray, 1924, reprinted 1951), p. 244; Ernest Thompson, *The Visigoths in the Time of Ulfila* (Oxford: Clarendon Press, 1966), p. xix. For a copy of the modified text see Socrates, *Historia Ecclesiastica* 2. 41.

11. Kopecek, 2:353–59; Sozomen *Hist. eccl.* 4. 24–26 and Theodoret *Hist. eccl.* 2. 23–25.

12. Manlio Simonetti, *Studi sul'Arianesimo* (Rome: Editrice Studium, [1965]), pp. 160–61.

13. Hans Lietzmann, *A History of the Early Church,* vol. 4 of *The Era of the Church Fathers,* 2d rev. ed., trans. Bertram Lee Woolf (London: Lutterworth Press, 1953), p. 57.

14. Gryson, *Scolies,* pp. 104–5.

15. See *Altercatio Heracliani laici cum Germinio episcopo Sirmiensi.* See the *Patrologia Latina. Supplementum,* vol. 1, cols. 345–50. This may be an interpolation of the actual debate, revised by a Nicene to caricature the bishop's doctrine. A profession of faith by Germinius from the same era reveals him as a partisan of the more moderate position espoused in the "Dated Creed," to which he subscribed in 359. It is, however, very likely genuine, since Ursacius and Valens of Mursa both accused him of setting aside the position of Rimini.

16. Gryson, *Scolies,* p. 106.

17. Ibid., pp. 107–120.

18. Meslin, pp. 86, 87.

19. Kopecek, 2:422.

20. Ibid., 2:425–29.

21. Ibid., 2:430, 431.

22. Ibid., 2:442–43.

23. See, for example, Basil, *Epistula* 338; Augustine, *De Civitate Dei* 18. 51; Epiphanius, *Panarion* 70. 1. 15; Ambrose, *In Lucam* 2.

24. Baus, p. 226.

25. See Thompson, pp. 79–81; Socrates *Hist. Eccl.* 1. 18. 4; cf. Sozomen *Hist. Eccl.* 2. 6. 1.

26. See Thompson, pp. 94–95; Revillout, pp. 33–35; *A Dictionary of Christian Biography,* s.v. "Anthropomorphitae" by Philip Schaff, "Audius or Audaeus," idem, "Uranius (2)" by G. T. Stokes.

27. Gryson, *Scolies,* p. 147.

28. This is probably the romanized form of the Germanic *Wolflein,* meaning "little wolf."

29. See Thompson, pp. 117–19.

30. Gryson, *Scolies,* p. 145.

31. Baus, p. 227; Daniel-Rops, p. 111.

32. Gryson, *Scolies,* p. 146.

33. Baus, p. 227; Daniel-Rops p. 110; Vogt, p. 219; Gryson, *Scolies,* p. 146.

34. Gwatkin, p. 27n.

35. Mierow, p. 164.

36. Thompson, p. 95. Monasticism had won a firm footing among them, as it had among the Audaeans.

37. Gryson, *Scolies,* p. 148.

38. Auxentius, *Scolia Arriana in Concilium Aquileiense* 37. The writer has chosen to use the texts, titles, and numbering systems found in *Corpus Christianorum. Series Latina* 87.1 for references to the *Collectio Veronensis, Scolia Arriana in Concilium Aquileiense, Fragmenta in Lucam Rescripta,* and the *Fragmenta Theologica Rescripta* instead of those found in the older and in many ways less adequate *Patrologiae Cursus Completus. Series Latina Supplementum.* Quotations from and references to the *Scolia Arriana in Concilium Aquileiense* as found in the *Corpus Christianorum. Series Latina,* which represent the writer's own assessment of Arianism, will be cited in the text as "Scol." Where appropriate, the citation will include an abbreviated form of the names of those Arians usually assumed to be the authors of the various *scolia.*

39. Socrates, *Hist. Eccl.* 4.33.

40. Sozomen, *Hist. Eccl.* 4.24. See Thompson, p. xix.

41. *Collatio cum Maximino Arianorum episcopo* 4. References to the *Collatio* will be cited in the text as "Coll." Where appropriate, an abbreviated form of Augustine or Maximinus will be used to indicate which of these bishops was speaking.

42. Gryson, *Scolies,* pp. 174, 175.

43. Ibid., 147.

44. Thompson, pp. 96, 97.

45. Gryson, *Scolies,* p. 149.

46. Sozomen, *Hist. Eccl.* 6.37; Theodoret, *Hist. Eccl.* 4. 33.

47. Revillout, p. 43.

48. Marcelino Menéndez y Pelayo, *Historia de los Heterodoxos Españoles,* ed. Felix F. Corso, tomo 1 (Corrientes: Editorial Glem, 1583; Buenos Aires, Argentina: Editorial Perlado, 1945), p. 487.

49. Baus, p. 228.

50. Mierow, p. 165.

51. Kopecek, 2:441.

52. *Codex Theodosianus* 16.5.6. All translations of the Theodosian Code are those of Clyde Pharr. Theodosius also provided a compendium of Nicene dogma (the formulations of Gregory of Nazianzus and Basil of Caesarea) as the test of true adherence to the Catholic religion. The Neo-Arians had, by this time, begun to be called Eunomians after their leader, the former disciple of Aetius. Following the advice of Meletius, Theodosius had invited only those Eastern bishops of a pronounced Nicene persuasion to a council in his capital.

53. See Council of Constantinople, A.D. 381, canon 1. Translation available in *A Select Library of Nicene and Post-Nicene Fathers of the Christian Church,* 2d series. 14:172.

54. See *Codex Theodosianus* 16.5.8.

55. Kopecek, 2:516.

56. Ibid., 2:517, 518.

57. *Codex Theodosianus* 16.5.11.

58. Lietzmann, pp. 60–61.

59. Ibid., p. 61.

60. Ibid.

61. Gryson, *Scolies,* pp. 121, 126, 127.

62. Ibid., p. 125.

63. Lietzmann, p. 62.

64. Gryson, *Scolies,* p. 121.

65. Yves M. Duval, "La présentation arienne du Concile d'Aquilée de 381: à propos des 'Scolies ariennes sur le concile d'Aquilée' par R. Gryson," *Revue d'Histoire ecclesiastique* 76, no. 2 (1981) p. 317.

66. Gryson, *Scolies,* pp. 133–35.

67. See Lietzmann, p. 62.

68. Ibid., pp. 62–63.

69. Ibid., p. 62; Gryson, *Scolies,* p. 165.

70. Lietzmann, p. 63.

71. *Codex Theodosianus* 16.1.4.

72. Kopecek, 2:572.

73. *Concise Oxford Dictionary of the Christian Church,* s.v. "Arianism."

74. Irénée Chevalier, *S. Augustin et la pensée Grecque les relations trinitaires,* Collectanea Friburgensia 33, n.s., 24. (Fribourg, Suisse: Librarie de l'Université, 1940), pp. 28–33.

75. Kopecek, 1:202–10.

76. *Adversus Orthodoxos et Macedonianos* 6; *Instructio Verae Fidei* 13.

77. R. D. Williams, "The Logic of Arianism," *Journal of Theological Studies* 34 (April 1983): 56–58; Gwatkin, *Studies*, p. 22.

78. Williams, pp. 59–60. This view could have been derived from the *Isagoge* or *Categories* of Porphyrian Aristotelianism. Williams quotes a number of passages illustrating the conceptual similarities between Porphyrian Aristotlelianism and Arianism.

79. *A Dictionary of Christian Theology*, s.v. "Ingeneracy," by H. E. W. Turner.

80. T. E. Pollard, "The Origins of Arianism," *Journal of Theological Studies* Oxford 9 (1958): 109–110. Pollard's characterization of this as "pure sophistry" is extremely uncharitable.

81. *A Dictionary of Christian Theology*, s.v. "Trinity," by H. E. W. Turner.

82. Williams, pp. 59–61.

83. Quoted in John Henry Newman, *The Arians of the Fourth Century*, 4th ed. (London: Pickering, 1876), p. 215.

84. Kopecek, 1:242–46.

85. Ibid., 2:321–22, 331, 459–64.

86. Chevalier, p. 33.

87. Kopecek, 1:280, 291, 294; 2:327, 330. See also Eunomius's *Apologia* 18.

88. Kelly, *Athanasian Creed*, p. 80.

89. Kopecek, *Neo-Arianism*, 1:197.

90. Ibid., 2:337–38.

91. See also *Contra Hereticos* 1, 5; *Adversus Orthodoxos et Macedonianos* fragm. 2, 5, 6; *Instructio Verae Fidei* 14, 17.

92. Meslin, p. 308.

93. Gryson, *Scolies*, p. 181.

94. Kelly, *Athanasian Creed*, p. 78.

95. Meslin, pp. 304–5.

96. Ibid., pp. 306–7.

97. Gwatkin, p. 24.

98. Newman, p. 209.

99. Robert C. Gregg and Dennis E. Groh, *Early Arianism: A View of Salvation* (Philadelphia: Fortress Press, 1981), p. 1.

100. Gwatkin, *Studies*, pp. 24–25.

101. Gregg and Groh, pp. 13–24.

102. Newman, p. 210.

103. Gwatkin, p. 24; Gregg and Groh, p. 81.

104. Ibid., pp. 6–11.

105. Ibid., pp. 26–30.

106. Ibid., pp. 101–2, 116–17.

107. *A Dictionary of Christian Theology*, s.v. "Anhomeans," by H. E. W. Turner.

108. Kopecek, 2:323, 484, 491.

109. Ibid., 2:477, 493.

110. See Gryson, *Scolies*, p. 185.

111. Kelly, *Athanasian Creed*, p. 79.

112. Gryson, *Scolies*, pp. 185, 186.

113. Ibid., p. 188.

114. *Adversus Orthodoxos et Macedonianos* fragm. 7.

115. See *Adversos Orthodoxos*, 2, 5, 6.

116. *Instructio Verae Fidei* 22.

117. Meslin, pp. 311–12.

118. Ibid., pp. 312–13.

119. Aloys Grillmeier, *Christ in the Christian Tradition,* vol. 1 of *From the Apostolic Age to Chalcedon (431),* 2d rev. ed., trans. John Bowden (London: Mowbrays, 1975), pp. 183–92.

120. *A Dictionary of Christian Theology,* s.v. "Christology," by George S. Hendry.

121. Quoted in Baus, p. 93.

122. Williams, pp. 59–61.

123. Pollard, "Origins," pp. 104–8.

124. Williams, pp. 59–61.

125. Gwatkin, p. 23.

126. See also *Instructio Verae Fidei* fragm. 20.

127. Meslin, p. 316.

128. *A Dictionary of Christian Theology,* s.v. "Trinity," by H. E. W. Turner.

129. Kopecek, 2:526.

130. See also *In Sancta Epiphania* 7.8.

131. See also *Instructio Verae Fidei* 21, 23.

132. See also *Contra Hereticos* 1.

133. Meslin, p. 322.

134. Gwatkin, p. 25.

135. Gregg and Groh, pp. 50, 51, 78, 117, 169.

136. See Kopecek, 1:11.

137. Gregg and Groh, pp. 58–67.

138. Kopecek, 2:486, 497, 522.

139. See, for example, *De Lectionibus Sanctorum Evangeliorum* 8.3; 19.4; *In Sancto Pascha* 1–5; *Fragmenta in Lucam* 1.31.

140. Gregg and Groh, pp. 1–12.

141. Chevalier, p. 28. See T. E. Pollard, "The Exegesis of Scripture and the Arian Controversy," *Bulletin of the John Rylands Library* 41 (1958–59): 416–17; J. Lebreton, *A History of the Dogma of the Trinity,* trans. A. Thorold (New York: Benziger Brothers, 1939), pp. 93–94.

142. Gwatkin, *Studies,* p. 20.

143. T. E. Pollard, "The Exegesis of John 10:30 in the Early Trinitarian Controversies," *New Testament Studies* 3 (1957): 339–42.

144. Chevalier, p. 33.

145. Kopecek, 2:324.

146. Quoted in Kopecek, 1:228.

147. Kopecek provides a translation and an illuminating discussion of Aetius's *Syntagmation* in 1:227–97.

148. Kopecek, 2:321–22, 459–61, 464, 472.

149. Thompson, p. 117.

150. Ibid., pp. 122, 141, 143, 149, 155.

151. Ibid., p. 152.

152. Ibid., p. 123.

153. Ibid., p. 126.

154. E. L. Woodward, *Christianity and Nationalism in the Later Roman Empire* (New York: Longmans, Green & Co., 1916), p. 68.

155. See also *Contra Hereticos* 1–5; *Adversus Orthodoxos et Macedonianos* fragm. 9–12.

156. Meslin, p. 235.

157. See Thompson, pp. 117, 121–26.
158. Meslin, p. 227.
159. *Opus imperfectum in Matthaeum* 909. There is still some dispute over the authorship of this work. Meslin gives probably the best guess by ascribing it to Maximinus. Meslin, p. 228.
160. Thompson, p. 154; see pp. 141–43.
161. Ibid., p. 152.
162. Ibid., p. 140; see pp. 135–44.
163. Meslin, pp. 230, 235.
164. See Meslin, p. 394.
165. Ibid., p. 230.
166. Thompson, p. 153.
167. Novation, for example, held this position.
168. Eugene Teselle, *Augustine, the Theologian* (New York: Herder & Herder, 1970), p. 227. See Augustine, *De Trinitate* 2.9.15.
169. See Alfred Schindler, *Wort und Analogie in Augustins Trinitätslehre* (J. C. B. Mohr; Tübingen, 1965), pp. 130–46.

# Chapter 3: Augustine and Arianism to the Time of His Debate with Maximinus

1. Warmington, pp. 55–57.
2. Ibid., p. 12.
3. Jones, 1:175, 183–84.
4. Warmington, pp. 5, 64–67, 108, 111; Brown, *Religion and Society*, p. 32.
5. Warmington, p. 15.
6. Peter Brown, *Augustine of Hippo* (Los Angeles: University of California Press, 1967), p. 421; Jones, 1:197, 653; Warmington, p. 26.
7. Frend, pp. 652, 653, 700.
8. Warmington, p. 75.
9. Brown, *Augustine of Hippo*, pp. 138–45, 197–201.
10. Daniel-Rops, pp. 77–78.
11. Markus, pp. 143, 149.
12. Brown, *Augustine of Hippo*, pp. 272–73.
13. Schindler, p. 2; Eugene Teselle, *Augustine the Theologian* (New York: Herder & Herder, 1970), p. 311; Duchesne, p. 121.
14. Besides the *Contra Sermonem Arianorum* and *Contra Maximinum Arianorum episcopum*, some of Augustine's other writings aimed specifically at combatting Arianism include *Sermones* 52, 118, 126, 135, 139, 140, 183, and 341; *Tractatus in Evangelium Joannis* 17, 18, 20, 27, 36, 37, 49, 59, and 71; and *Epistulae* 171, 238, 239, 241, and 242. Portalié, p. 347.
15. Pierre de Labriolle, *History and Literature of Christianity from Tertullian to Boethius*, trans. Herbert Wilson (New York: Alfred A. Knopf, 1925), p. 408; Schindler, p. 5.
16. See Peter Brown, *Augustine of Hippo*, pp. 81, 82.
17. See Peter Brown, *Augustine of Hippo*, pp. 81–84; Meslin, p. 233.
18. Kelly, *Athanasian Creed*, pp. 80–82.
19. Ibid., pp. 80, 85.
20. See Kelly, *Athanasian Creed*, pp. 22, 86, 87.
21. Ibid., p. 80.

22. See Schindler, p. 4.

23. *Tractatus in Joannis Evangelium* will be abbreviated as "Tract. in Joan."

24. Each of Augustine's *Epistula* will be abbreviated as "Ep."

25. Augustine also displayed a great deal of knowledge of some basic Early Arian doctrines in his *De symbolo ad catechumenos* 2.26. Appendix 3, *Corpus Scriptorum Ecclesiasticorum Latinorum,* vol. 58, p. 35.

27. See Anne Marie La Bonnardière, *Recherches de chronologie augustiénne* (Paris: Études Augustiénnes, 1965), pp. 165–78.

28. See Teselle, p. 235 and Robert J. O'Connell, *The Origin of the Soul in Saint Augustine's Later Works* (New York: Fordham University Press, 1987).

29. Ibid., p. 10.

30. La Bonnardière, pp. 165–78.

31. Ibid., pp. 81, 83.

32. Ibid., pp. 63–118.

33. See Brown, *Augustine of Hippo,* pp. 81–84, 103. See also Meslin, p. 233.

34. Teselle, p. 311. See also Manlio Simonetti, "S. Agostino e gli Ariani," *Revue des études augustiniennes* 13 (1967): 55–84.

35. For example, Portalié notes its anonymity (p. 59). Revillout believes that Maximinus was the author of this "catechism" (p. 98). Revillout also calls it a catechism.

36. Chevalier, pp. 28–32.

37. A more complete discussion of this will appear below.

38. Teselle, pp. 294–96.

39. Chevalier, pp. 15–28; Teselle, p. 116.

40. Ibid., p. 294.

41. See, for example, Teselle, p. 294.

42. O'Connell, p. 1 footnote; for example see J. N. D. Kelly, *Early Christian Doctrines,* rev. ed. (San Francisco: Harper & Row, 1978), p. 271; Justo L. González, *A History of Christian Thought,* vol. 1 of *From the Beginnings to the Council of Chalcedon* (Nashville, TN: Abingdon Press, 1970), p. 336; Rusch, *Controversy,* p. 1; Teselle, p. 311; Schindler, p. 10; et al.

43. Van der Meer, p. 119.

44. Martindale, p. 536.

45. The abbreviation for the *Contra Sermonem Arianorum* will be "CS" and the abbreviation for the *Retractationes* will be "R."

46. See, for example, Portalié, p. 59.

47. Othmar Perler and Jean-Louis Maier, *Les Voyages de Saint Augustin* (Paris: Études Augustinniennes, 1969), pp. 340–50, 465, 466.

48. Meslin, p. 133; please note *Sermones* 151–56; *Epistula* 200.

49. Perler, pp. 351, 352, 359, 360.

50. See La Bonnardière, p. 73.

51. Meslin, pp. 130–32.

52. The abbreviation for the *Sermo Arianorum* will be "S."

53. Tarsicius Van Bavel has a very helpful discussion of this in his *Recherches sur La Christologie de Saint Augustin,* pp. 57–63.

54. See, for example, *In Johannis Epistula* 3.

55. Bonner, p. 142.

56. Van der Meer, pp. 119–20. See *Epistula* 171.

57. La Bonnardière p. 98.

58. O'Connell, p. 8.

59. See discussion of her position in section on early contacts.

60. Portalié, p. 72.
61. Perler, p. 263.
62. Chevalier, p. 20; Schindler, p. 5; Meslin, p. 58. Bentley-Taylor and Mary Inez Bogan place it between the *Contra Sermonem Arianorum* and the *Collatio cum Maximino* but do not discuss their reasons for doing so. Bentley-Taylor, p. 214; Mary Inez Bogan, "Translator's Note," in *The Retractations*, The Fathers of the Church Series, vol. 60 (Washington, D.C.: Catholic University of America Press, 1968), p. 235.
63. Martindale, pp. 834, 835.
64. Brown, *Augustine of Hippo*, p. 141.
65. Van der Meer, p. 120.
66. The account of this conference, given below, is based on Augustine's *Epistula* 238.
67. Bonner, p. 142.
68. See, for example, *Scolia* 23–31, 40.
69. Van der Meer, p. 120.

# Chapter 4. Augustine and Maximinus

1. Brown, *Augustine of Hippo*, p. 241.
2. Bury, *Empire*, p. 36.
3. Martindale, p. 238.
4. MacNamara, *Friendship in St. Augustine* (Fribourg, Switzerland: University Press, [1958]), p. 173.
5. Martindale, p. 238.
6. MacNamara, p. 175.
7. Perler, pp. 366–69.
8. See Bentley-Taylor, p. 211.
9. See MacNamara, p. 175.
10. See Martindale, pp. 237–39.
11. Bury, *Empire*, pp. 237–38.
12. Martindale, p. 239.
13. Edward N. Luttwak, *Grand Strategy of the Roman Empire* (Baltimore: Johns Hopkins University Press, 1976), pp. 81–83.
14. See MacNamara, *Friendship*, p. 177.
15. Warmington, p. 14.
16. See Perler, *Voyages*, pp. 18, 387–89.
17. Ibid., p. 387.
18. Edgar Nathaniel Johnson and James Westfall Thompson, *An Introduction to Medieval Europe 300–1500* (New York: W. W. Norton & Company, 1937), p. 95.
19. Jones, 1:189.
20. Johnson, p. 95.
21. Jones, 1:195; Courcelle, p. 123.
22. Ibid., p. 117.
23. MacNamara, p. 177. See Possidius *Vita Augustini* 28.
24. Bury, *Invasions*, p. 118.
25. Courcelle, p. 118. Courcelle claims that an inscription at Altava provides a rather detailed account of the journeys of Gaiseric's forces all the way to the capture of Carthage. Ibid., pp. 117–18.
26. Daniel-Rops, p. 64.

27. Courcelle, p. 118.

28. Perowne, p. 75.

29. Courcelle, pp. 122, 123.

30. See Courcelle, pp. 122, 123.

31. Ibid., p. 124.

32. Portalié, p. 35; Perler, p. 388.

33. Courcelle, p. 125. For the story of what happened later to Boniface and the Vandals, see the historical narrative in chapter 1.

34. Meslin, pp. 95–96; Van der Meer, p. 123; Bentley-Taylor, p. 215.

35. Gryson, *Scolies,* p. 67.

36. Meslin, p. 93.

37. Gryson, *Scolies,* p. 66.

38. Hammond C. P. Bammel, "From the School of Maximinus: The Arian material in Paris Ms. Lat. 8907," *Journal of Theological Studies* 31 (October 1980): 400.

39. Meslin, pp. 92–94.

40. See *Sermones* 140.

41. Otto Bardenhewer, *Geschichte der Altkirchlichen Literatur,* 4 vols. (Darmstadt: Wissenschaftliche Buchgesellschaft, 1962) 4:479.

42. Courcelle, p. 137, n. See *Opus imperfectum in Matthaeum.*

43. Gryson, *Scolies,* p. 67; Thompson, p. 119, n. 2.

44. Ibid., pp. 119–20; Meslin, p. 96.

45. Gryson, *Scolies,* p. 67.

46. Meslin, p. 93.

47. See Concinnata *Vita sancti Augustini episcopi* 8. 8.4; Meslin, pp. 94–95; Van der Meer, p. 122. The abbreviation for the *Contra Maximinum Arianorum episcopum* will be "CM."

48. Meslin, p. 95.

49. *Sermones* 140. 4; see CM 2.22; Van der Meer, p. 123, 206; Bentley-Taylor, p. 213; Bonner, p. 144.

50. Concinnata *Vita Sancti Augustini Episcopi* 8.8.4.

51. Augustine, in order to spare his city the trials of an election after his death, had insisted on the election of the deacon Heraclius in 426 to serve as his auxiliary with the right of succession and had already handed over to him the external administration of the church. Portalié, p. 35. For an official account of the election in which Heraclius was chosen as Augustine's successor, see Ep. 213.

52. Giovanni Papini, *Saint Augustine,* trans. Mary Prichard Agnetti (New York: Harcourt, Brace & Company, 1930), p. 282; Bentley-Taylor, p. 215.

53. For a complete listing of scriptural references for this work, and for the *Sermo Arianorum,* the *Contra Sermonem Arianorum,* and the *Contra Maximinum Arianorum episcopum,* see the Appendix on Scripture References.

54. Kelly, *Athanasian Creed,* pp. 70–72.

55. Ibid., p. 77.

56. Ibid., p. 79.

57. Ibid., p. 81.

58. What he actually said was that he would continue to hold these views even if strapped to the *equuleum.* The *equuleum* was a Roman instrument of torture made of metal and shaped roughly like a horse. It was used primarily in Roman Africa. The person to be tortured was stripped naked and strapped to it. Then, hot coals were placed around its metal base.

59. Kelly, *Athanasian Creed,* p. 80.

60. See Bentley-Taylor, p. 215; Bonner, p. 144.
61. See Bentley-Taylor, p. 215.
62. Van der Meer, p. 123.
63. Bonner, p. 144; Van der Meer, p. 123.
64. Meslin, p. 96.
65. Ibid.; Gryson, *Scolies,* p. 68.
66. Bammel, p. 401.
67. Meslin, p. 96.
68. Gryson, *Scolies,* p. 68.
69. Bardenhewer, 4:480.
70. See Appendix of Scripture References.
71. Tarsicius J. Van Bavel, *Recherches sur la christologie de saint Augustin; l'humain et le divin dans le Christ d'apres saint Augustin* (Fribourg, Switzerland: Editions Universitaires, 1954), p. 169.
72. Ibid., p. 169.

# Chapter 5. Augustine against the Gothic Arians: A Theological Review and Exposition

1. See Portalié, p. 130.
2. González, p. 337.
3. William Pearson Tolley, *The Idea of God in the Philosophy of St. Augustine* (New York: R. R. Smith, 1930), p. 185.
4. See the discussion under "Christology" for a more complete exposition of this view.
5. *De diversas quaestiones* 9.69.1.
6. Howard J. Lowen, "The Use of Scripture in Augustine's Theology," *Scottish Journal of Theology* 34, no. 3 (1981): 221.
7. See Teselle, pp. 175–76. For a complete listing of scriptural references for the *Sermo Arianorum,* the *Contra Sermonem,* the *Collatio cum Maximino,* and the *Contra Maximinum* see Appendix 1 (compiled by the researcher).
8. Robert H. Ayers, "Language Theory and Analysis in Augustine," *Scottish Journal of Theology* 29, no. 1 (1976): 7–9.
9. Ibid., p. 62.
10. *Dictionary of Christian Theology,* s.v. "Trinity, Doctrine of the," by H. E. W. Turner.
11. Chevalier, p. 28.
12. Ayers, pp. 66–67.
13. For an excellent general study of Augustine's use of rhetoric, see M. L. Clarke, *Rhetoric at Rome: A Historical Survey* (London: Cohen & West, 1953; reprint ed., London: Lowe & Brydone, 1962).
14. Fortman, p. 140.
15. Paul Henry, *Saint Augustine on Personality,* Saint Augustine Lecture Series (New York: Macmillan, 1960), p. 10.
16. Ibid., pp. 8, 9.
17. Fortman, pp. 148–49.
18. See Tolley, p. 193.
19. References to Psalms are in the chapter and verse numbers of the Protestant system rather than that of the Vulgate.
20. See Portalié, p. 153.

21. See Teselle, p. 152.

22. Tavard, p. 268.

23. *Opus Imperfectum Contra Julianum* 1.138. This is one of the very last works by Augustine, probably written late A.D. 429 or early A.D. 430.

24. Teselle, p. 148. See Origen, *De Principiis* 2.6.

25. *De Peccatorum Meritis et Remissione* 1.21.60.

26. *De diversis quaestionibus* 9.69.1.

27. See Van Bavel, p. 103.

28. See *De natural et gratia contra Pelagium* 55.3, 4 and *De gratia Christi et peccato originali* 1.13.25.

29. *De nuptiis et concupiscentia* 1.28.

## Conclusion

1. Both Gerald Bonner, in his *St. Augustine,* and Frederick Van der Meer, in *Augustine the Bishop,* made the less important debate with Pascentius the centerpiece of their all-too-brief discussions of Augustine's anti-Arian works.

2. *In Ioannis Evangelium* 15.9.

## Appendix 2. A Few Notes on Important Western Texts

1. Labriolle, p. 253.

2. Ibid., p. 254.

3. Revillout, pp. 95–96.

4. Menéndez, 1:497–504.

5. Meslin, p. 103. Meslin gives a good summary of the history of the critical study of these texts on pages 103 through 110.

6. Roger Gryson, "Introduction," in *Scripta Arriana Latina. Pars I,* ed. Roger Gryson, *Corpus Christianorum. Series Latina,* vol. 87. (Turnholti: Typographi Brepols Editores Pontificii, 1982), p. xviii.,

7. *Patrologiae Cursus Completus. J. P. Migne Editus et Parisiis, Anno Domini 1844 Excusus. Series Latina. Supplementum,* Accurante Adaberto Hamman (Paris, Editions Garnier Frères) 1:326. See also *Patrologiae Cursus Completus. Series Latina,* ed. J. P. Migne, 221 vols. (Paris, 1844–64) 13:593, 631.

8. Labriolle, p. 255.

9. Gryson, "Introduction," in *Scripta Arriana,* p. xxi.

10. Berthold Altaner, *Patrology,* trans. Hilda C. Graef, (Edinburgh: Nelson, 1960), p. 437.

11. Gryson, *Scolies,* pp. 58–59.

12. Ibid., pp. 79, 80.

13. Waitz, *Ueber das Leben und des Lehre des Ulfila,* Bruchstrüke eines ungedruckten Werkes aus dem Ende des 4. Jahrhunderts (Hanover, 1840); Bessell, *Ueber das Leben des Ulfilas und die Bekehrung der Gothen zum Christenthum* (Göttingen, 1860).

14. Bammel, pp. 392–93.

15. For example Kauffmann, D. B. Capelle, Otto Bardenhewer 3:595–96; Michel Meslin (See pp. 101–250 for all the works he attributes to Maximinus); Altaner, p. 335; Bammel, p. 401; E. Dekkers, *Clavis Patrum Latinorum* (Steenbrugge, 1961), pp. 159ff. nos. 692ff; Dirksen, *Elementary Patrology,* p. 272, Schindler, p. 3; Duchesne, p. 121; Hamman, *Patrologia Latina Supplementum* 1:693. Waitz, however, rejected this view (pp. 26, 27).

16. *Patrologia Latina Supplementum* 1:691–93.
17. Gryson, *Scolies,* pp. 64, 66.
18. Ibid., pp. 69–75.
19. Bammel, pp. 396–97.
20. Ibid., p. 398.
21. Ibid., pp. 399–400.
22. Ibid., p. 400; See *Patrologia Latina Supplementum* 1:709, no. 71.
23. Meslin, pp. 104–5.
24. Bammel, pp. 395–96, 399.
25. Labriolle, p. 256.
26. *Patrologia Latina Supplementum* 1:326.
27. Bardenhewer, p. 412.
28. Gryson, "Introduction," in *Scripta Arriana,* p. xxiii.
29. Thompson, p. 119, n. 2.
30. Labriolle, p. 254.
31. Gryson, "Introduction," in *Scripta Arriana,* pp. xxiii, xxiv.
32. Labriolle, p. 254.
33. Meslin, pp. 101–250.
34. Gryson, "Introduction," in *Scripta Arriana,* p. xxiv.

# Appendix 3. Gothic Arian Worship: Practices and Organizations

1. Revillout, p. 49.
2. See Socrates, *Hist. eccl.* 5.23.
3. Meslin, p. 325.
4. Baus, p. 229.
5. Revillout, p. 48.
6. Ibid., p. 96. See also *Collatio* 4.
7. M. A. Smith, *Church Under Siege* (Leicester, England; Inter-Varsity Press, 1976), p. 167.
8. See Thompson, p. 155.
9. Augustine *De Civitate Dei* 1.1; Orosius, *Historia* 7.39; Jerome, *Epistulae* 27.13; also see Revillout, p. 110.
10. Daniel-Rops, p. 112.
11. Revillout, pp. 107–8.
12. Daniel-Rops, p. 111.
13. Meslin, pp. 382, 383, 387.
14. Ibid., p. 512, 513.
15. Menéndez, 1:512–14.
16. Meslin, p. 389. See Revillout, p. 100.

# BIBLIOGRAPHY

## Collections

*Corpus Christianorum. Series Latina.* Turnholti: Typographi Brepols.

*Monumenta Germaniae historica inde ab anno Christi quinqentismo usque ad annum millesi-mum.* Edited by the Societas Aperiendis Fontibus Rerum Germanicarum Medii Aevi. 15 vols. in 13 Vols. Berlin: Weidmannsche Verlagsbuchhandlung, 1892; reprint ed., Berlin: Drukerei Hildebrand, 1961.

*Patrologiae Cursus Completus. Series Latina.* Edited by Jacques Paul Migne. 221 vols. Paris: 1844–64.

*Patrologiae Cursus Completus a J. P. Migne Editus et Parisiis, Anno Domini 1844 Excu-sus. Series Latina. Supplementum.* Accurante Adaberto Hamman. Paris: Editions Garnier Frères.

## Reference Works

*The Concise Oxford Dictionary of the Christian Church.* 2d ed. Edited by Elizabeth A. Livingstone. Oxford: University Press, 1977.

*A Dictionary of Christian Biography, Literature, Sects, and Doctrines during the First Eight Centuries.* Edited by William Smith and Henry Wace. London: John Murray, 1882.

*A Dictionary of Christian Theology.* Edited by Alan C. Richardson. Philadelphia: Westminster Press, 1969.

## Books

Altaner, Berthold. *Patrology.* Translated by Hilda C. Graef. Edinburgh: Nelson, 1960.

Anderson, James F. *St. Augustine and Being: A Metaphysical Essay.* The Hague: Martinus Niehoff, 1965.

Arnheim, M. T. W. *The Senatorial Aristocracy in the Late Roman Empire.* Oxford: Clarendon Press, 1972.

Ayers, Robert Hyman. *Language, Logic, and Reason in the Church Fathers: A Study of Tertullian, Augustine, and Aquinas.* New York: G. Olms, 1979.

Bardenhewer, Otto. *Geschichte der altkirchlichen Literatur.* 4 vols. Darmstadt: Wis-senschaftliche Buchgesellschaft, 1962.

Battenhouse, Roy W., ed. *A Companion to the Study of St. Augustine.* Oxford University Press, 1959; reprint ed., Grand Rapids, MI: Baker Book House, 1979.

Baus, Karl, Hans-Georg Beck, Eugen Ewig, and Herman Josef Vogt. *The Imperial Church from Constantine to the Early Middle Ages*. Translated by Anselm Biggs. Vol. 2 of *History of the Church*, Hubert Jedin and John Dolan, gen. eds. New York: Seabury Press, 1980.

Bentley-Taylor, David. *Augustine, Wayward Genius: The Life of St. Augustine of Hippo*. Grand Rapids, MI: Baker Book House, 1980.

Berkhof, Louis. *The History of Christian Doctrines*. Grand Rapids, MI: Baker Book House, 1937.

Bessell, Wilhelm. *Ueber das Leben des Ulfilas und die Bekehrung der Gothen zum Christenthum*. Göttigen, 1860.

Boak, Arthur Edward Romiley. *The Master of Offices in the Later Roman and Byzantine Empires*. New York: Macmillan, 1919. Reprint, New York: Johnson Reprint Corporation, 1972.

Bonner, Gerald. *St. Augustine of Hippo: Life and Controversies*. Philadelphia: Westminster Press, 1963.

Boyle, Isaac. *A Historical View of the Council of Nice with a Translation of Documents*. Philadelphia: J. B. Lippincott & Co., 1879.

Brown, Peter. *Augustine of Hippo*. Los Angeles: University of California Press, 1967.

———. *Religion and Society in the Age of Saint Augustine*. London: Faber and Faber, 1972.

———. *The World of Late Antiquity A.D. 150–750*. London: Harcourt Brace Jovanovich, 1971.

Burnaby, John. *Augustine: Later Works*. Selected and translated by John Burnaby. Philadelphia: Westminster Press, 1955.

Burke, Kenneth. *The Rhetoric of Religion: Studies in Logology*. Boston: Beacon Press, 1961.

Bury, John Bagnell. *History of the Later Roman Empire from the Death of Theodosius I to the Death of Justinian*. 2 vols. London: Macmillan, 1923.

———. *The Invasion of Europe by the Barbarians*. New York: Macmillan, 1928. Reprint. New York: Russell & Russell, 1963.

Cantor, Norman F. *Medieval History: The Life and Death of a Civilization*. London: Collier-Macmillan, 1969.

Chevalier, Irénée. *S. Augustin et la pénsee Grecque les relations trinitaires*. Collectanea Friburgensia 33, n. s., 24. Fribourg, Switzerland: Librairie de l'Université, 1940.

Clarke, M. L. *Rhetoric at Rome: A Historical Survey*. London: Cohen & West, 1953. Reprint. London: Lowe & Brydone, 1962.

Courcelle, Pierre Paul. *Histoire littéraire grandes invasion germaniques*. 3d ed. Paris: Études Augustiniennes, 1965.

Daniel-Rops, Henri. *The Church in the Dark Ages*. Translated by Audrey Butler. New York: E. P. Dutton & Co., 1959.

Dekkers, Ernst. *Clavis Patrum Latinorum*. Steenbrugge, 1961.

Diesner, Hans Joachim. *Der Untergang der römischen Herrschaft in Nordafrika*. Weimar: Hermann Böhlaus Nachfolger, 1964.

Dill, Samuel. *Roman Society in the Last Century of the Western Empire*. 2d revised ed. New York: Meridian Books, 1958.

Duchesne, Louis. *Early History of the Christian Church from Its Foundation to the End of the Fifth Century.* Vol. 3 of *The Fifth Century.* Translated by Claude Jenkins. London: John Murray, 1924; reprinted 1951.

DuRoy, Olivier. *L'Intelligence de la foi en la Trinitate selon saint Augustin: genèse de sa theologie trinitaire jusqu'er 391.* Paris: Etudes Augustiniennes, 1961.

Fortman, Edmund J. *The Triune God: A Historical Study of the Doctrines of the Trinity.* Corpus Instrumentorum, 1972. Reprint. Grand Rapids, MI: Baker Book House, 1982.

Frend, W. H. C. *The Rise of Christianity.* Philadelphia: Fortress Press, 1984.

Gadamer, Hans-Georg. *Truth and Method.* Translation of *Wahrheit und Methode* published by J. C. B. Mohr in Tübingen in 1960. Translation edited by Garret Barden and John Cumming from the 2d ed. [1965]. New York: Seabury Press, 1975.

Geerlings, Wilhelm. *Christus Exemplum: Studien zur Christologie und Christusverkündigung Augustins.* Tübingen Theologische Studien. Band 13. Mainz: Mathias-Grunwald Verlag, 1978.

Gilson, Etienne. *Introduction à l'etude de saint Augustin.* 2d ed. Paris: J. Vrin, 1941.

Goffart, Walter. *Barbarians and Romans A.D. 418–584: The Techniques of Accommodation.* Princeton, NJ: Princeton University Press, 1980.

González, Justo L. *A History of Christian Thought.* Vol. 1 of *From the Beginnings to the Council of Chalcedon.* Nashville, TN: Abingdon Press, 1970.

Gregg, Robert C. and Dennis E. Groh. *Early Arianism: A View of Salvation.* Philadelphia: Fortress Press, 1981.

Grillmeyer, Aloys. *Christ in the Christian Tradition.* Vol. 1 of *From the Apostolic Age to Chalcedon (431).* 2d revised ed. Translated by John Bowden. London, Oxford: Mowbrays, 1975.

Gryson, Roger, ed. *Scolies Ariennes sur le Concile d'Aquilée: Introduction, Texte Latin, Traduction et Notes.* Sources Chrétiennes, no. 267. Paris: Les Editions du Cerf, 1980.

Gwatkin, Henry Melvill. *Studies of Arianism.* 2d ed. Cambridge: Deighton Bell and Co., 1900.

Gummerus, J. *Die Homöusianische Partei bis zum Tode des Konstantius: Ein Beitrag zur Geschichte des Arianischen Streites in dem Jahren 356–361.* Leipzig: Georg Böhme, 1900.

Henry, Paul. *Saint Augustine on Personality.* Saint Augustine Lecture Series. New York: Macmillan, 1960.

Hilgarth, J. N., ed. *The Conversion of Western Europe, 350–750.* Englewood Cliffs, NJ: Prentice-Hall, 1969.

Hollister, C. Warren. *Medieval Europe: A Short History.* 2d ed. New York: John Wiley & Sons, 1968.

Johnson, Edgar Nathaniel and James Westfall Thompson. *An Introduction to Medieval Europe 300–1500.* New York: W. W. Norton & Company, 1937.

Jones, A. H. M. *The Later Roman Empire 284–602: A Social, Economic and Administrative Survey.* 2 vols. Norman: University of Oklahoma Press, 1964.

Keating, Bern. *The Invaders of Rome.* New York: G. P. Putnam Sons, 1966.

Kelly, J. N. D. *The Athanasian Creed: The Paddock Lectures for 1962–3.* New York: Harper & Row, 1964.

———. *Early Christian Doctrines.* San Francisco: Harper & Row, 1978.

Kopecek, Thomas A. *A History of Neo-Arianism.* 2 vols. Cambridge, MA: Philadelphia Patristic Foundation, 1979.

Labriolle, Pierre de. *History and Literature of Christianity from Tertullian to Boethius.* Translated by Herbert Wilson. New York: Alfred A. Knopf, 1925.

La Bonnardière, Anne Marie. *Recherches de Chronologie Augustienne.* Paris: Études Augustiniennes, 1965.

Lamirande, Emilien. *Church, State and Toleration: An Intriguing Change of Mind in Augustine.* Villanova, PA: Villanova University Press, 1975.

Latouche, Robert. *Caesar to Charlemagne.* Translated by Jennifer Nicholson. New York: Barnes & Noble, 1968.

———. *Les Grandes invasions et la crise de l'Occident au Ve siècle.* Paris: Aubier, 1946.

Lebreton, J. *A History of the Dogma of the Trinity.* Translated by A. Thorold. New York: Benziger Brothers, 1939.

Lietzmann, Hans. *A History of the Early Church.* Vol. 4 of *The Era of the Church Fathers.* 2d revised ed. Translated by Bertram Lee Woolf. London: Lutterworth Press, 1953.

Lot, Ferdinand. *The End of the Ancient World and the Beginnings of the Middle Ages.* Translated by Philip Leon and Mariette Leon. New York: Harper Torchbooks, 1961.

Luttwak, Edward N. *The Grand Strategy of the Roman Empire: From the First Century A.D. to the Third.* Baltimore: Johns Hopkins University Press, 1976.

———. *Early Christian Doctrines.* San Francisco: Harper & Row, 1978.

Kopecek, Thomas A. *A History of Neo-Arianism.* 2 vols. Cambridge, MA: Philadelphia Patristic Foundation, 1979.

Labriolle, Pierre de. *History and Literature of Christianity from Tertullian to Boethius.* Translated by Herbert Wilson. New York: Alfred A. Knopf, 1925.

La Bonnardière, Anne Marie. *Recherches de Chronologie Augustienne.* Paris: Études Augustiniennes, 1965.

Lamirande, Emilien. *Church, State and Toleration: An Intriguing Change of Mind in Augustine.* Villanova, PA: Villanova University Press, 1975.

Latouche, Robert. *Caesar to Charlemagne.* Translated by Jennifer Nicholson. New York: Barnes & Noble, 1968.

———. *Les Grandes invasions et la crise de l'Occident au Ve siècle.* Paris: Aubier, 1946.

Lebreton, J. *A History of the Dogma of the Trinity.* Translated by A. Thorold. New York: Benziger Brothers, 1939.

Lietzmann, Hans. *A History of the Early Church.* Vol. 4 of *The Era of the Church Fathers.* 2d revised ed. Translated by Bertram Lee Woolf. London: Lutterworth Press, 1953.

Lot, Ferdinand. *The End of the Ancient World and the Beginnings of the Middle Ages.* Translated by Philip and Mariette Leon. New York: Harper Torchbooks, 1961.

Luttwak, Edward N. *The Grand Strategy of the Roman Empire: From the First Century A.D. to the Third.* Baltimore: Johns Hopkins University Press, 1976.

MacMullen, Ramsey. *Enemies of the Roman Order: Treason, Unrest, and Alienation in the Empire.* Cambridge: Harvard University Press, 1967.

———. *Soldier and Civilian in the Later Roman Empire.* Cambridge: Harvard University Press, 1963.

MacNamara, Marie Aquinas. *Friendship in St. Augustine*. Fribourg, Switzerland: University Press, [1958].

Mandouze, André. *Saint Augustin. L'Aventure de la raison et de la grace*. Paris: Études Augustiniennes, 1968.

Markus, Robert Austin. *Christianity in the Roman World*. London: Thames and Hudson, 1974.

Marrou, Henri Irénée. *Saint Augustin et la fin de la culture antique*. Paris: Editions E. de Boccard, 1938.

Martindale, R. J. *The Prosopography of the Later Roman Empire*. Vol. 2 of *A.D. 395–527*. Cambridge: Cambridge University Press, 1980.

Meslin, Michel. *Les Ariens d'Occident: 335–430*. Patristica Sorbonensia. Paris: Editions du Seuil, 1967.

Menéndez y Pelayo, Marcelino. *Historia de los Heterodoxos Españoles*. Edited by Felix F. Corso. Vol. 1. Buenos Aires: Argentina Editorial Perlado, 1945.

Mierow, Charles Christopher, ed. *The Gothic History of Jordanes in English Version with an Introduction and Commentary*. New York: Barnes & Noble, 1966.

Monceaux, Paul. *Historie litteraire de l'Afrique chrétienne depuis les origines jusqu'a l'invasion Arabe*. 7 vols. Bruxelles: Culture et Civilisation, 1963.

Newman, John Henry. *The Arians of the Fourth Century*. 4th ed. London: Pickering, 1876.

O'Connell, Robert J. *The Origin of the Soul in St. Augustine's Later Works*. New York: Fordham University Press, 1987.

Painter, Sidney. *A History of the Middle Ages 284–1500*. New York: Alfred A. Knopf, 1961.

Papini, Giovanni. *Saint Augustine*. Translated by Mary Prichard Agnetti. New York: Harcourt, Brace and Company, 1930.

Perler, Othmar and Jean-Louis Maier. *Les Voyages de Saint Augustin*. Paris: Études Augustiniennes, 1969.

Perowne, Stewart. *The End of the Roman World*. New York: Thomas Y. Crowell Company, 1967.

Picard, G. Charles. *La Carthage de saint Augustin*. [Paris:] Fayard, [1956].

Piganiol, A. *L'Empire Chrétien*. Paris: Presses universitaires de France, 1947.

Polman, Andries Derk Rietema. *The Word of God according to St. Augustine*. Translated by A. J. Pomerans. Grand Rapids, MI: Eerdmans, 1961.

Portalié, Eugene. *A Guide to the Thought of St. Augustine*. Translated by Ralph J. Bastian. Chicago: Henry Regnery, Co., 1960.

Revillout, Charles Jules. *De l'arianisme des peuples germaniques qui evahi l'empire Romain*. Paris: Madame Veuve Joubert, Libraire, 1850.

Rottmanner, Odilo. *Geistesfrüchte aus der Klosterzelle*. München: J. J. Lentner, 1908.

Rusch, William G. *The Later Latin Fathers*. London: Gerald Duckworth & Co., 1977.

———. *The Trinitarian Controversy*. Sources of Early Christian Thought. Philadelphia: Fortress Press, 1980.

Schindler, Alfred. *Wort und Analogie im Augustins Trinitätslehre*. Tübingen: J. C. B. Mohr, 1965.

Sidonius Apollinaris, *Letters*. Translated by O. M. Dalton. 2 vols. Oxford: University Press, 1915.

Simonetti, Manlio. *Studi sull'Arianesimo*. Rome: Editrice Studium, [1965].

Smith, M. A. *Church Under Siege*. Leicester, England: Inter-Varsity Press, 1976.

Stephenson, Carl. *Medieval History: Europe from the Second to the Sixteenth Century*. 3d ed. New York: Harper & Brothers, 1951.

Teselle, Eugene. *Augustine, the Theologian*. New York: Herder & Herder, 1970.

*The Theodosian Code and Novels and the Sirmondian Constitutions*. A Translation with Commentary, Glossary, and Bibliography by Clyde Pharr in collaboration with Theresa Sherrer Davidson and Mary Brown Pharr. Princeton, NJ: University Press, 1952.

Thompson, Ernest A. *The Visigoths in the Time of Ulfila*. Oxford: Clarendon Press, 1966.

Tolley, William Pearson. *The Idea of God in the Philosophy of St. Augustine*. New York: R. R. Smith, 1930.

Torrance, Thomas Forsyth. *Reality and Evangelical Theology*. The Payton Lectures. Philadelphia: Westminster Press, 1982.

Van Bavel, Tarsicius J. *Recherches sur la christologie de saint Augustin; l'humain et le divin dans le Christ d'apres saint Augustin*. Fribourg, Switzerland: Editions Universitaires, 1954.

Van der Meer, Frederick. *Augustine the Bishop: Religion and Society at the Dawn of the Middle Ages*. Translated by Brian Battershaw and G. R. Lamb. New York: Harper & Row, 1961.

Vogt, Joseph. *The Decline of Rome*. Translated by Janet Sondheimer. New York: New American Library, 1967.

Waitz, George. *Ueber das Leben und des Lehre des Ulfila*. Bruchstrüke eines ungedruckten Werkes aus dem Ende des 4. Jahrhunderts. Hanover, 1840.

Warmington, B. H. *The North African Provinces from Diocletian to the Vandal Conquest*. Cambridge: University Press, 1954.

Wallace-Hadrill, J. M. *The Barbarian West 400–1000*. 3d revised ed. New York: Hutchinson & Co., 1967.

Woodward, E. L. *Christianity and Nationalism in the Later Roman Empire*. New York: Longmans, Green, and Co., 1916.

## Journals

Bammel, Hammond C. P. "From the School of Maximinus: the Arian material in Paris Ms. Lat. 8907." *Journal of Theological Studies* 31 (October 1980): 390–402.

Burkhard, J. D. "Les Ariens d'Occident." *Revue d'Histoire et de Philosophie Religieuse* 51, no. 2 (1971): 169–74.

Daniels, Donald E. "The Argument of the *De Trinitate* and Augustine's Theory of Signs" *Augustinian Studies* 8 (1977): 33–54.

Duval, Yves M. "La présentation arienne du Concile d'Aquilée de 381: à propos des 'Scolies ariennes sur le concile d'Aquilée' par R. Gryson" *Revue d'Histoire ecclesiastique* 76, no. 2 (1981): 317–31.

Loewen, Howard J. "The Use of Scripture in Augustine's Theology." *Scottish Journal of Theology* 34, no. 3 (1981): 201–24.

O'Leary, Joseph S. "Dieu-esprit et dieu-substance chez Saint Augustin" *Recherches de Science religieuses* 69 (July 1981): 357–91.

Pollard, T. E. "The Exegesis of John X, 30 in the Early Trinitarian Controversies." *New Testament Studies* 3 (1957): 334–49.

———. "The Exegesis of Scripture and the Arian Controversy." *Bulletin of the John Rylands Library* 41 (1958/59): 414–29.

———. "The Origins of Arianism" *Journal of Theological Studies* 9 (1958): 103–11.

Ravicz, Marilyn E. "St. Augustine: Time and Eternity." *The Thomist* 22 (October 1959): 542–54.

Simonetti, Manlio. "S. Agostino e gli Ariani." *Revue des études Augustiennes* 13 (1967): 55–84.

Stead, George C. "The *Thalia* of Arius and the Testimony of Athanasius." *Journal of Theological Studies* 29 (April 1978): 20–52.

Tavard, George H. "The Christological Tradition in the Latin Fathers." *Dialog* (Autumn 1979): 265–70.

Von Stritzky, M. B. "Beobachtungen zur Verbindung zwischen Gregor von Nyssa und Augustin." *Vigiliae Christianae* 28, no. 3 (1974): 176–85.

Wassmer, T. A. "The Trinitarian Theology of Augustine and His Debt to Plotinus" *Scottish Journal of Theology* 14 (1961): 248–55.

Williams. R. D. "The Logic of Arianism." *Journal of Theological Studies* 34 (April 1983): 56–81.

# INDEX